THE WWII ERA COMIC ART OF E. SIMMS CAMPBELL

THE WWII ERA COMIC ART OF E. SIMMS CAMPBELL

Cuties in Arms
More Cuties in Arms

Coachwhip Publications
Landisville, Pennsylvania

The WWII Era Comic Art of E. Simms Campbell
Elmer Simms Campbell (1906-1971)

Cuties in Arms published 1941
More Cuties in Arms published 1943

ISBN 1-61646-133-0
ISBN-13 978-1-61646-133-1

CoachwhipBooks.com

E. Simms Campbell was the first African-American cartoonist to be published in nationally distributed magazines. His watercolor comic art was published in *Esquire*, *Cosmopolitan*, *The New Yorker*, and many other magazines, and his artistic talent was sought out by numerous advertisers. *Cuties* was his gag panel, and this volume brings together his two *Cuties in Arms* collections from 1941 and 1943, during those war years when soldier-oriented humor was particularly popular.

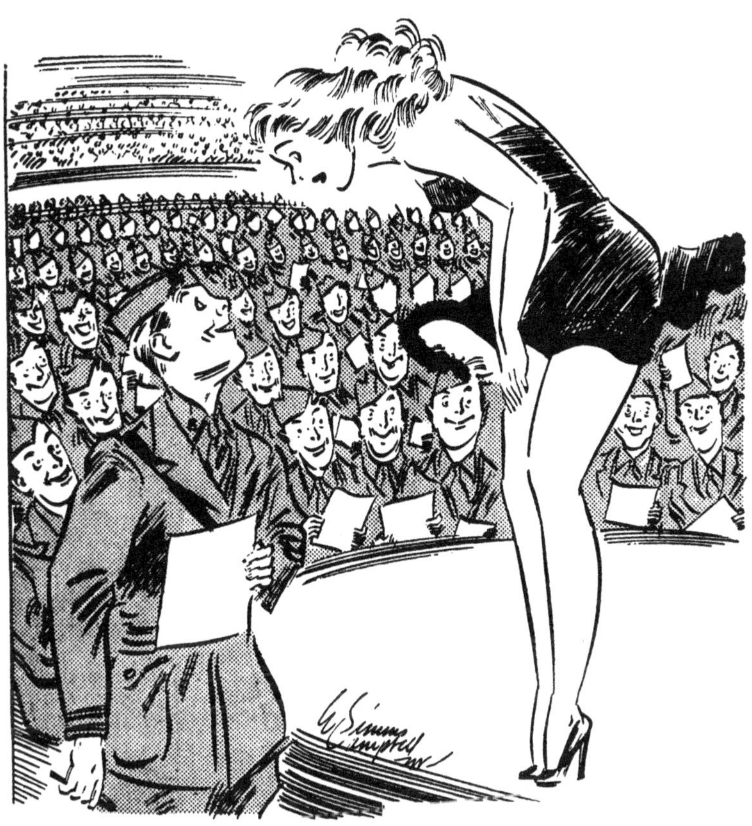

"Speaking for a few of the boys, the 7th, 8th and 9th Tank Corps and the 91st and 92nd Divisions, we'd each like your autograph!"

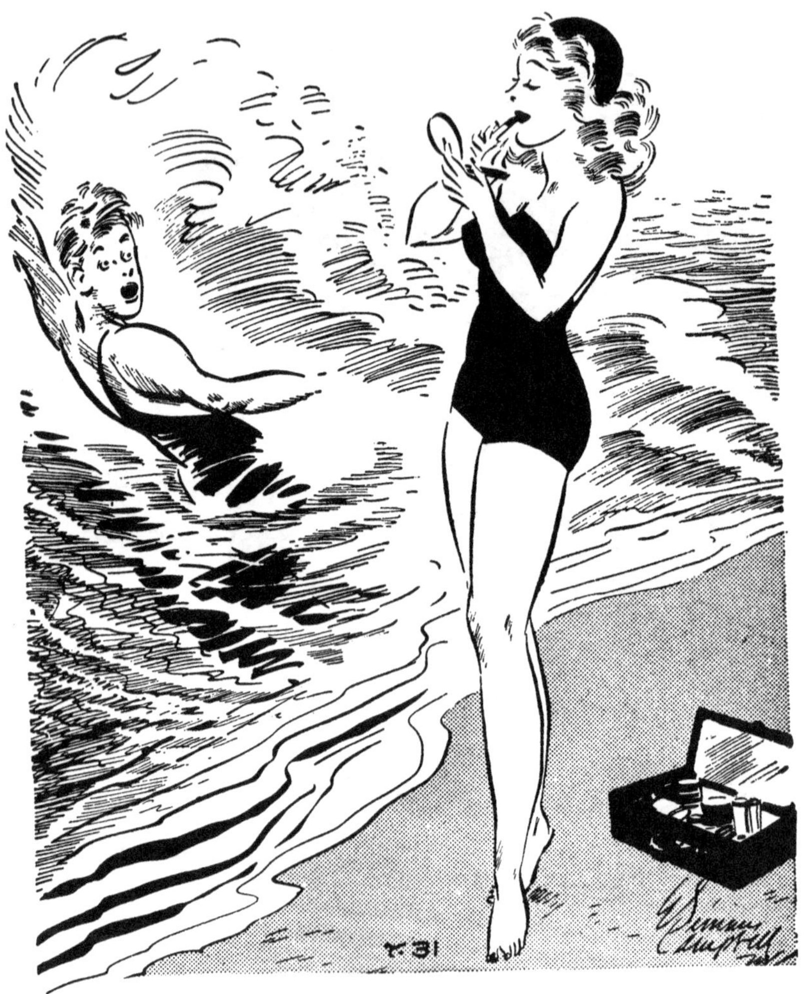

"I'll join you in a minute, dear . . . Just as soon as I put on my makeup!"

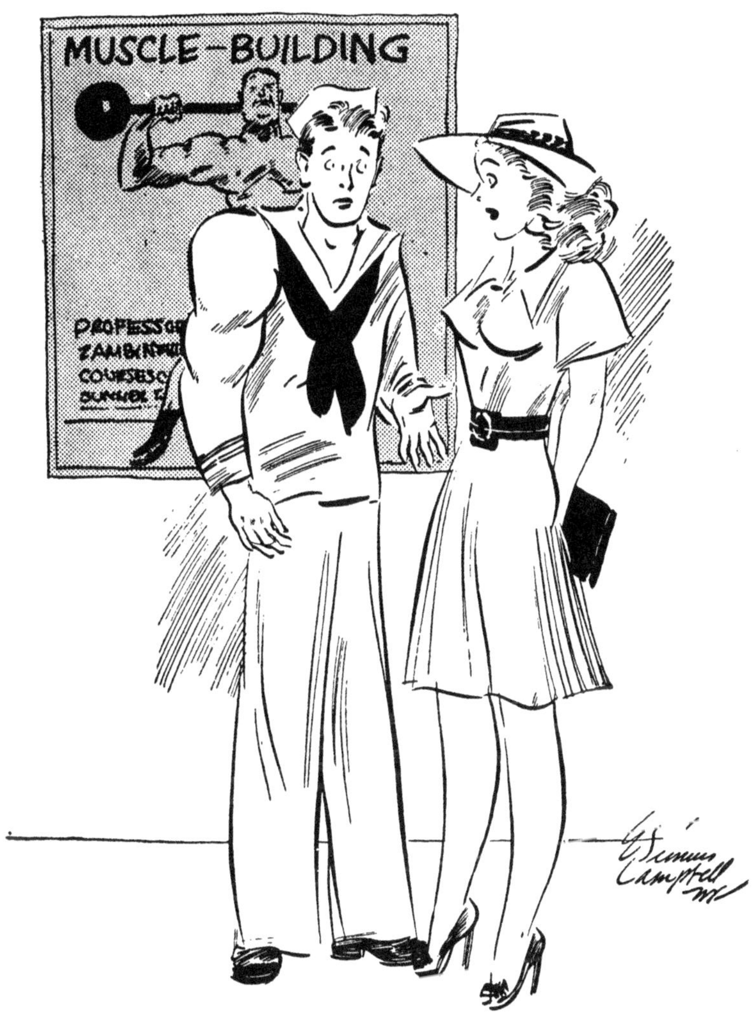

"Well, y'see, Mamie, I could only afford to take HALF the course!"

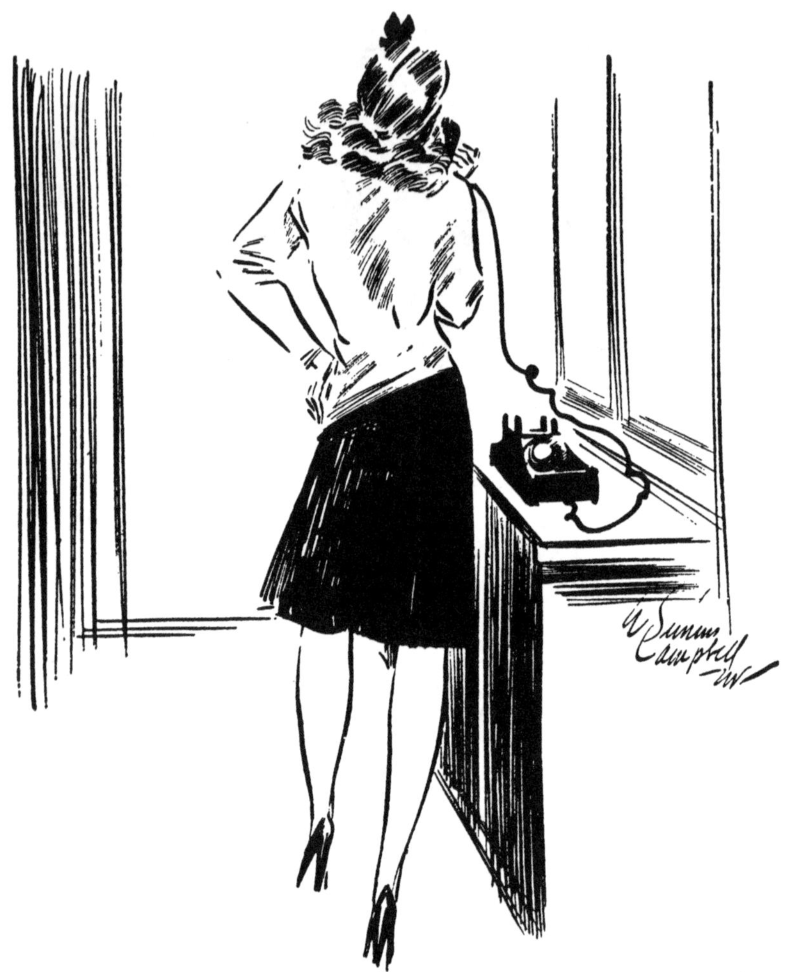

"Well, of course, if you've got pneumonia, I won't expect you tonight! But don't stand me up TOMORROW night!"

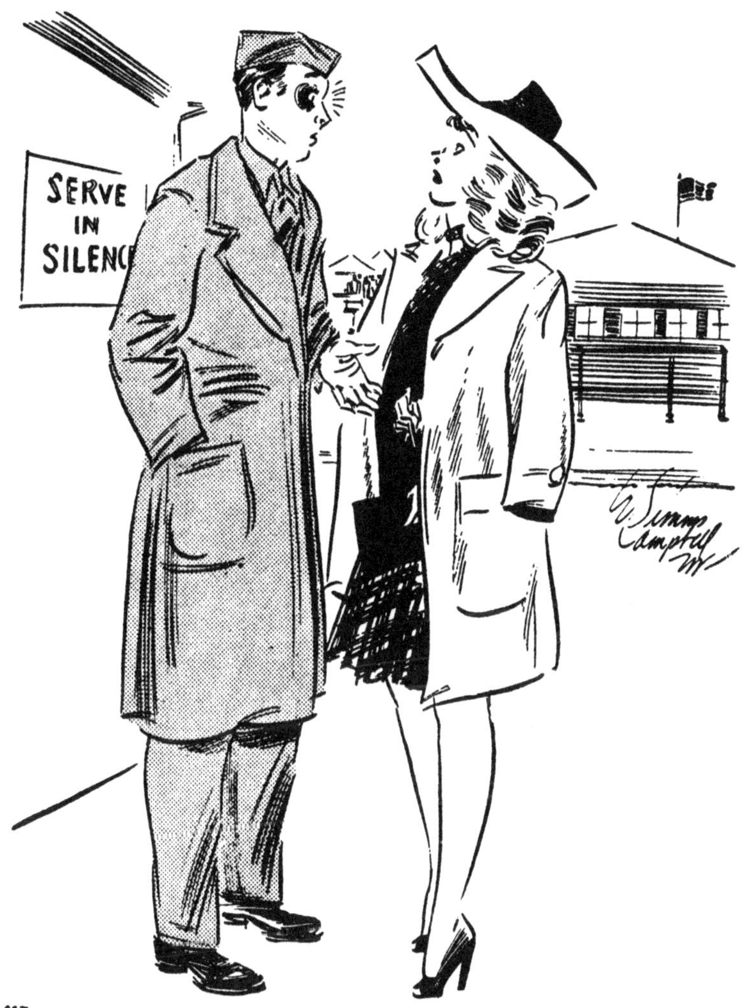

"I was simply saluting the shavetail, when I had to scratch my nose with my thumb!"

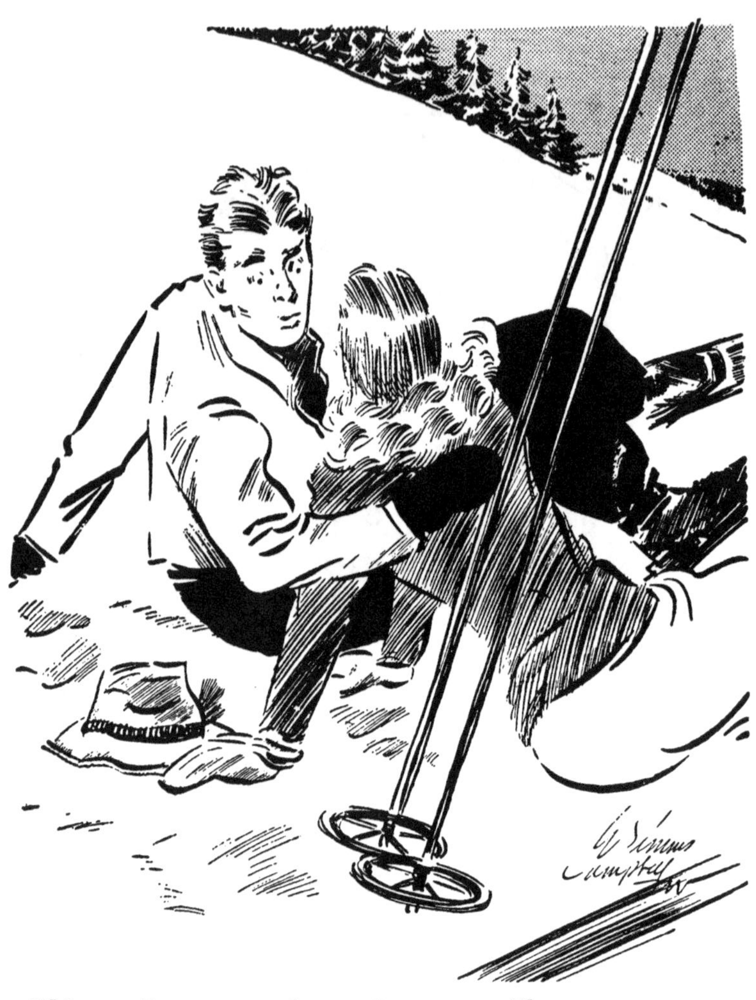

"My mother warned me about men like you . . . **you** darling!"

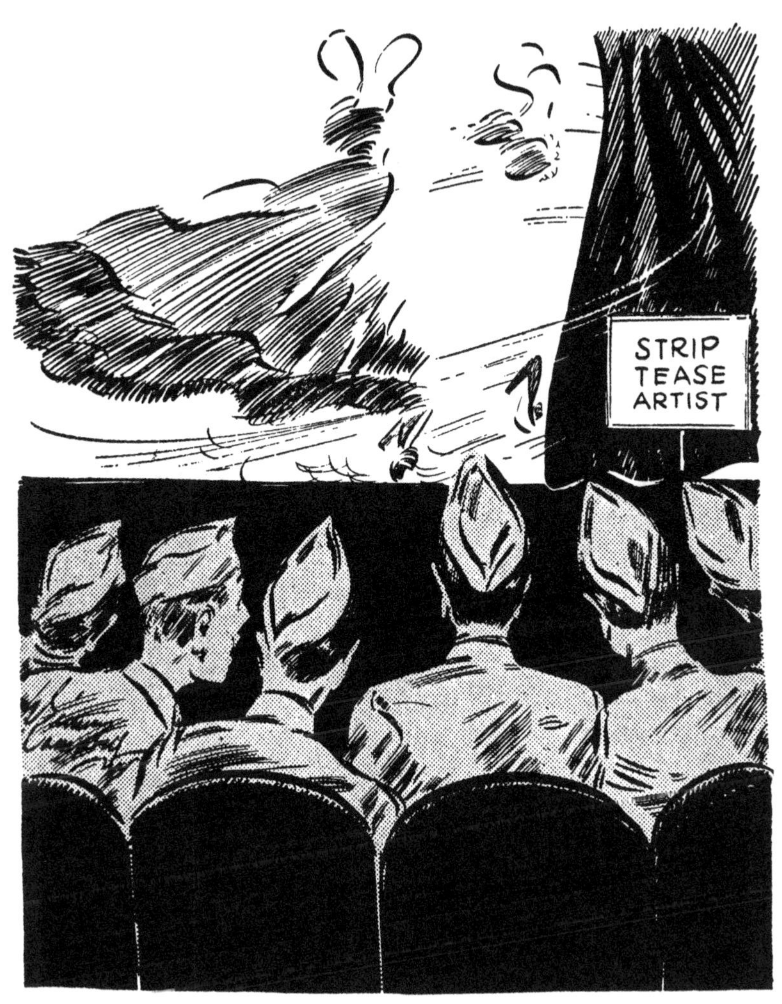

"She's a little TOO sensational!"

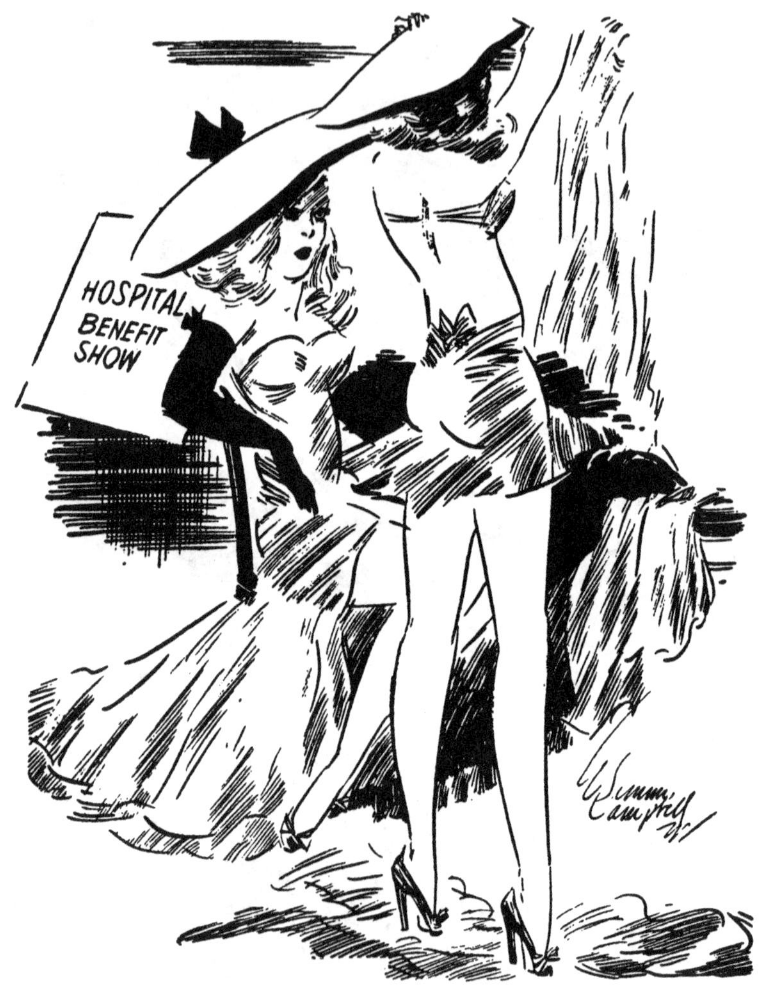

"I'm gonna faint at the benefit tonight. I think one of the internes likes me!"

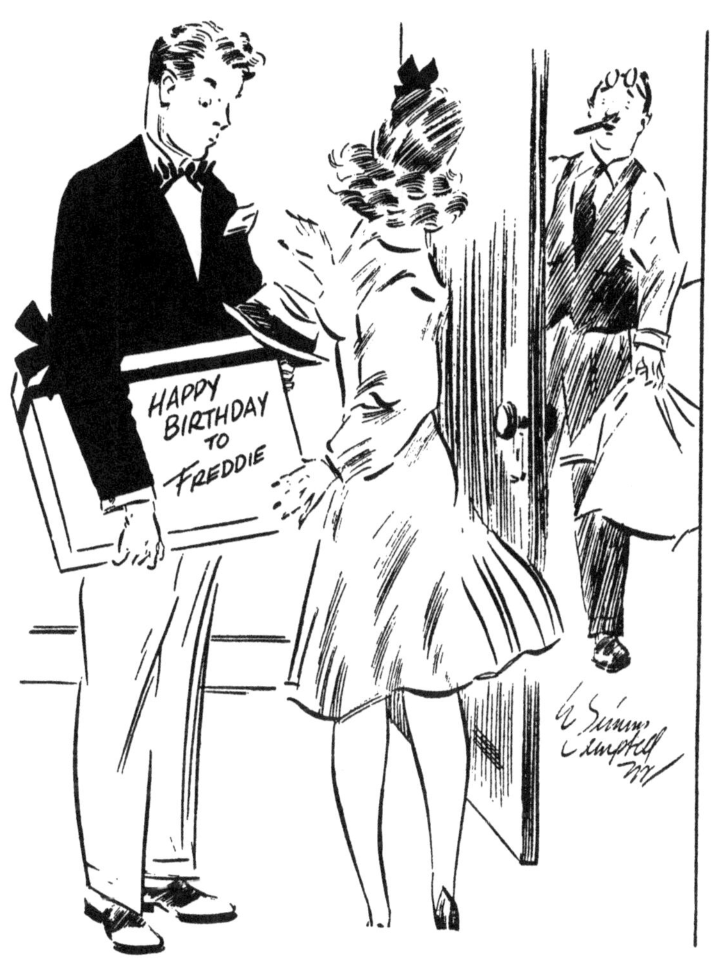

"It's chilly in here, daughter. Have you got that sweater the Army and Navy both returned to you?"

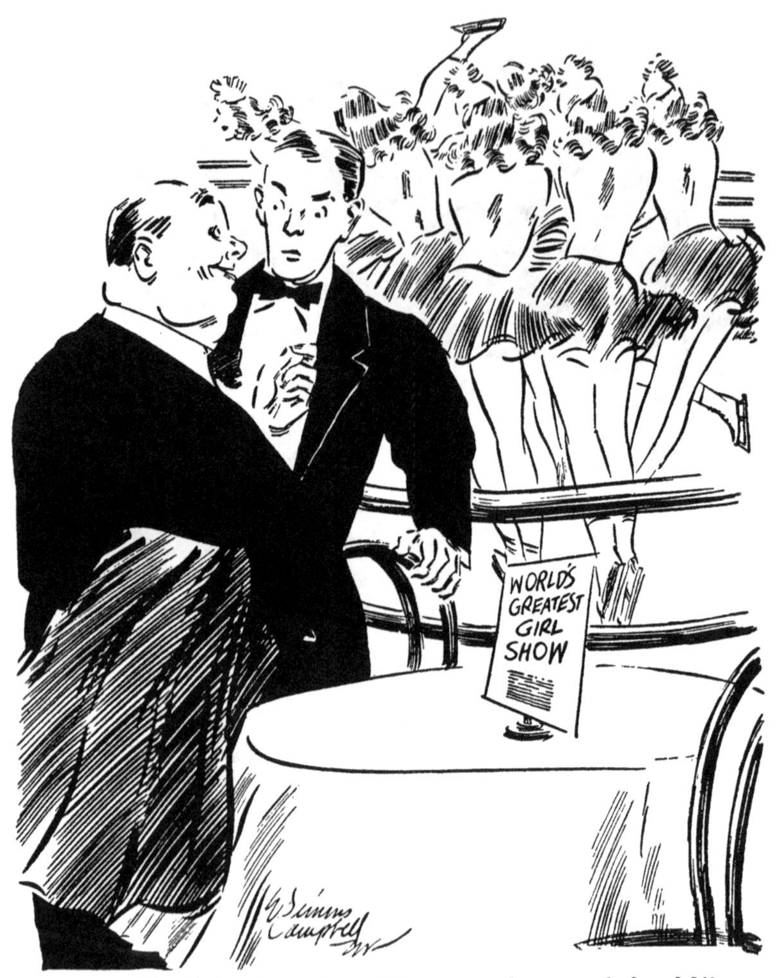

"Is this the place that has the good food?"

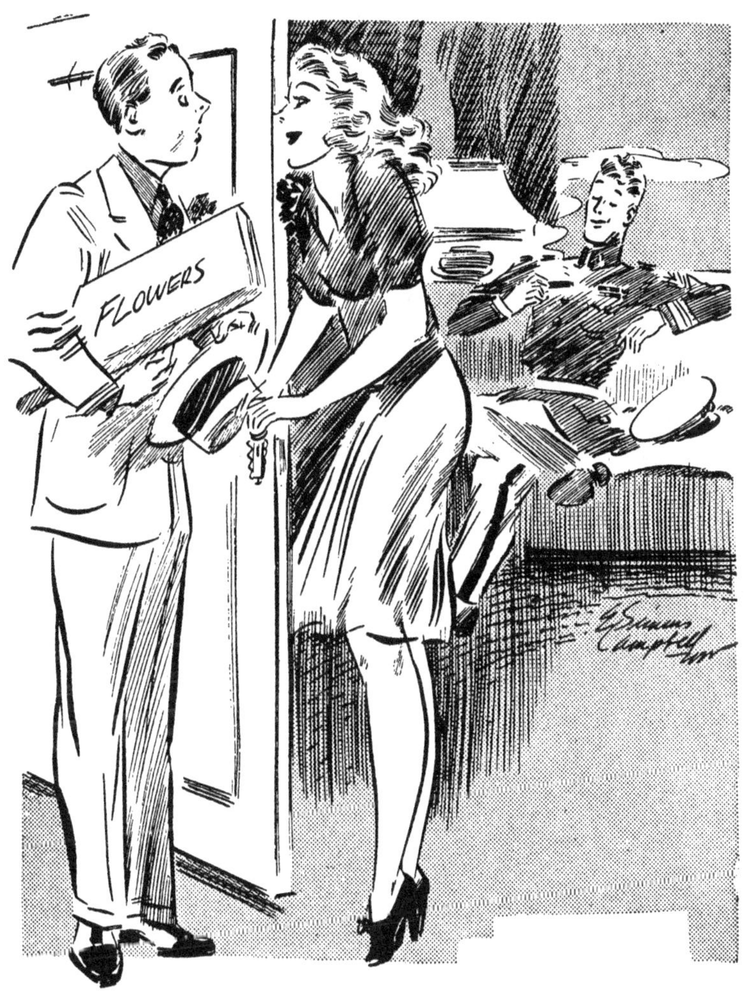

"I can't see you tonight, Tom. The Marines have landed and the situation is well in hand!"

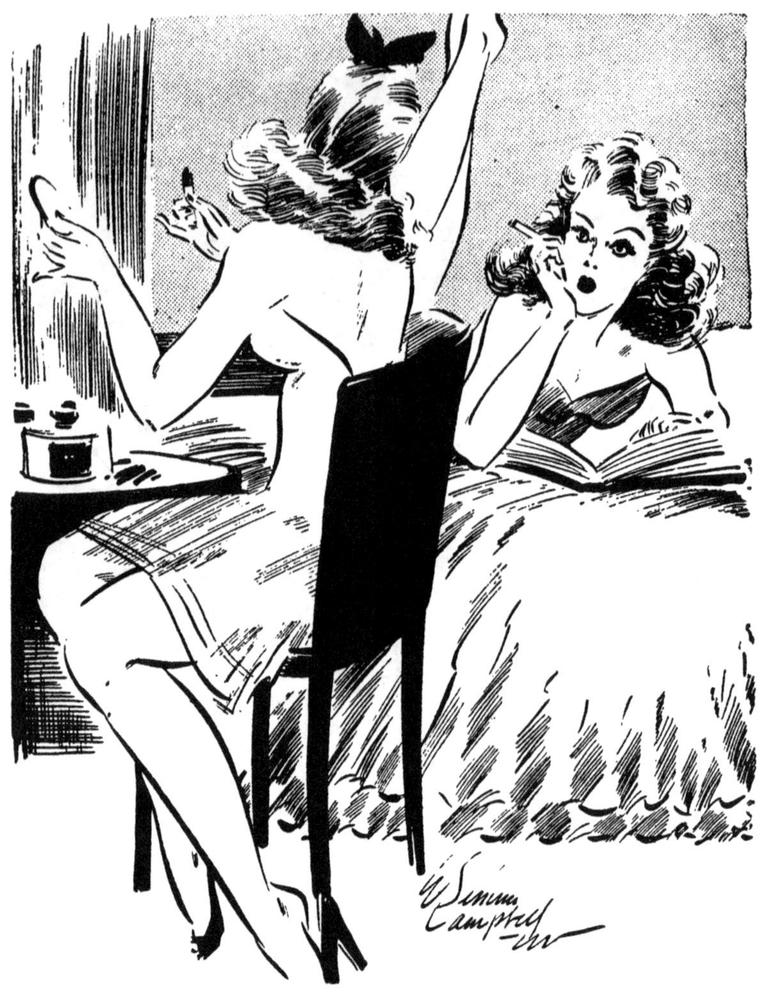

"I'll have to start putting make-up on at night! I meet the most wonderful men in my dreams!"

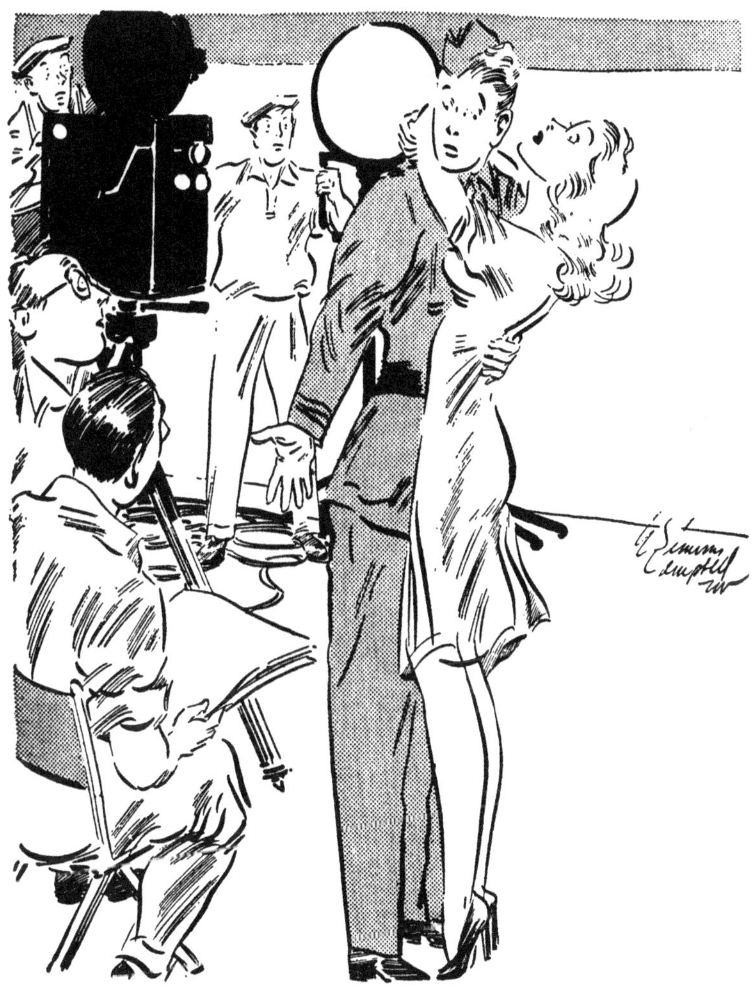

"I'm sorry, Mr. Brannick, but what do I do now?"

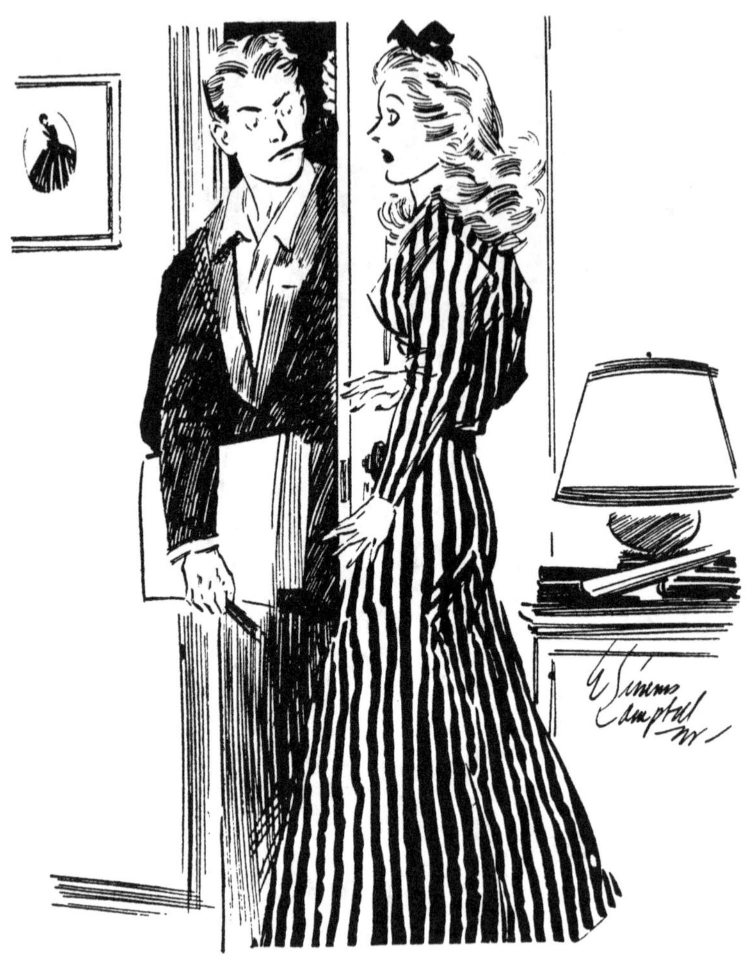

"—And DON'T come in to inspire me! I've got a heck of a lot of writing to do tonight!"

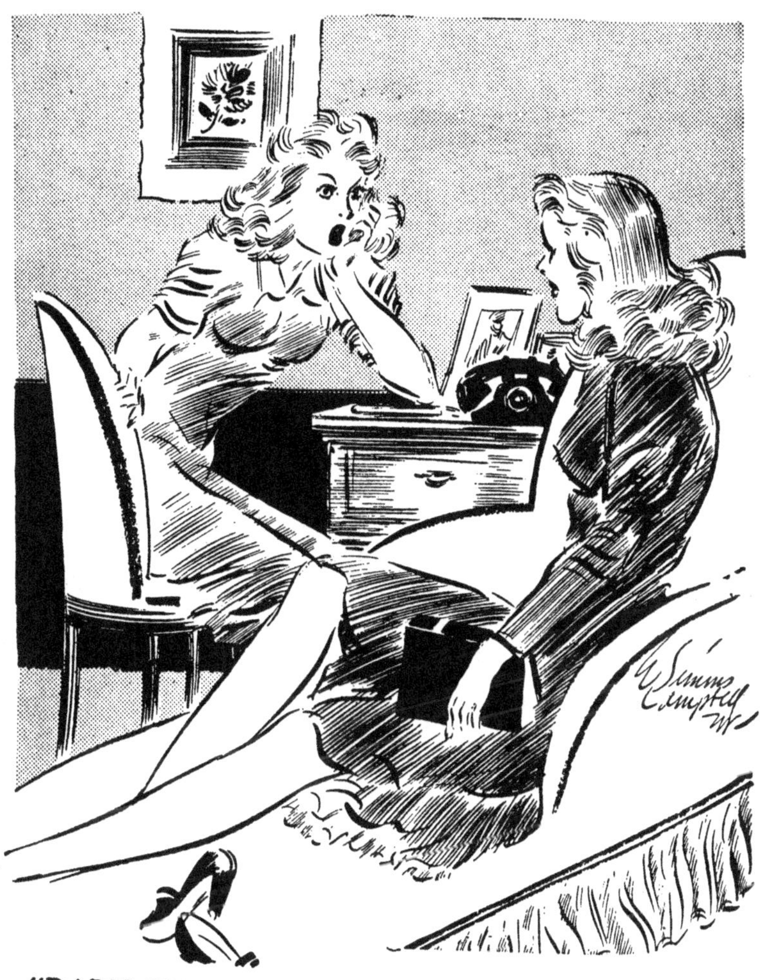

"DARN HITLER! Our 'phone was ALWAYS ringing before this war started!"

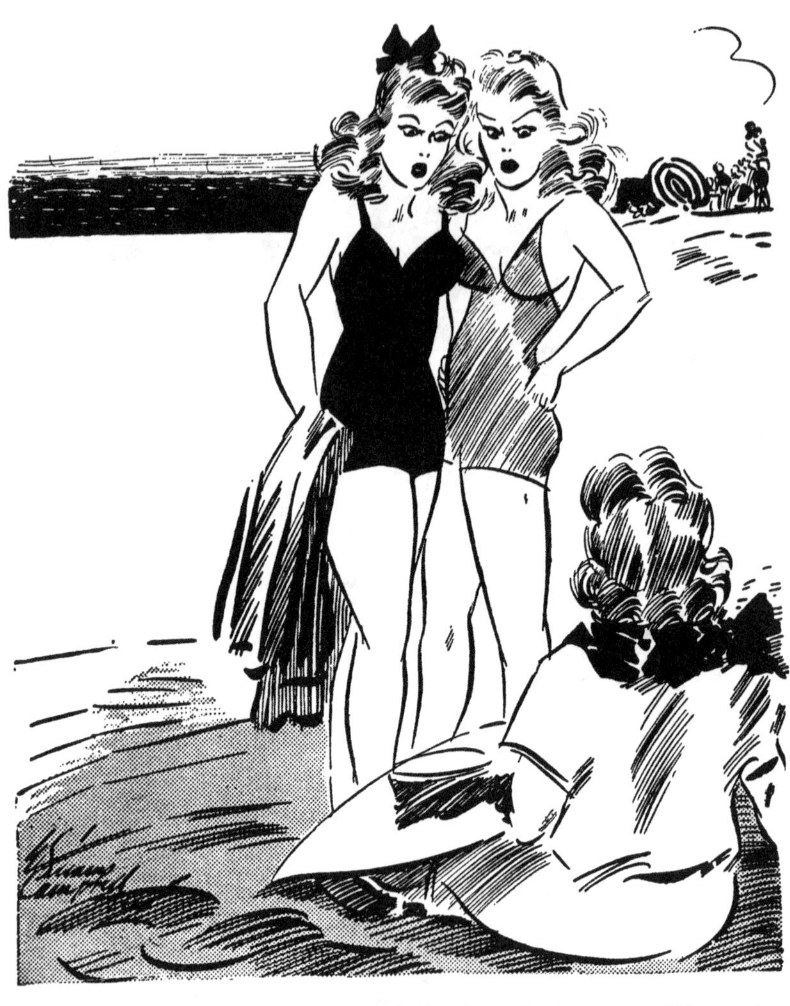

"What! Stay at this end of the beach, because it's cool and comfortable—with no men?"

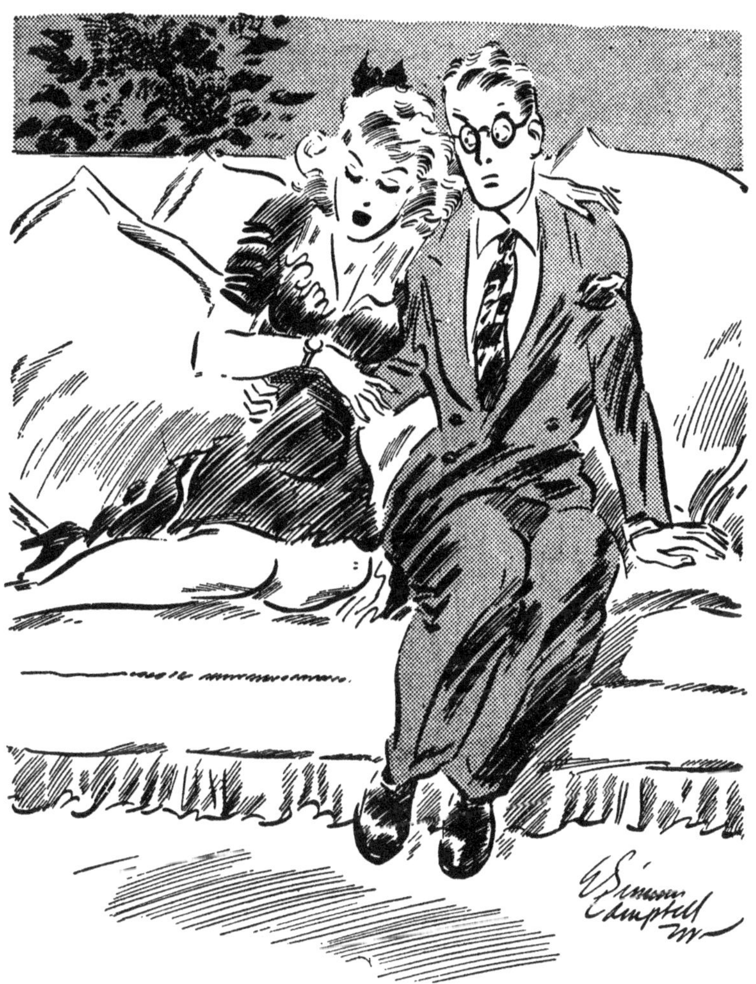

"You'll have to leave now, Henry. I promised Jack I'd be in bed every night by ten, while he's at camp."

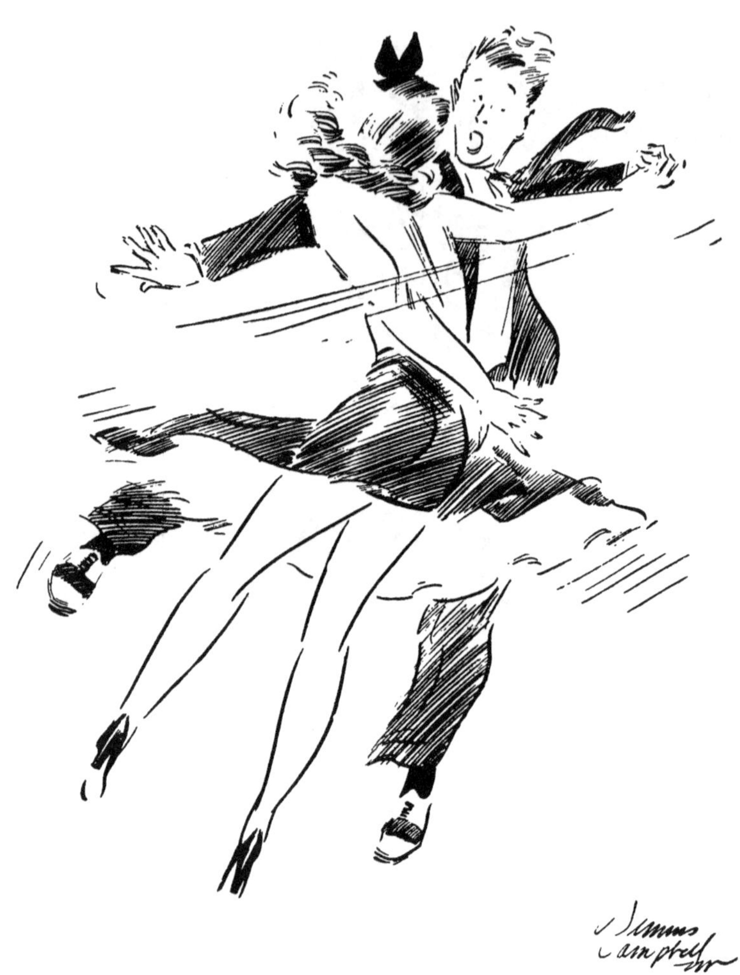

"Well, of all things—they're playin' a WALTZ!"

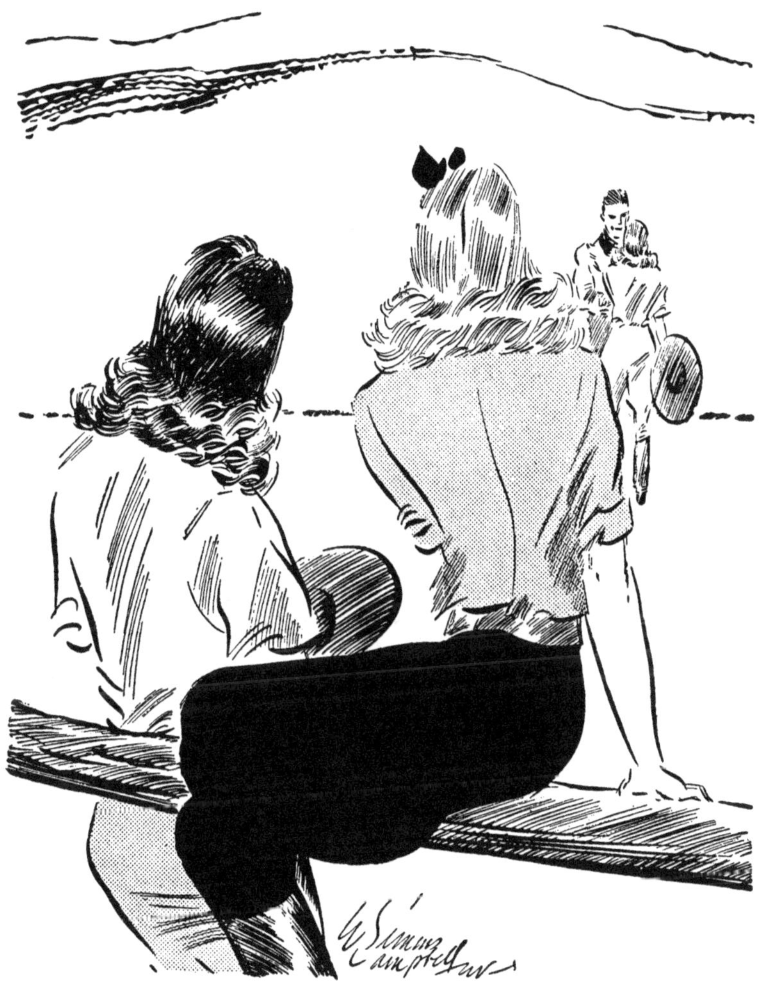

"She met him in a rather casual manner. She dropped her handkerchief in the park with her 'phone number on it!"

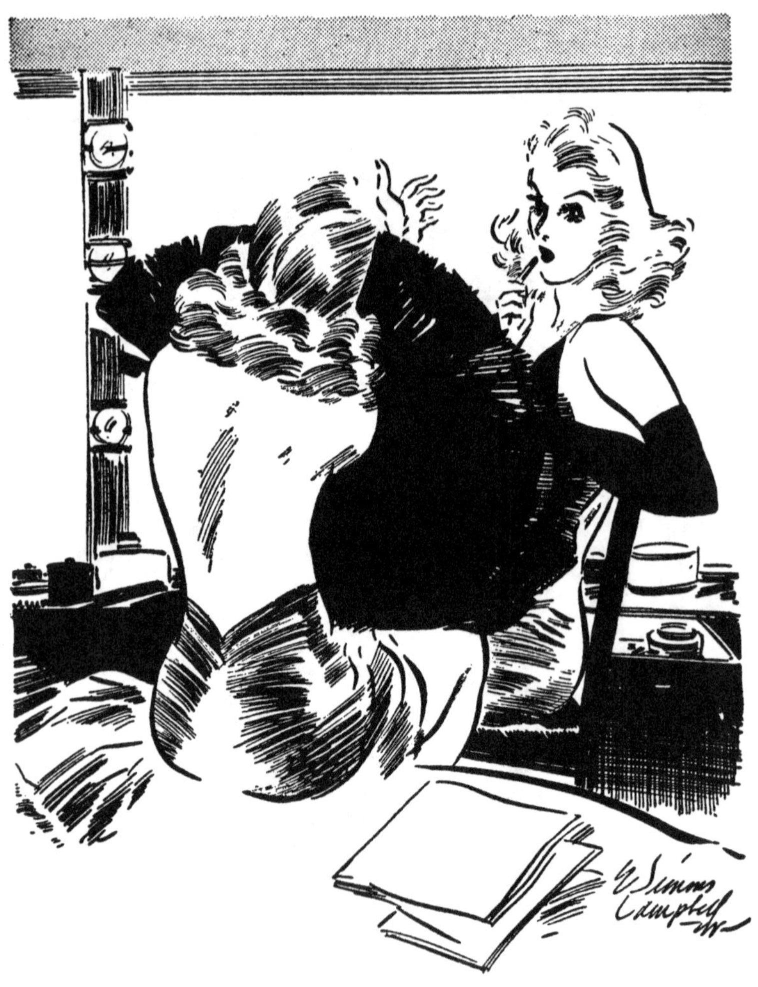

"My new boy friend is just like Tyrone Power—
WITHOUT the power!"

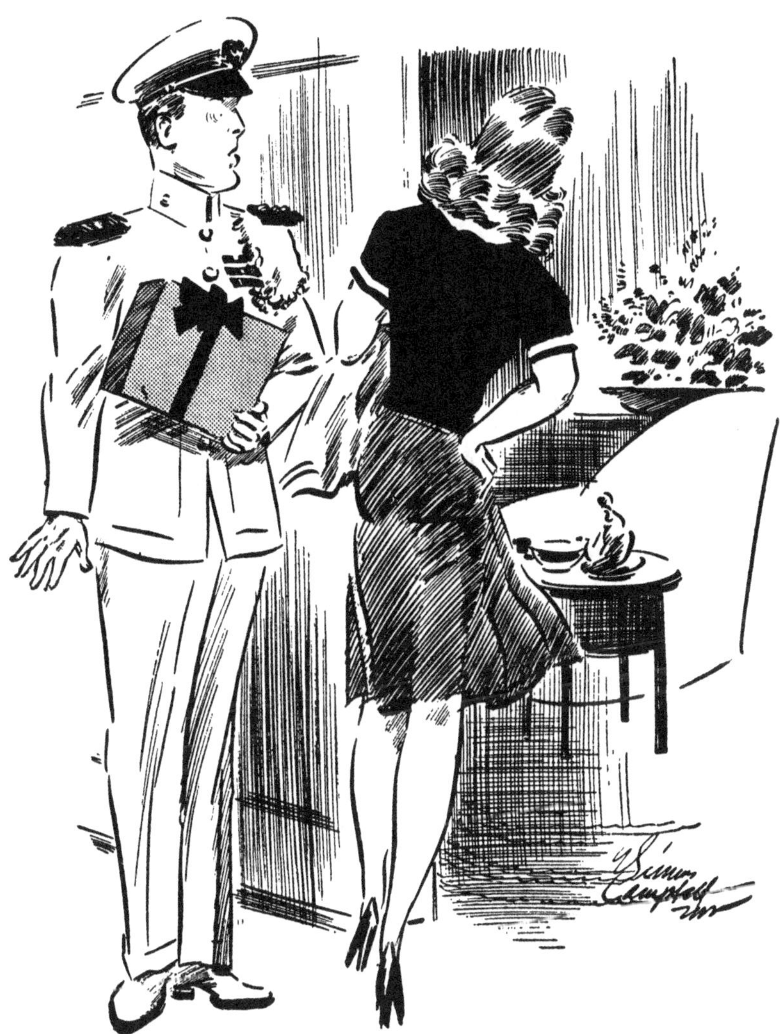

"Oh, Mabel! There's a gob here to see you."

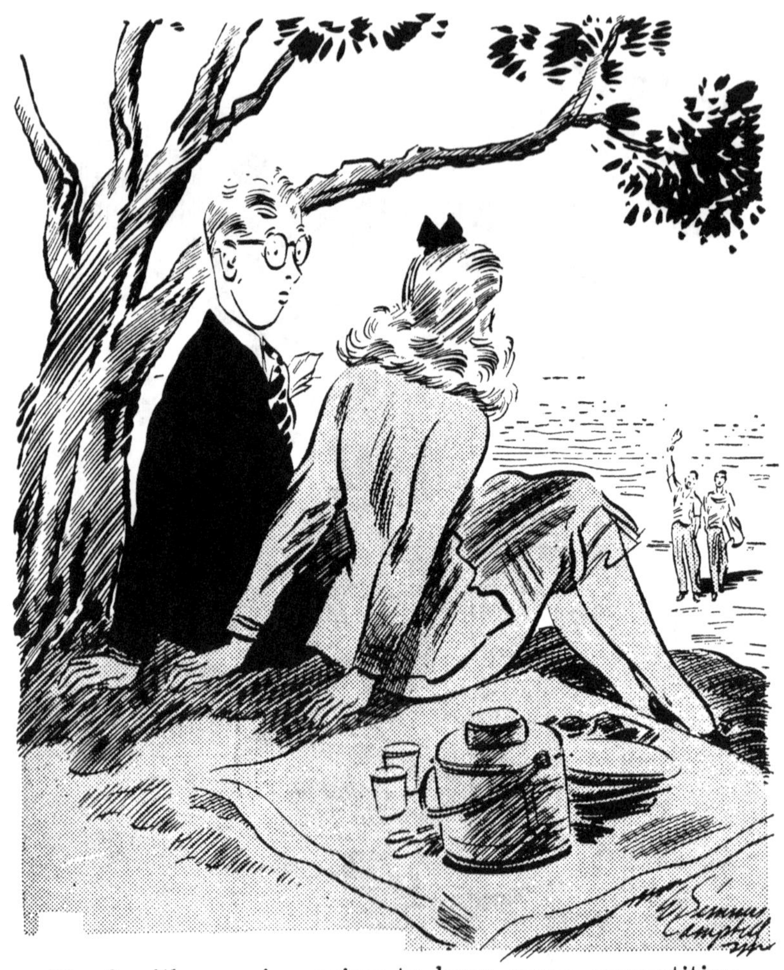

"Looks like you're going to have some competition, Clarence. Here come Joe and Harry, thank goodness."

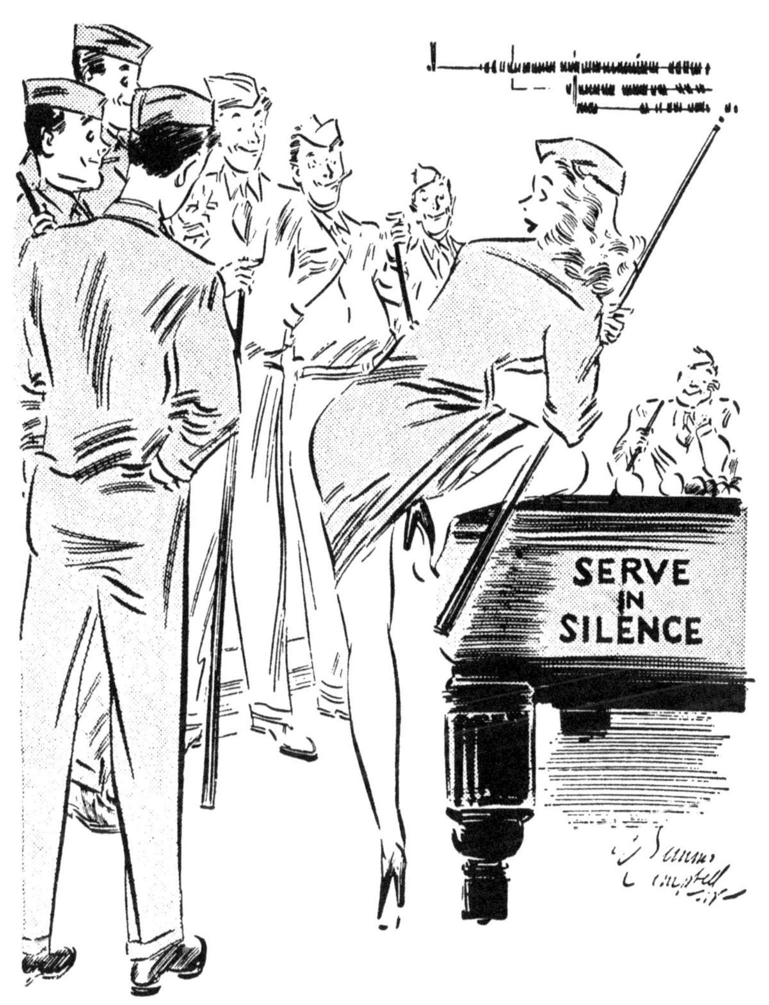

"Now don't be bashful. I want you boys to tell me, if I'm playing wrong!"

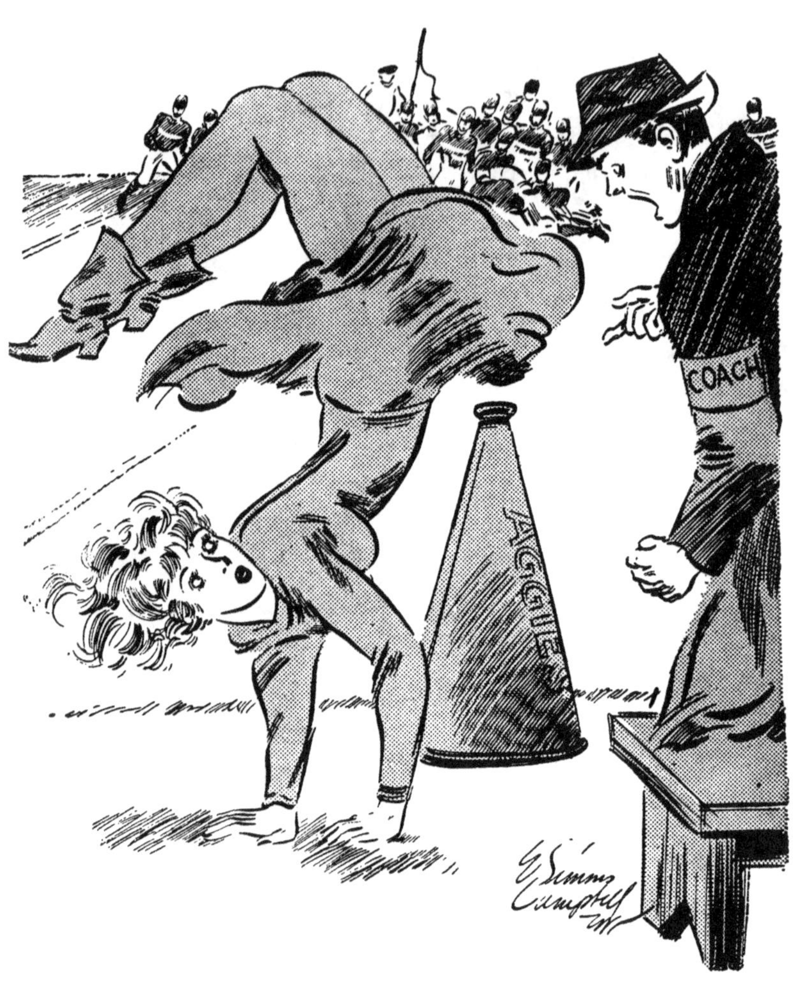

"Every time you do a cartwheel, we lose ten yards!"

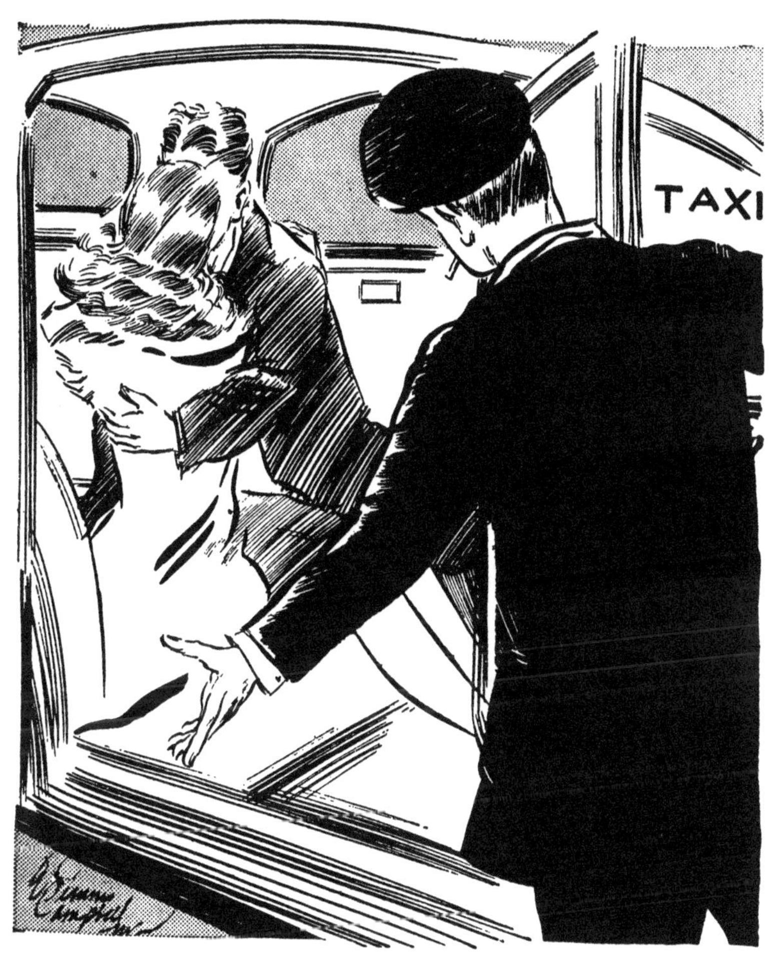

"Listen, I'm an air-raid warden! Don't you two HEAR them sirens?"

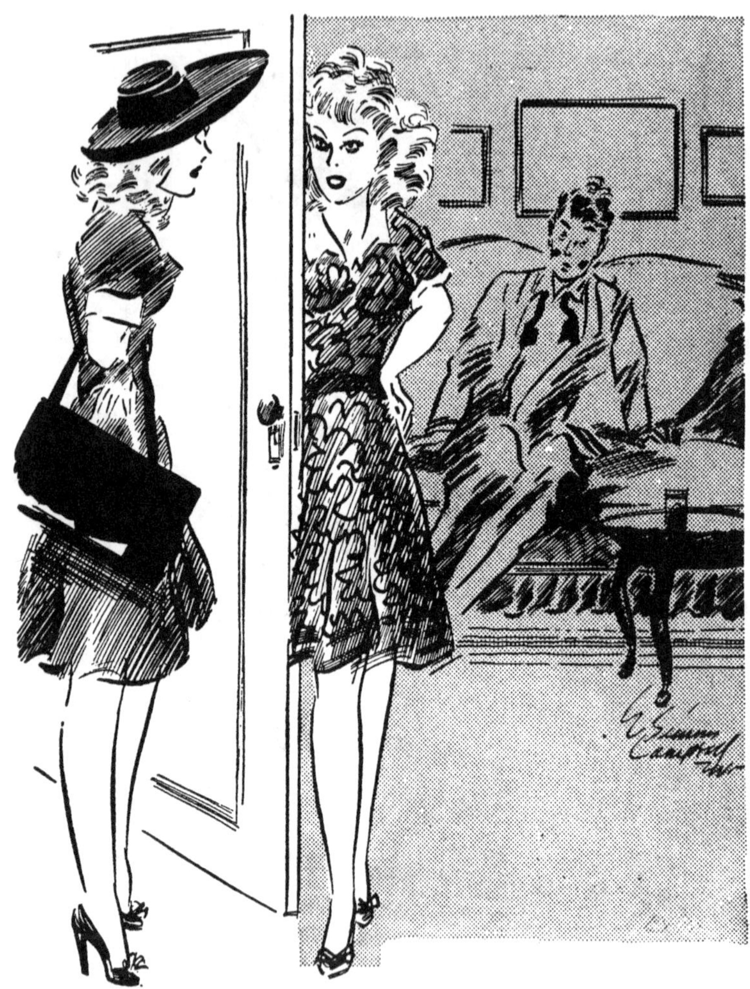

"Your boy friend called while you were out, darling, so I tried to entertain him like you would!"

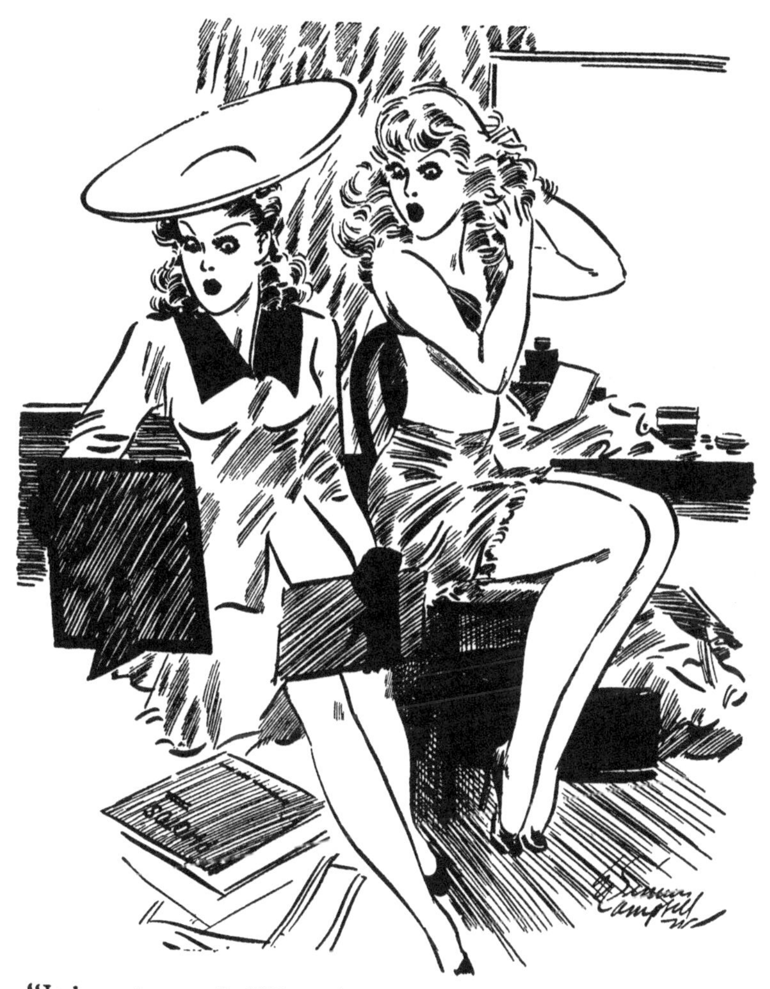

"Is he a tramp? Why, if he were battling the flu, everybody would root for the germs!"

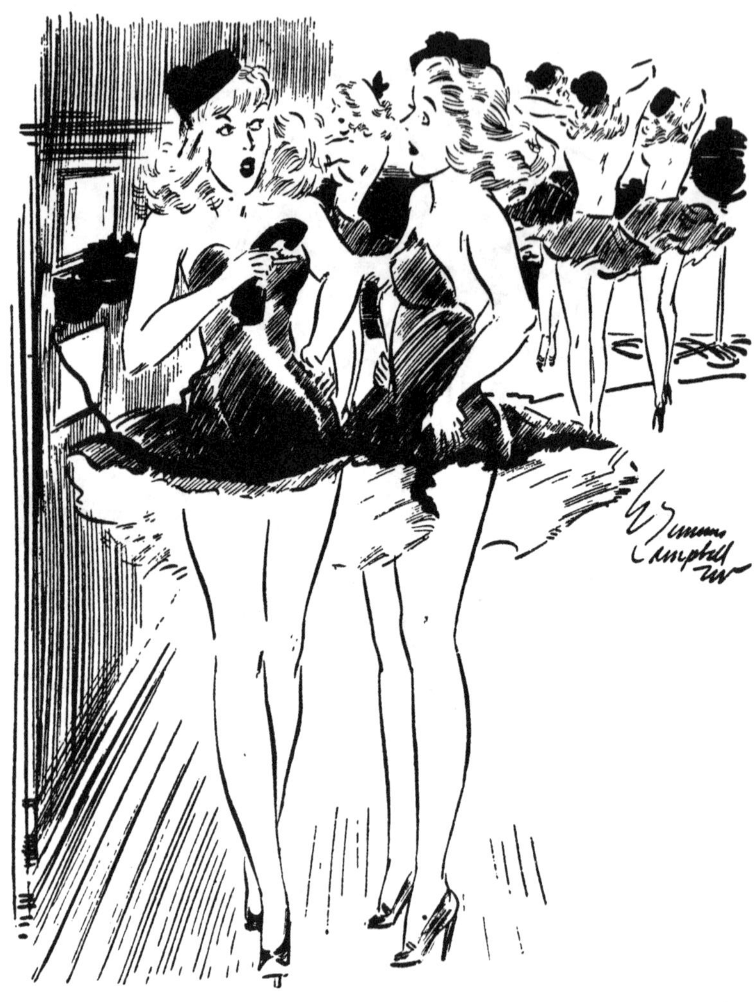

"What a husband! I left the baby's milk formula right on top of the breakfast dishes. If he'd have cleaned the kitchen, he'd have found it!"

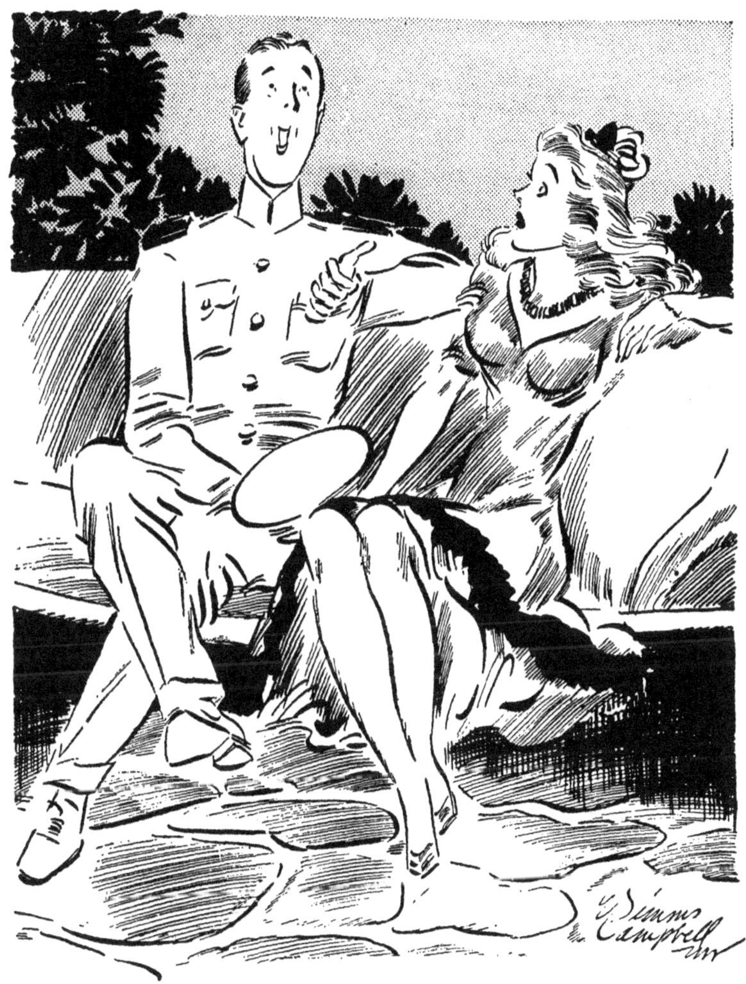

"What a gorgeous night, Miss Jones. Have you got a telescope?"

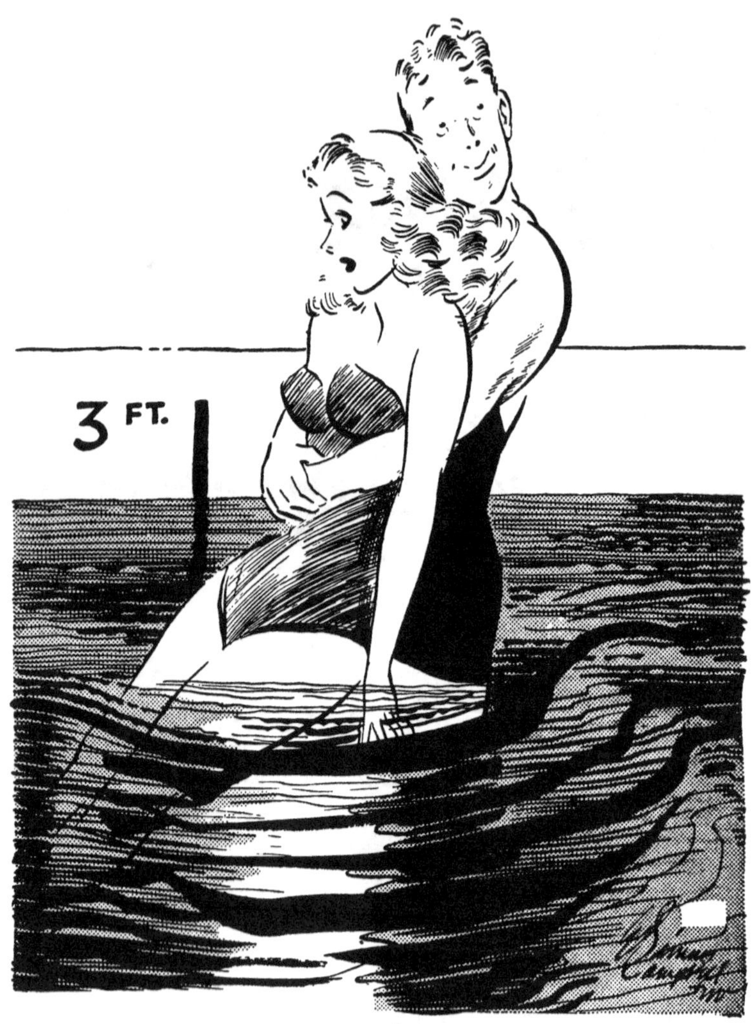

"But if you don't let me in the water, Mr. Ferguson, how am I going to learn to swim?"

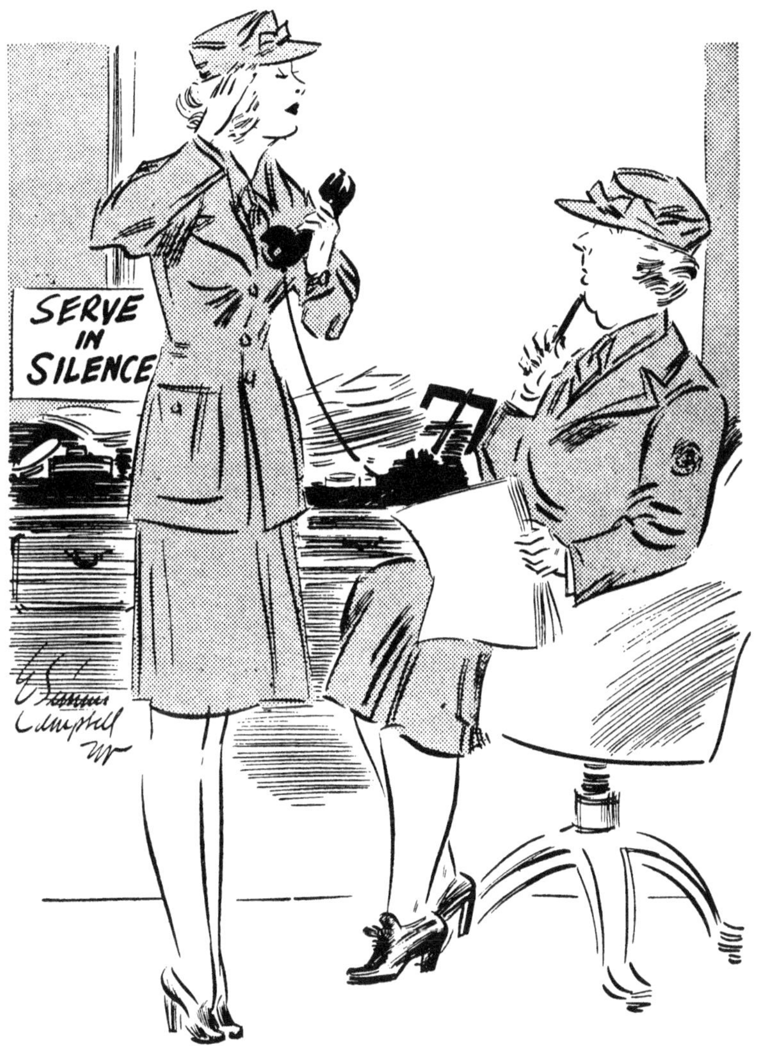

"Your husband said when you're through feeding 15,000 recruits, he'd appreciate your coming home and feeding the family!"

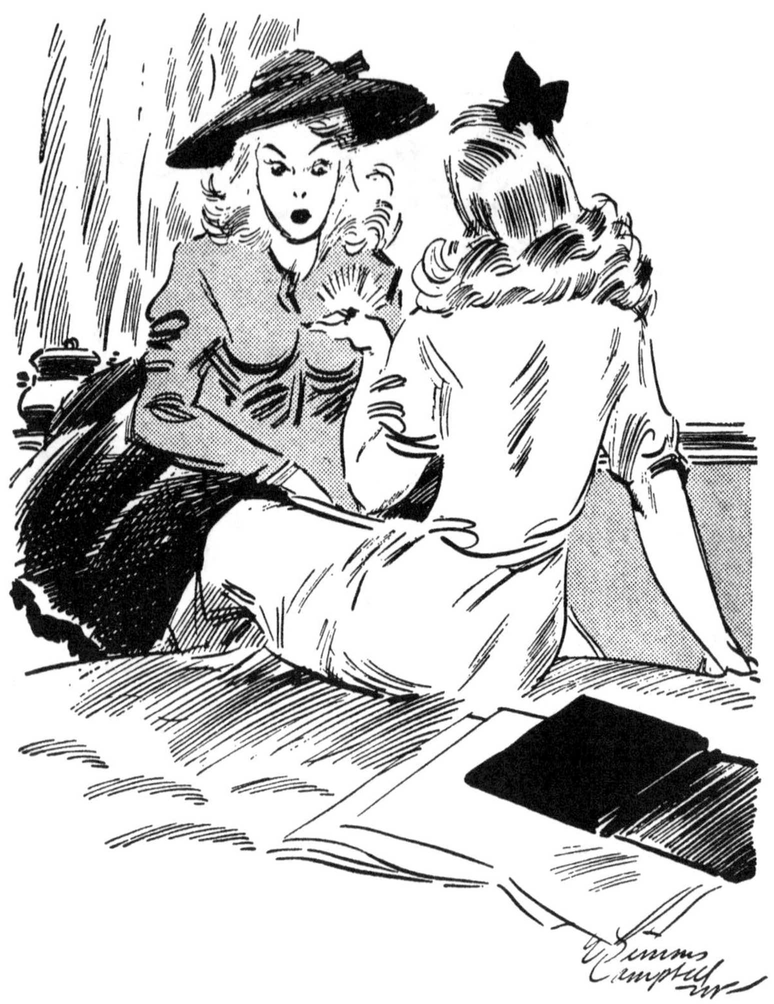

"I was never more embarrassed in my life. I was just about to slap him, when he gave me this ring!"

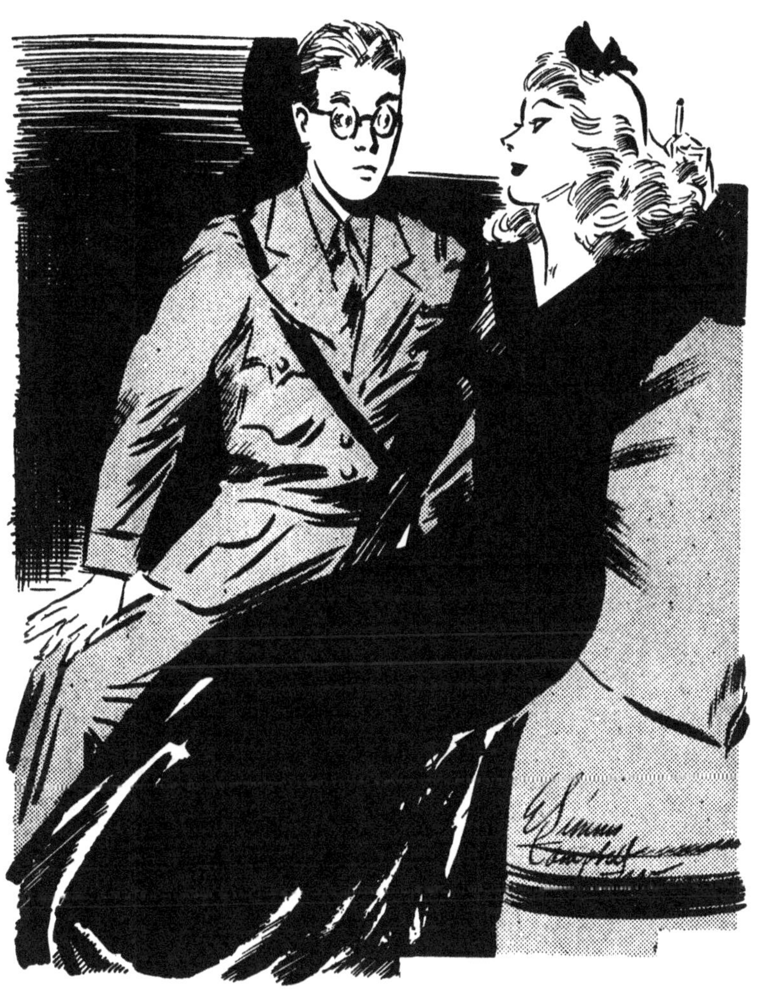

"I'm rationing my kisses. You'll have to get a card, just like the other fellows do!"

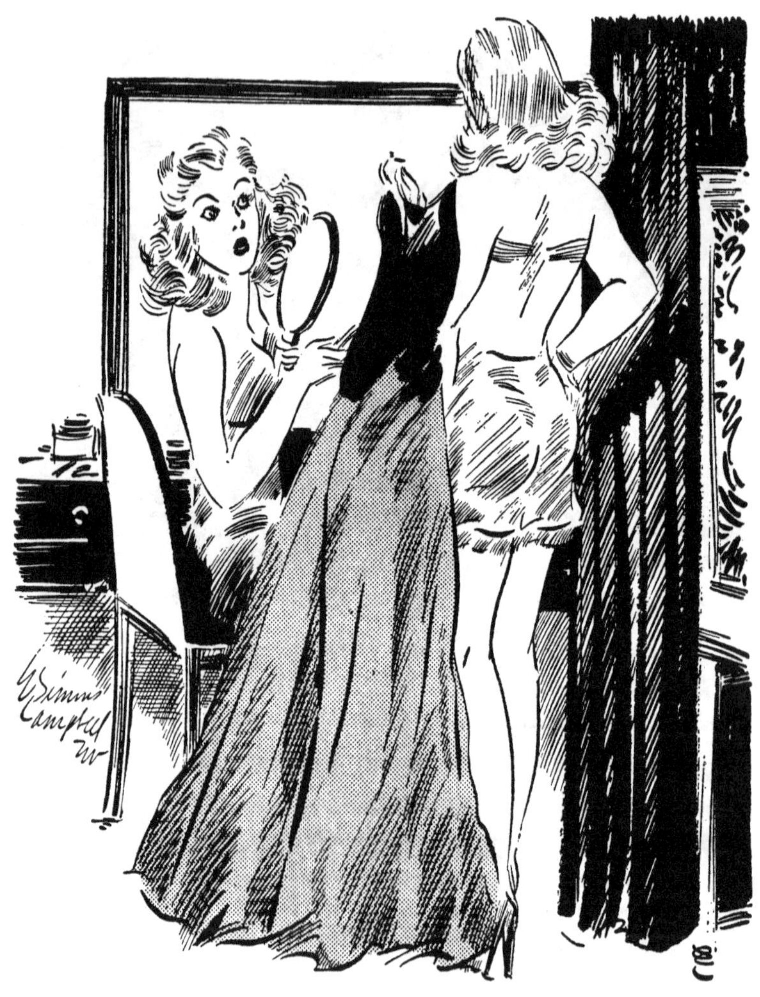

"If I wear my hostess gown, he might propose, and then again he might just want to sit in the house all evening!"

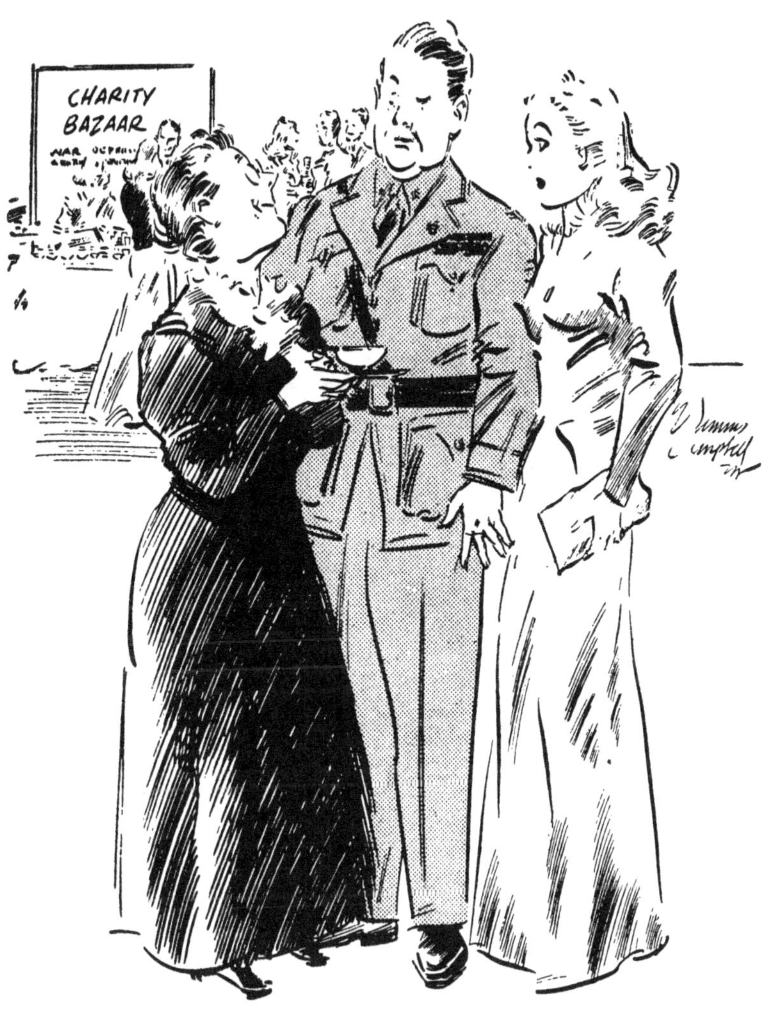

"My, but it's nice to see so many young men joining up. Even YOU are in the service, Colonel!"

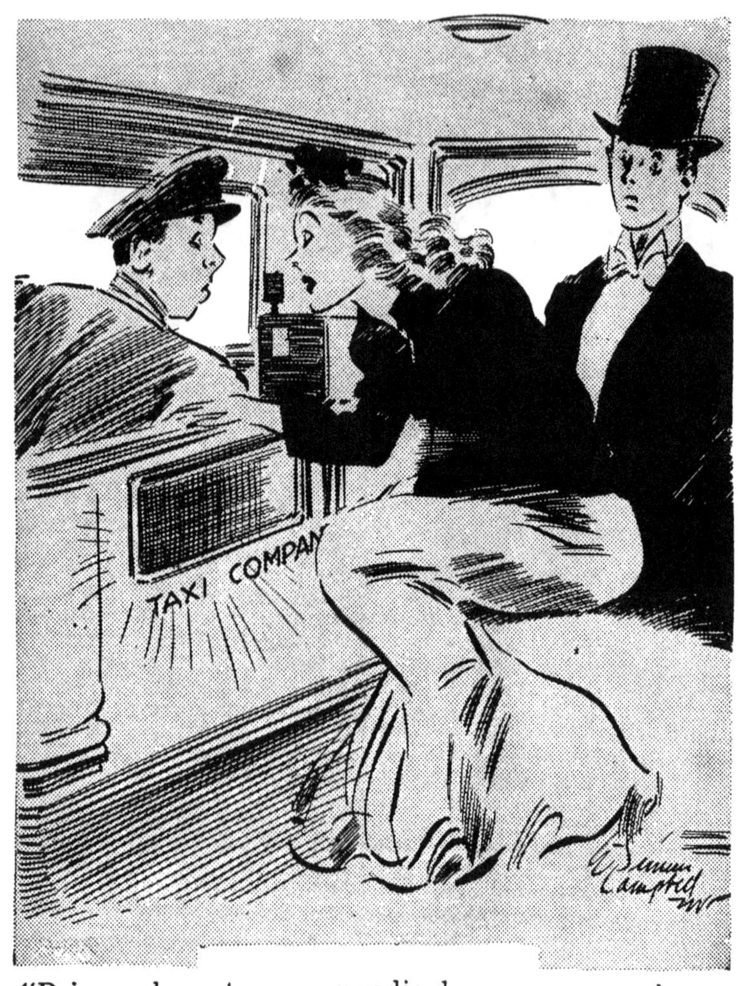

"Driver, please tune your radio down so you can hear me if I should yell for help!"

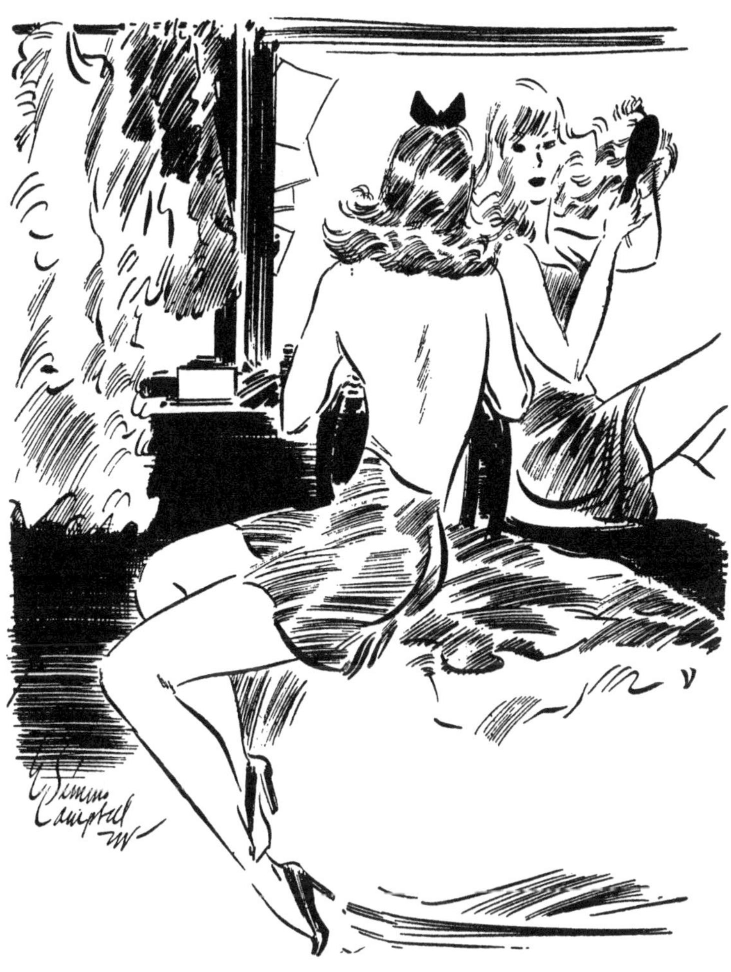

"I don't mind the shortage of men. It's the surplus of women that has me worried!"

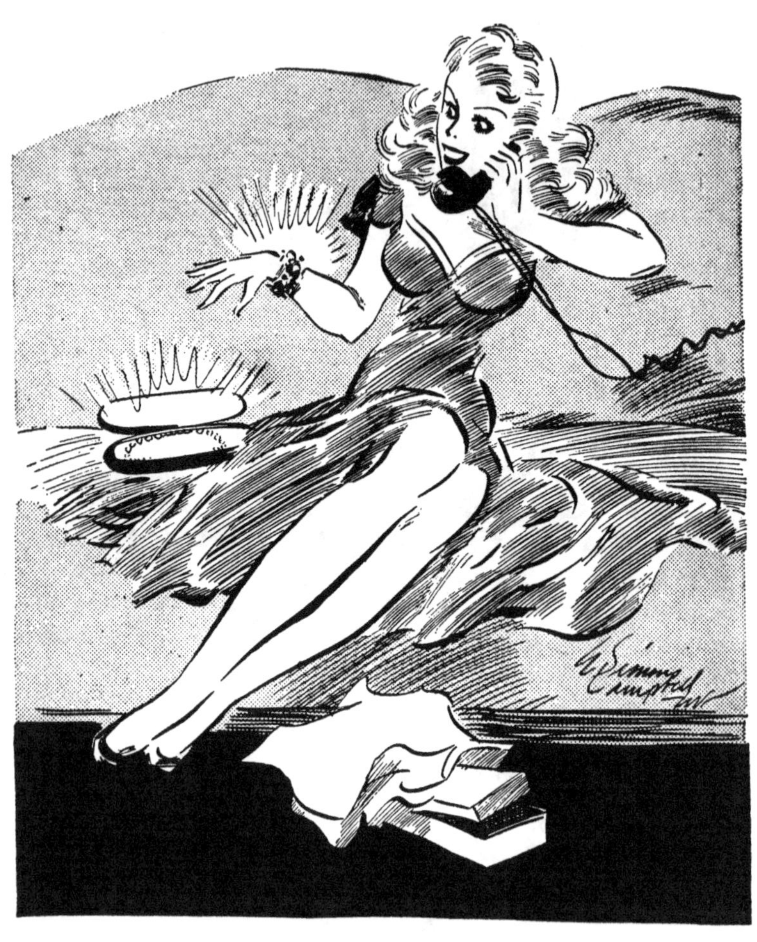

"Stop worrying. I'll let you know when I'm in love with you. Just keep on sending gifts like this!"

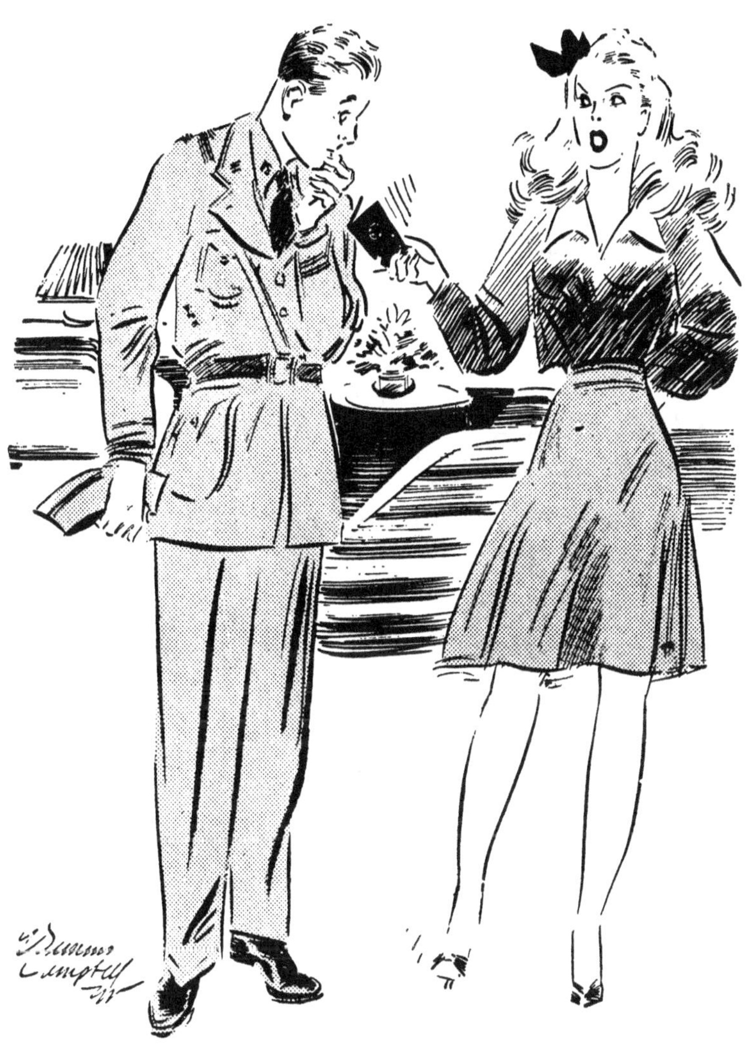

"—And I suppose this list of telephone numbers you forgot last night is a CODE, huh?"

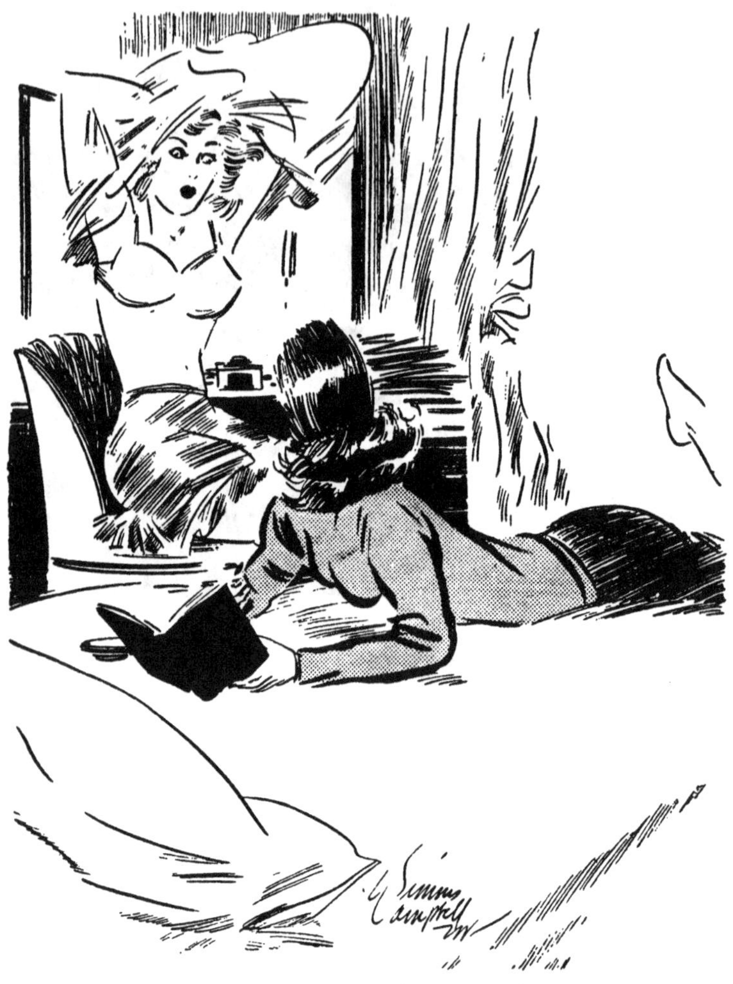

"What a book! For fifteen chapters they go together and when he kisses her, she SLAPS him!"

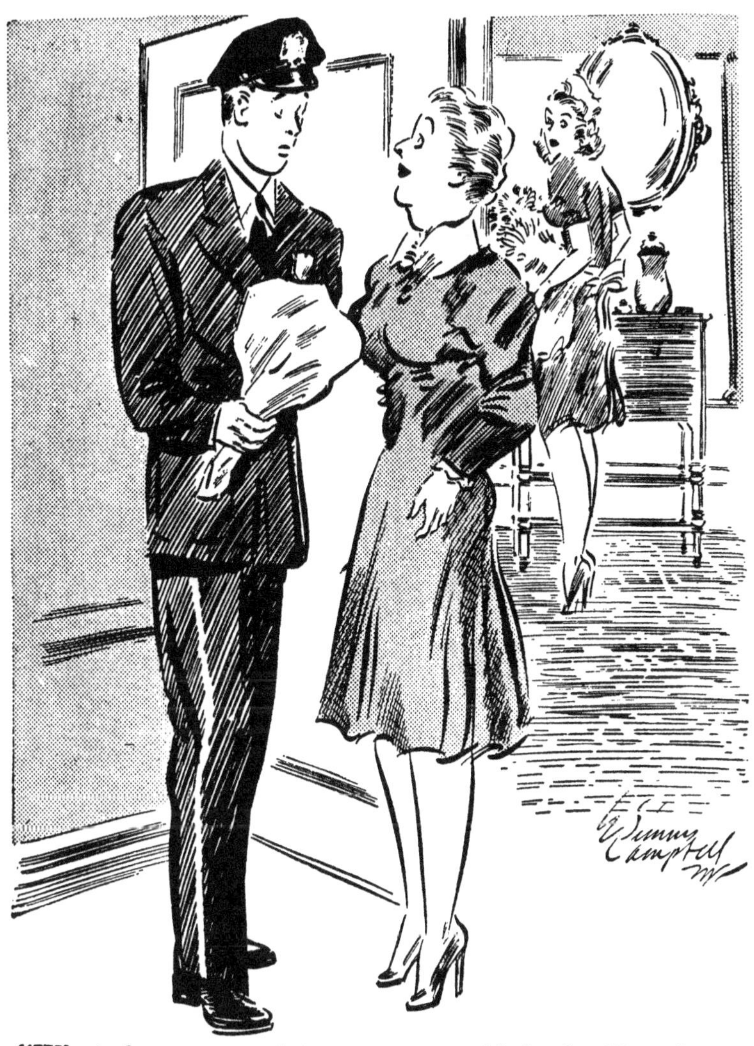

"What do you want to see my maid for? Has she done something, or is it love?"

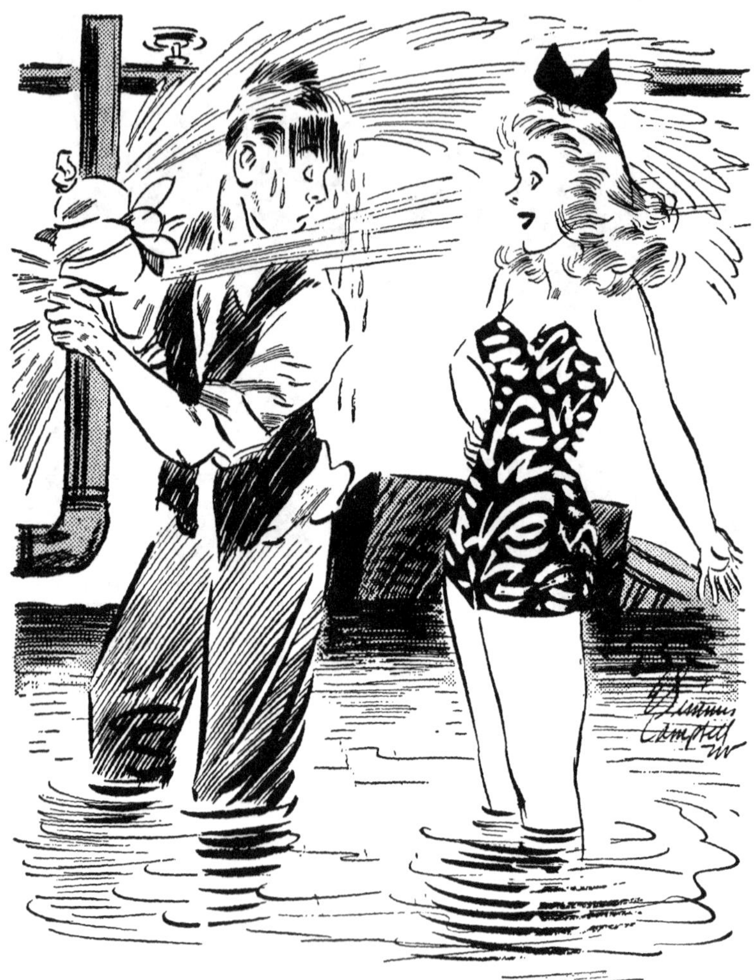

"I decided to slip on my bathing suit, dear. We've no idea when that plumber will get here."

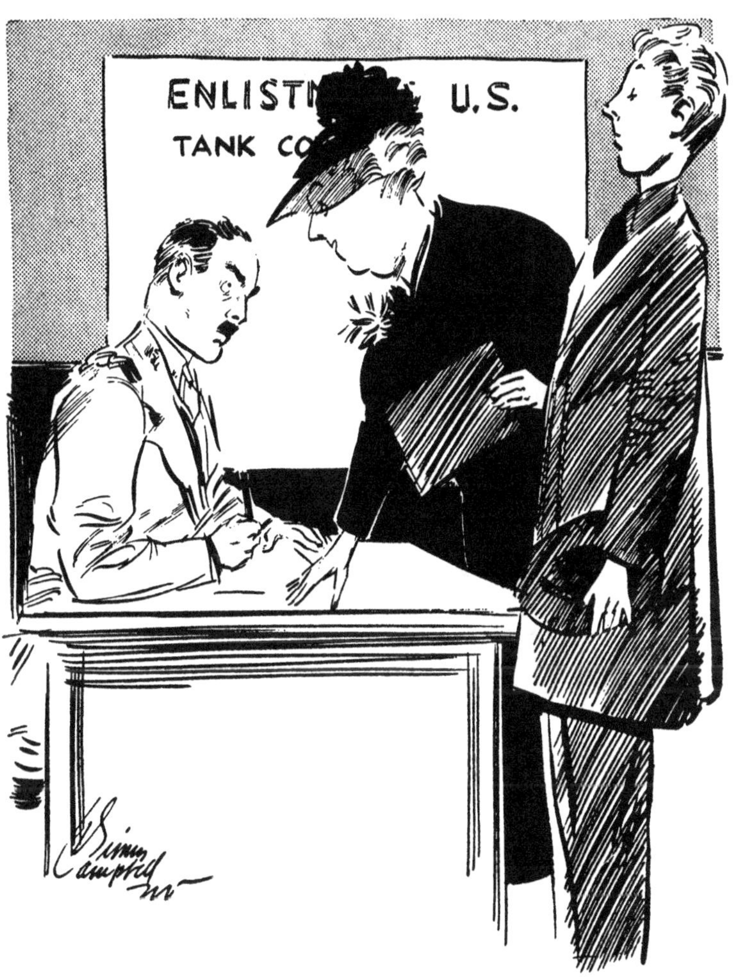

"Oh, and another thing, Colonel, Elwood is awfully fussy about his eggs at breakfast!"

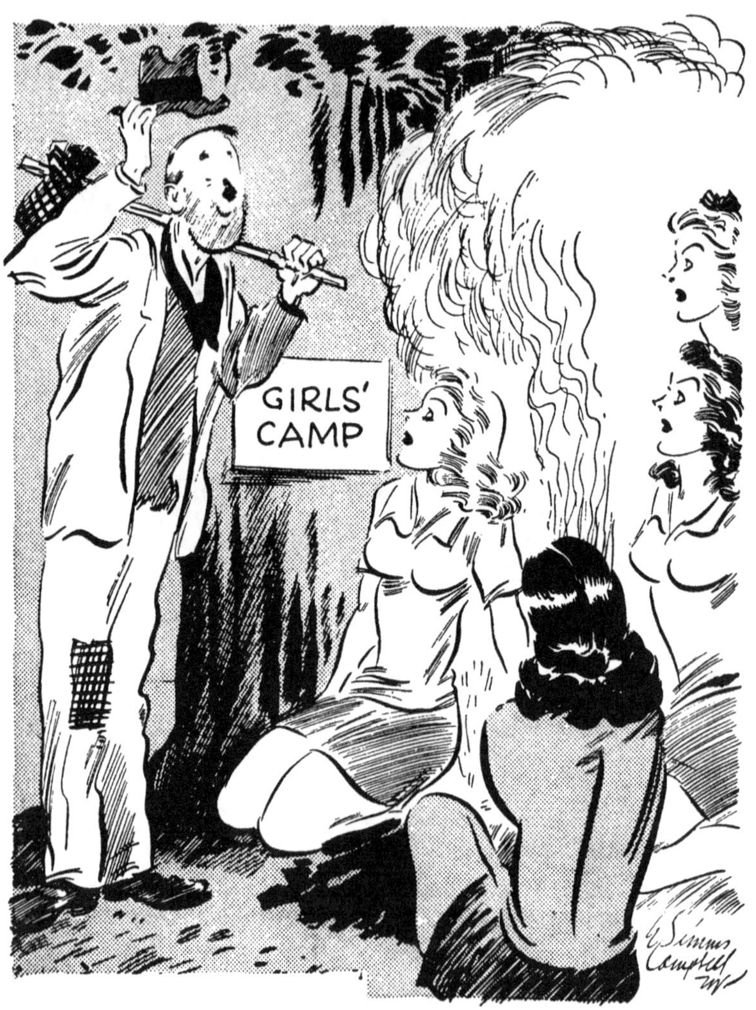

"Ahem—May I join you ladies? I see we're both interested in the same thing—the great outdoors."

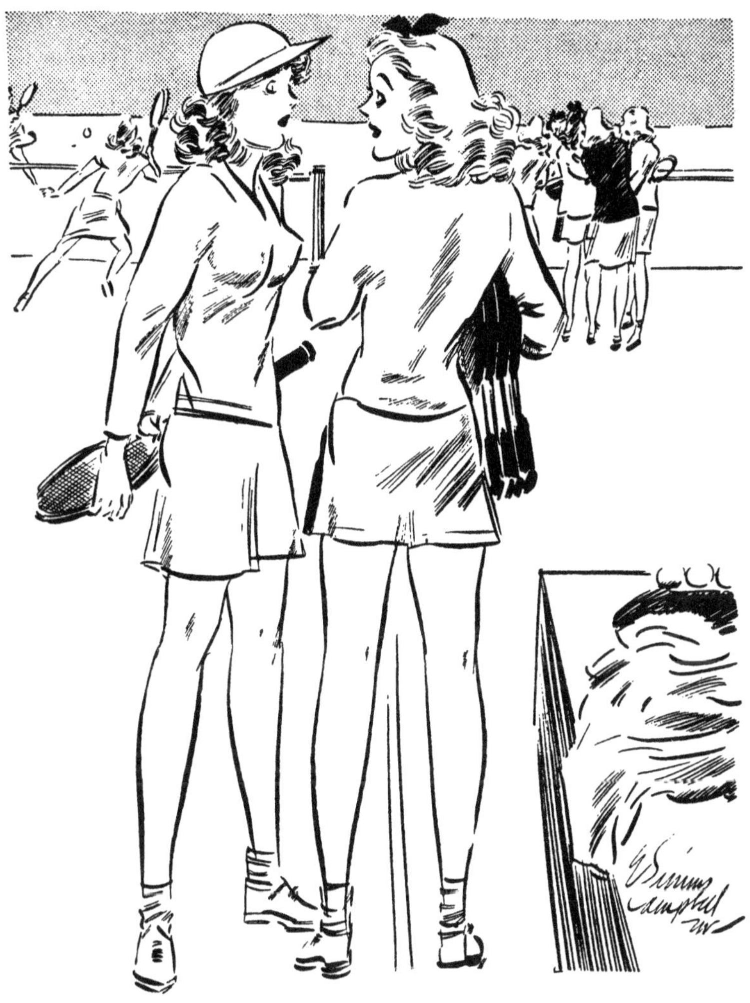

"I always loved tennis, but with so many women on the courts this year, it's not very interesting!"

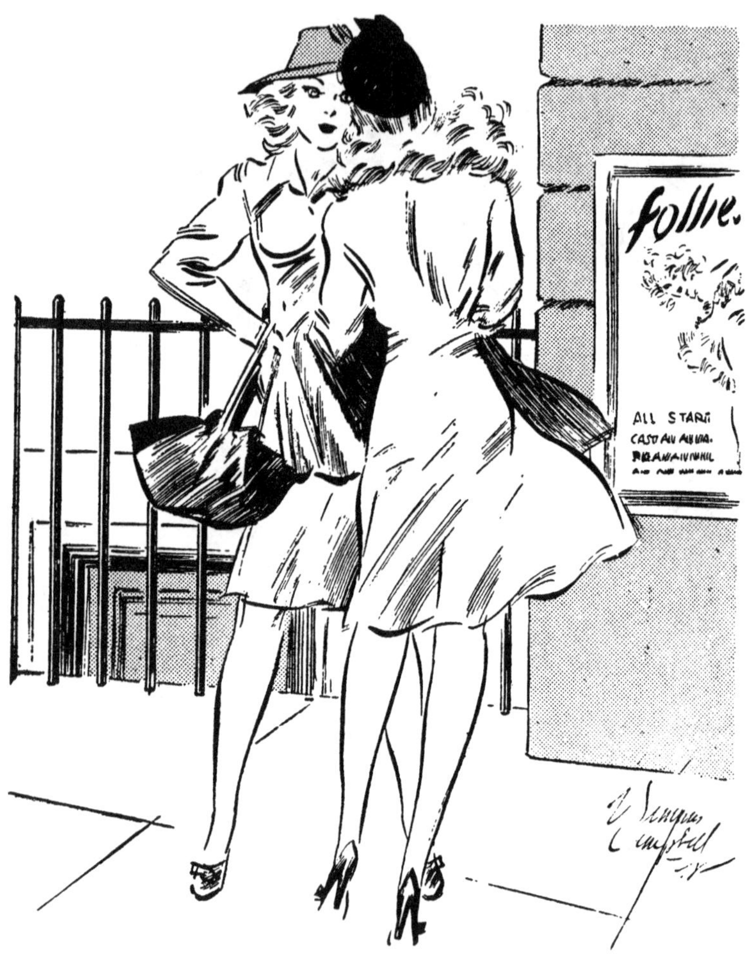

"—So I told him, 'Listen, I've been in show business five years and with my figure, I don't HAVE to know how to act!' "

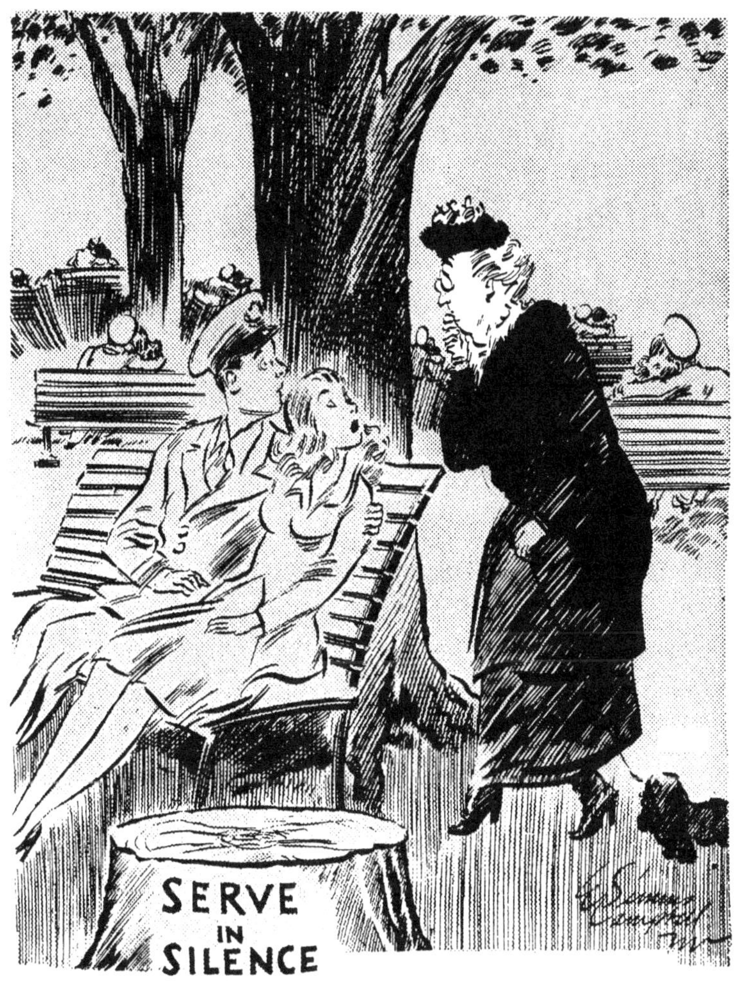

"Oh, I beg your pardon. I didn't know this was a military zone!"

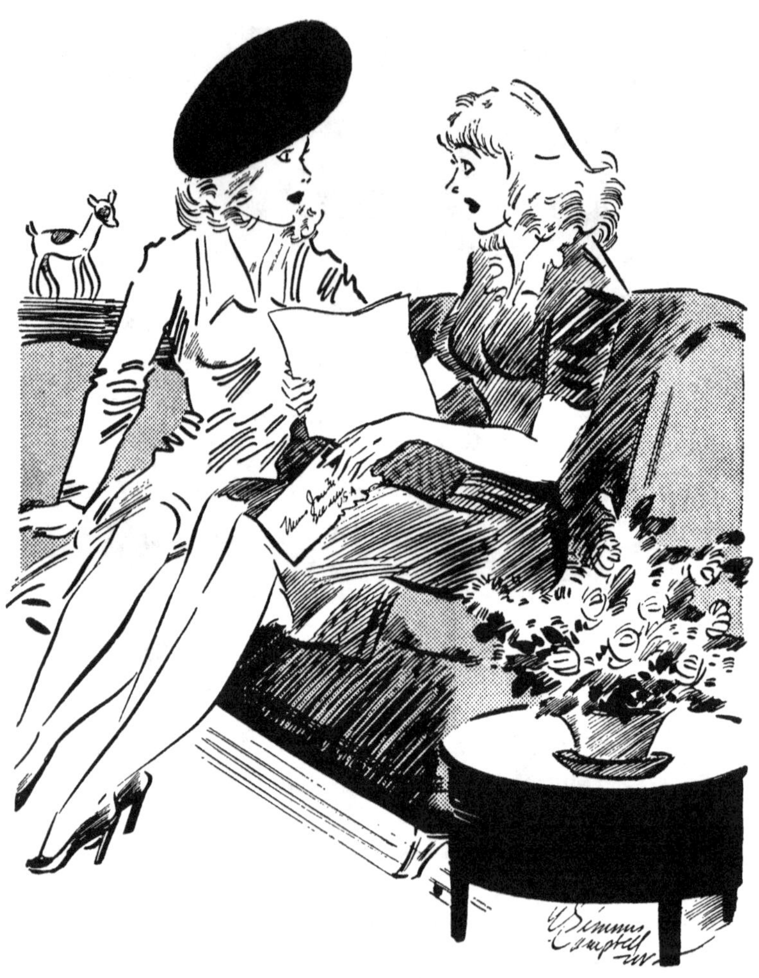

"I don't suppose there's anything to worry about—
that is, from Eskimo women?"

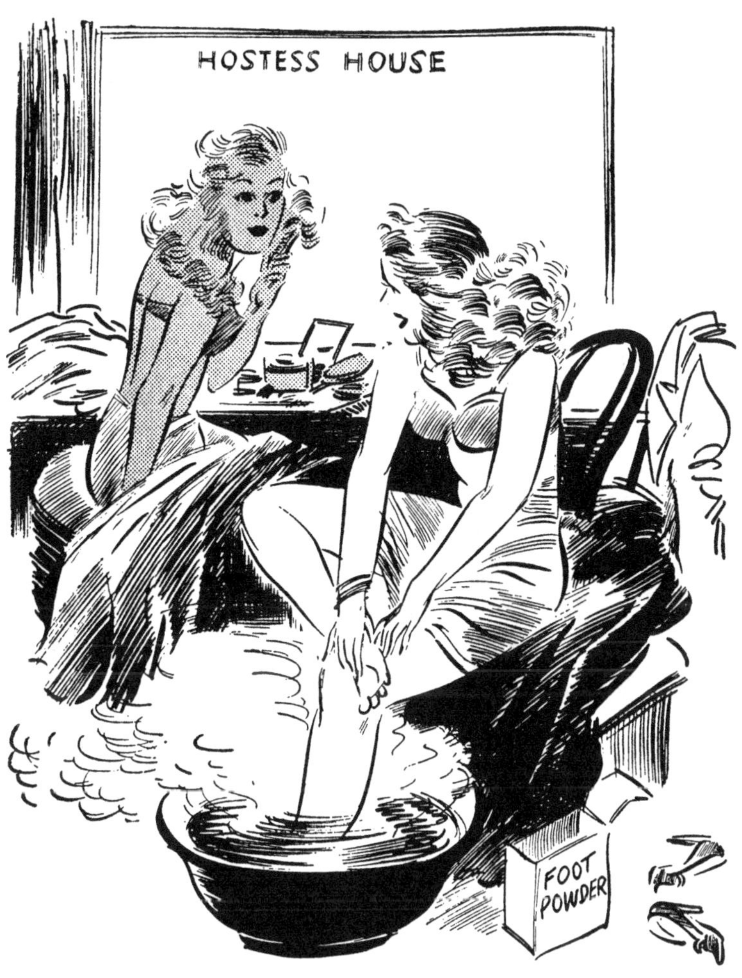

"I KNOW we'll win this war! Those soldiers will TRAMPLE them to death!"

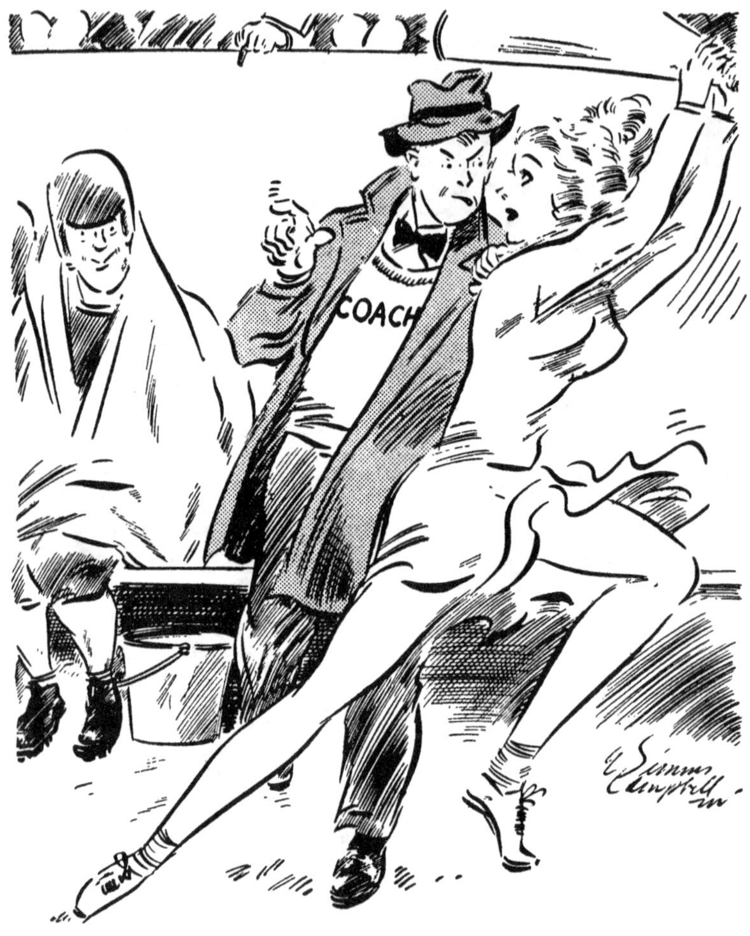

"Listen, Goldenlocks. Kindly stop cheering the team. They're paying more attention to YOU than they are to ME!"

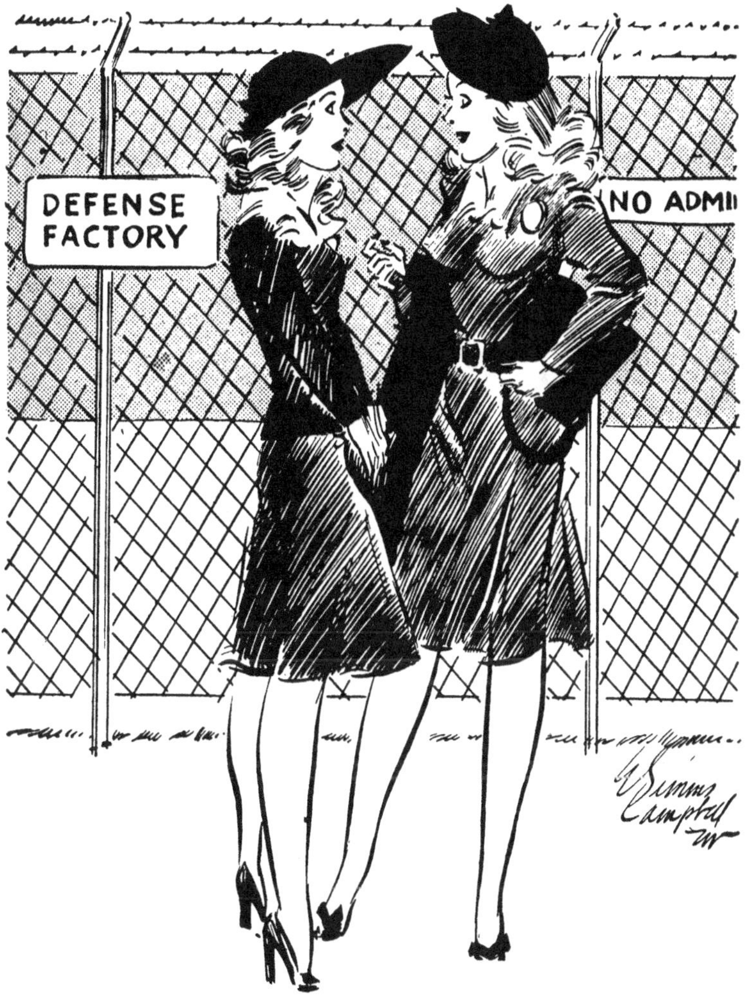

"The work is wonderful! I've already worked up to going out with the plant manager!"

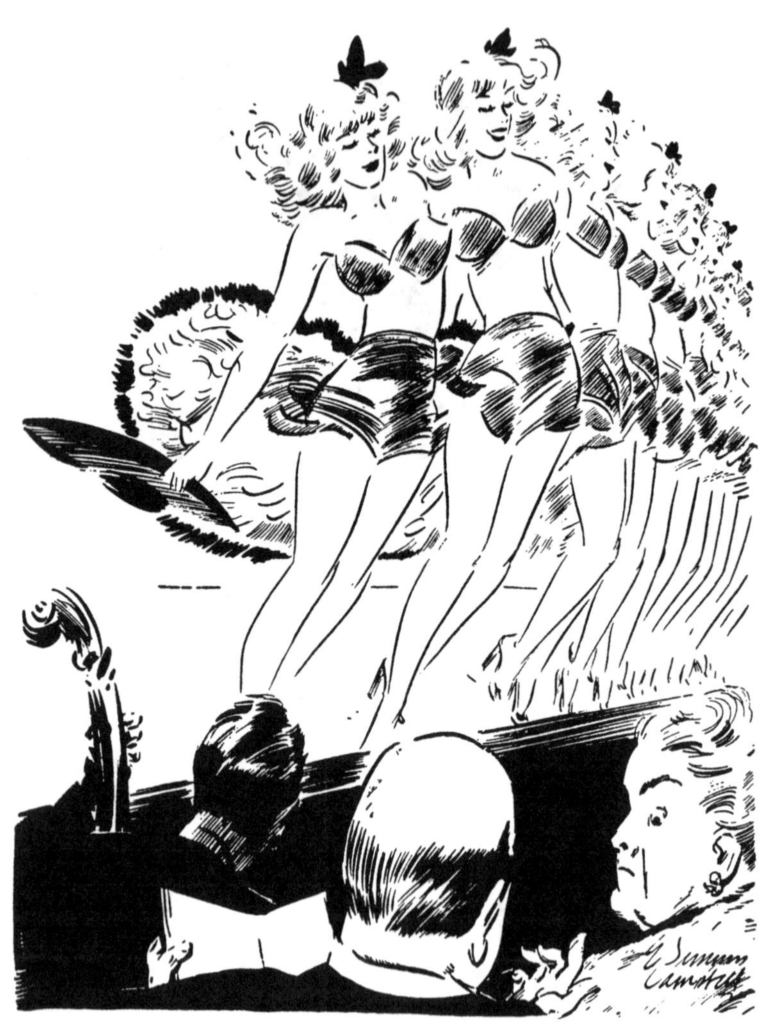

"By the way, darling, did you bring opera glasses?"

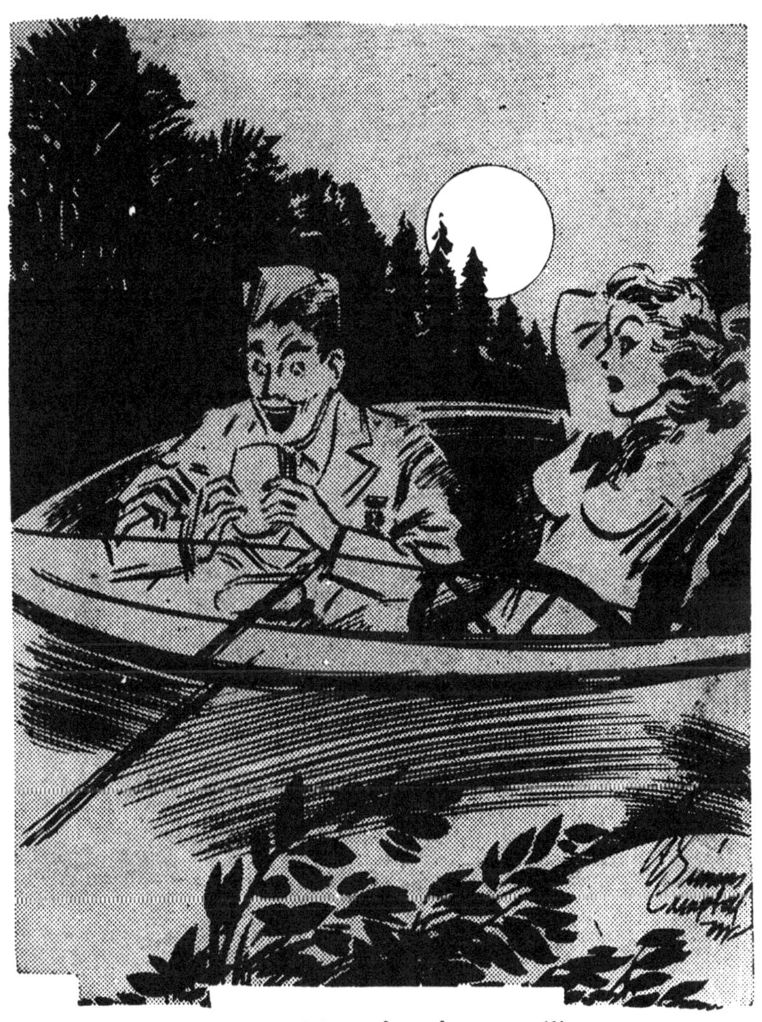

"Boy! Do I love hamburgers!"

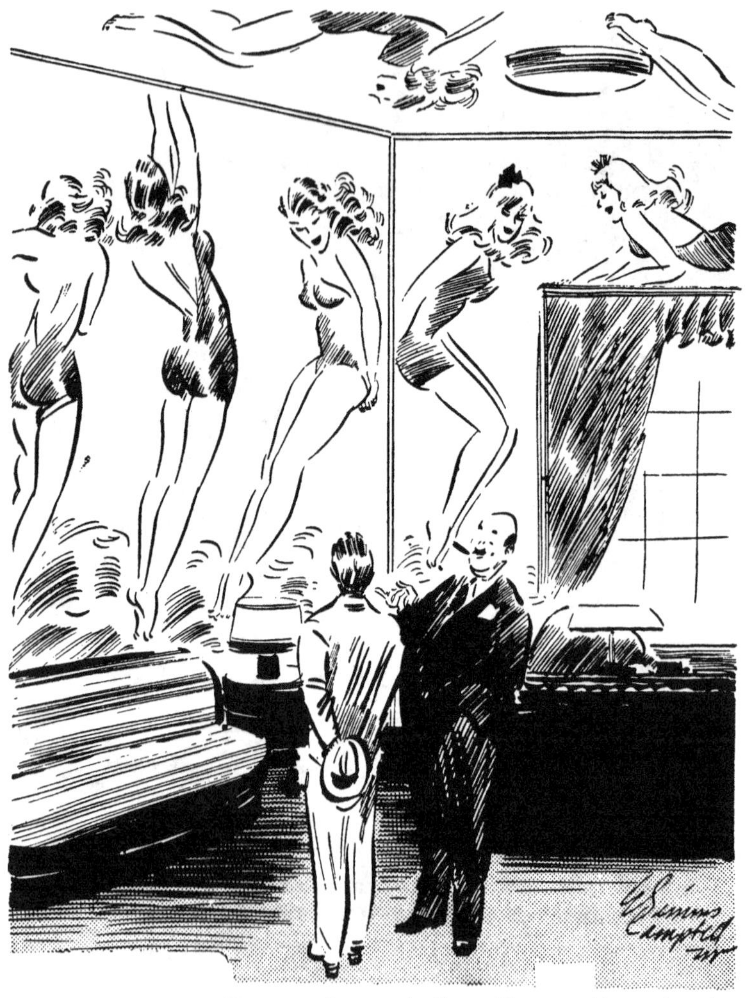

"I had my office redecorated. I'm nutty about swimming!"

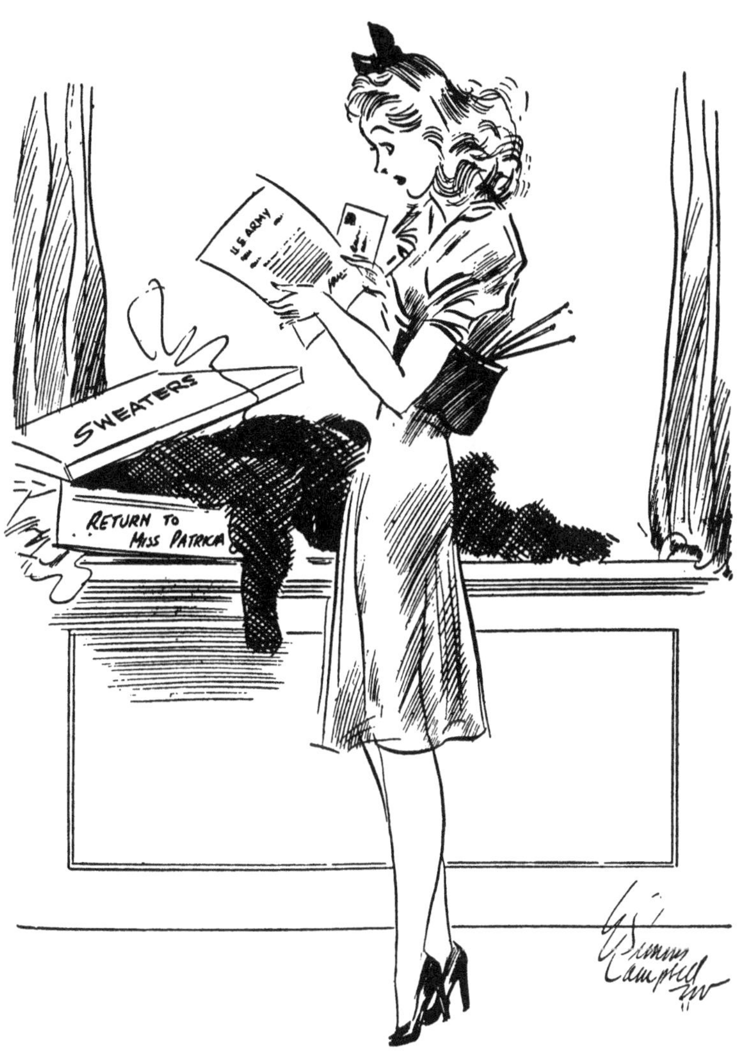

"— and in the future, we'd appreciate your leaving the sleeves and neck open!"

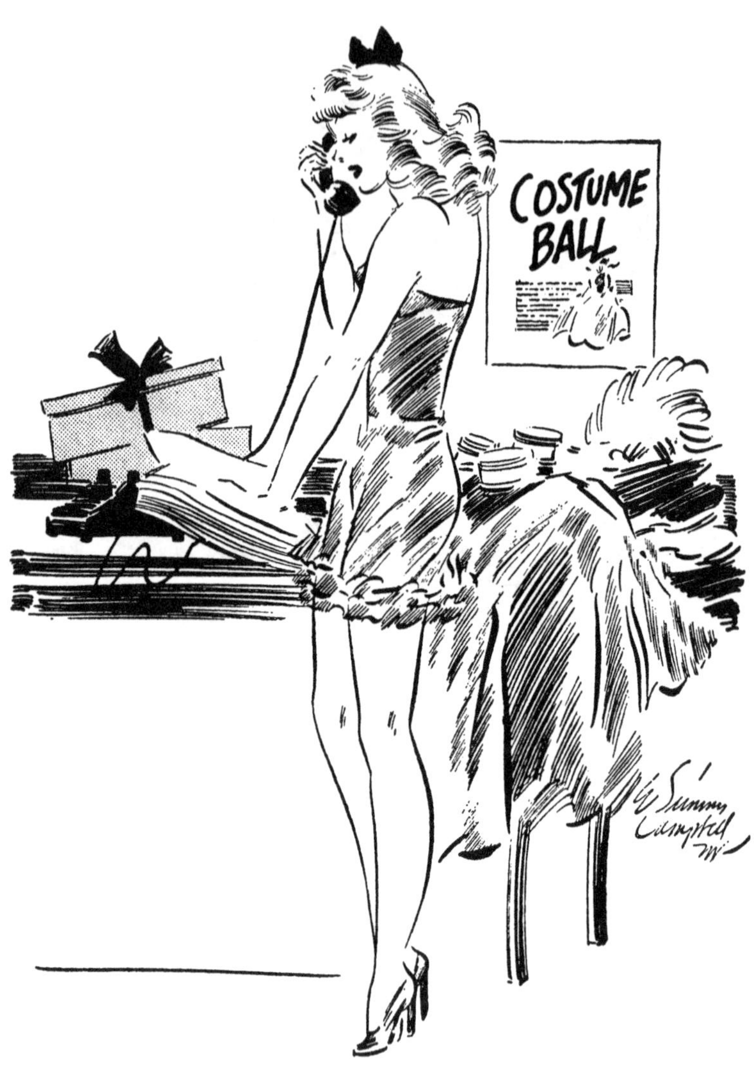

"I'm going as Lady Godiva this year. The only thing that worries me is finding a horse!"

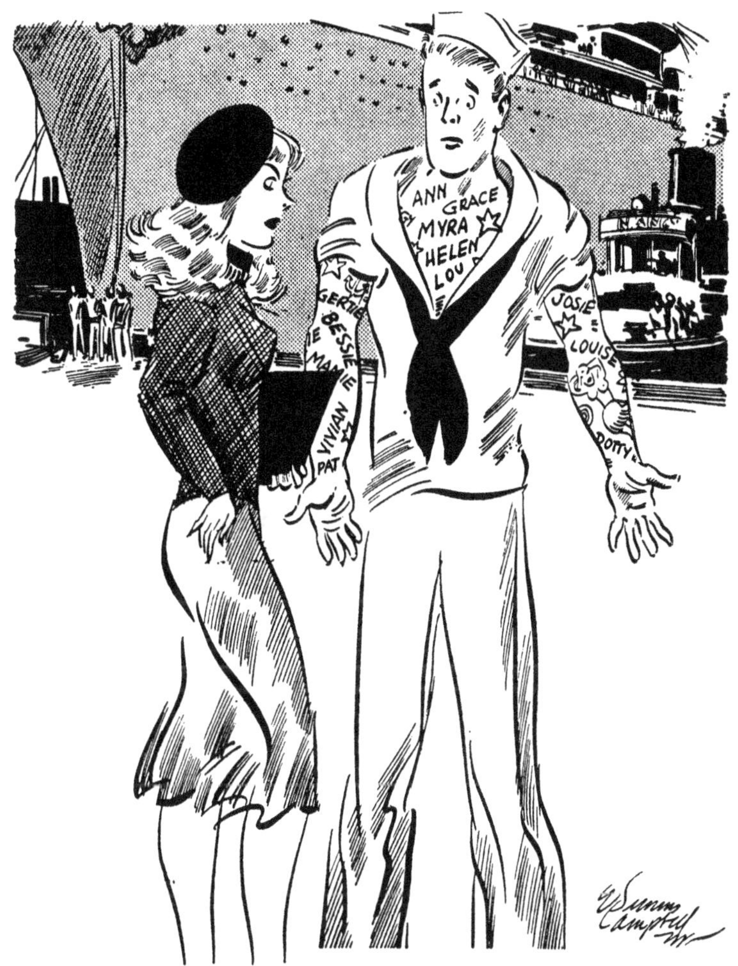

"Honest, Marie, I'd love to have you as my girl friend, but I haven't got room."

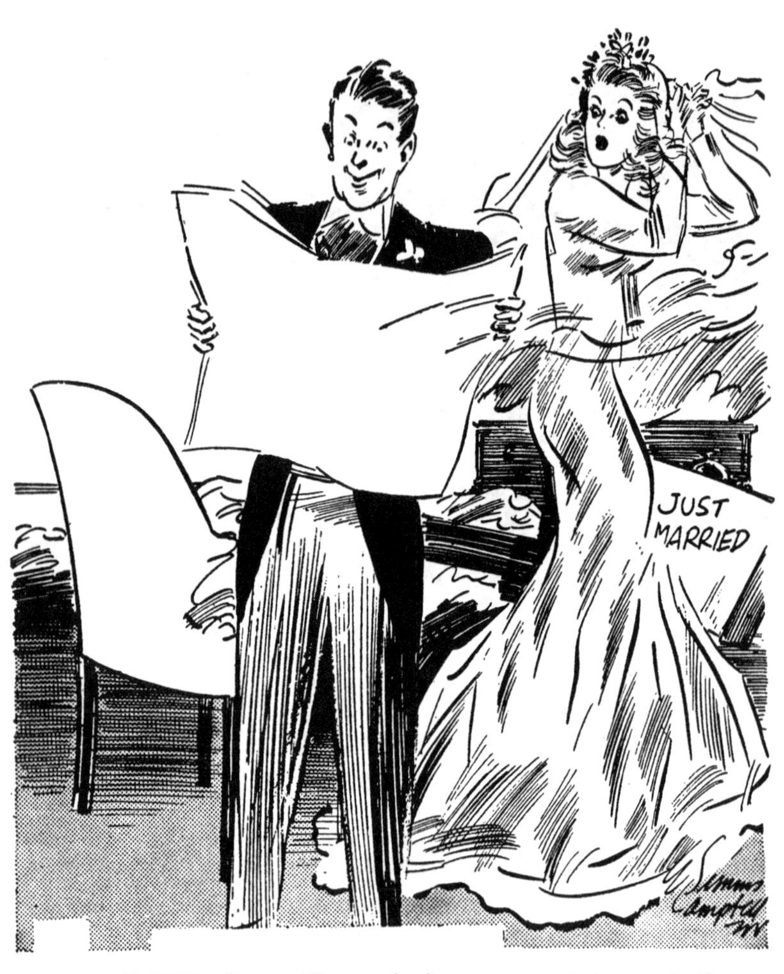

"OH, BOY! Lana Turner's in a new picture at the Orpheum tonight!"

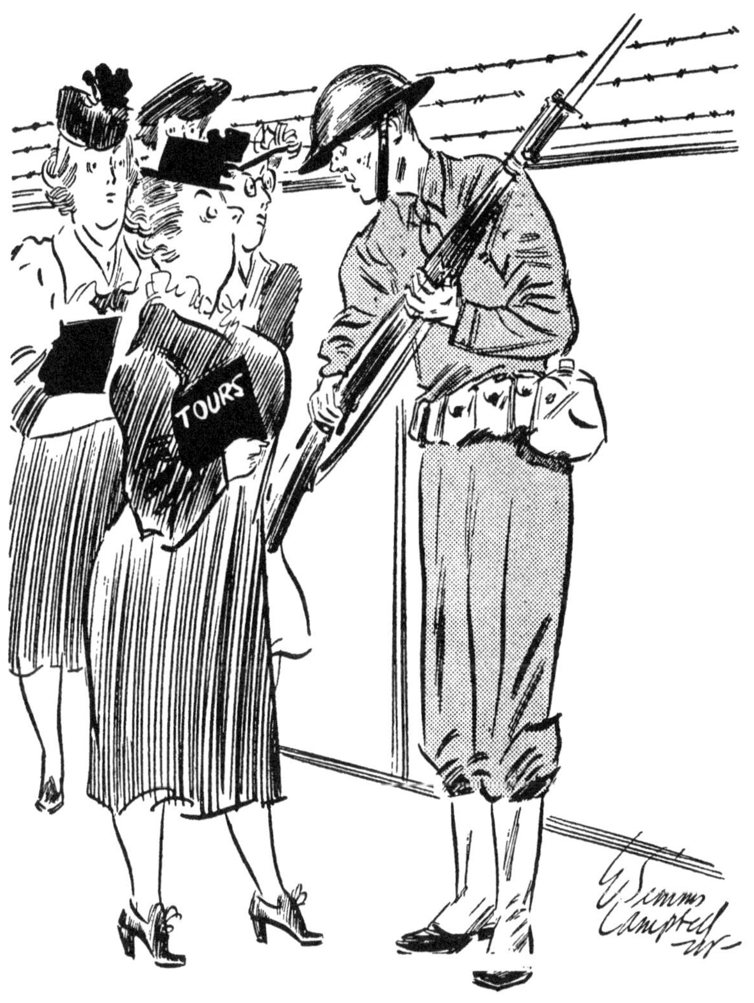

"I'm awfully sorry, ma'am, but I can't let ANYBODY in. Ladies come under that heading, too!"

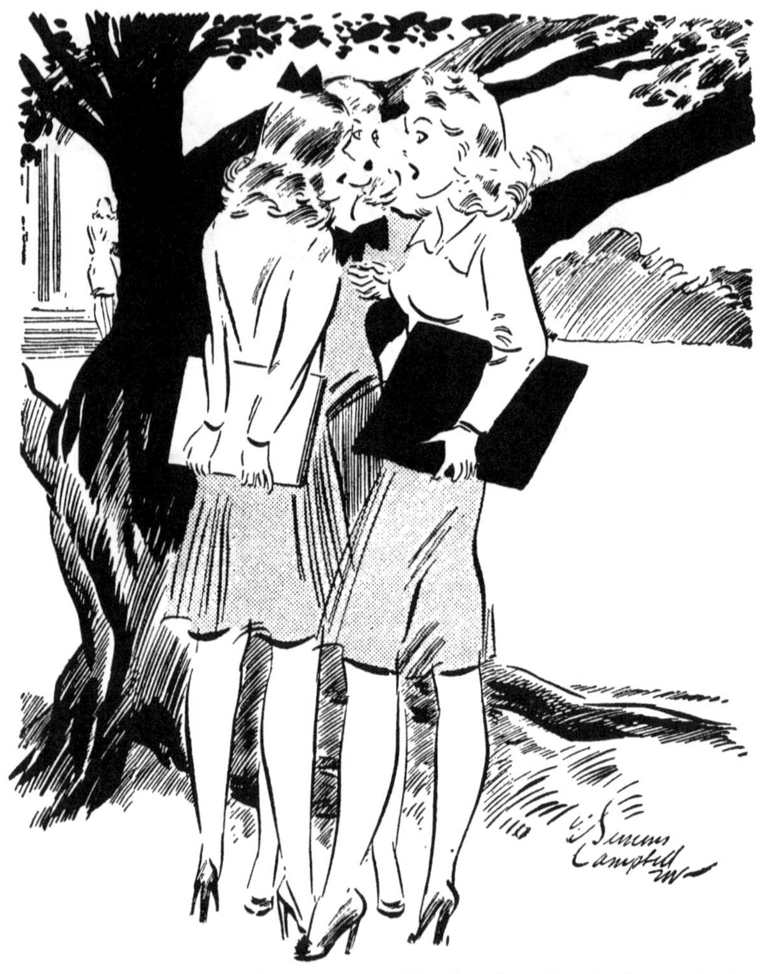

"I'm marrying that young Prof. who flunked me last term—and just wait 'til I get him home!"

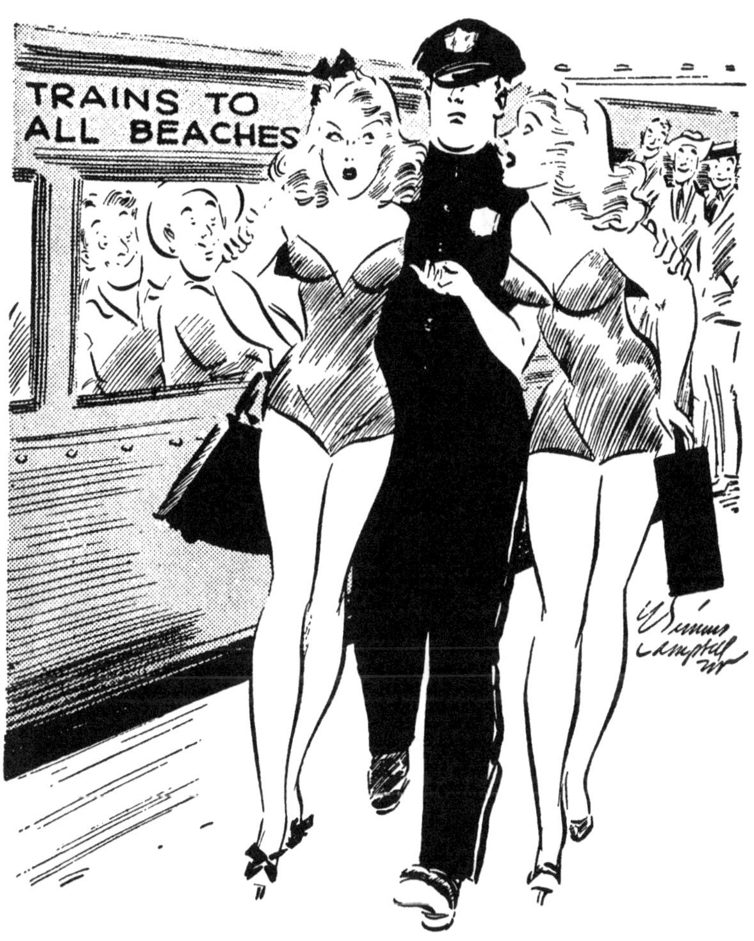

"— But, Officer! We only tried to save the locker-fee by dressing at home!"

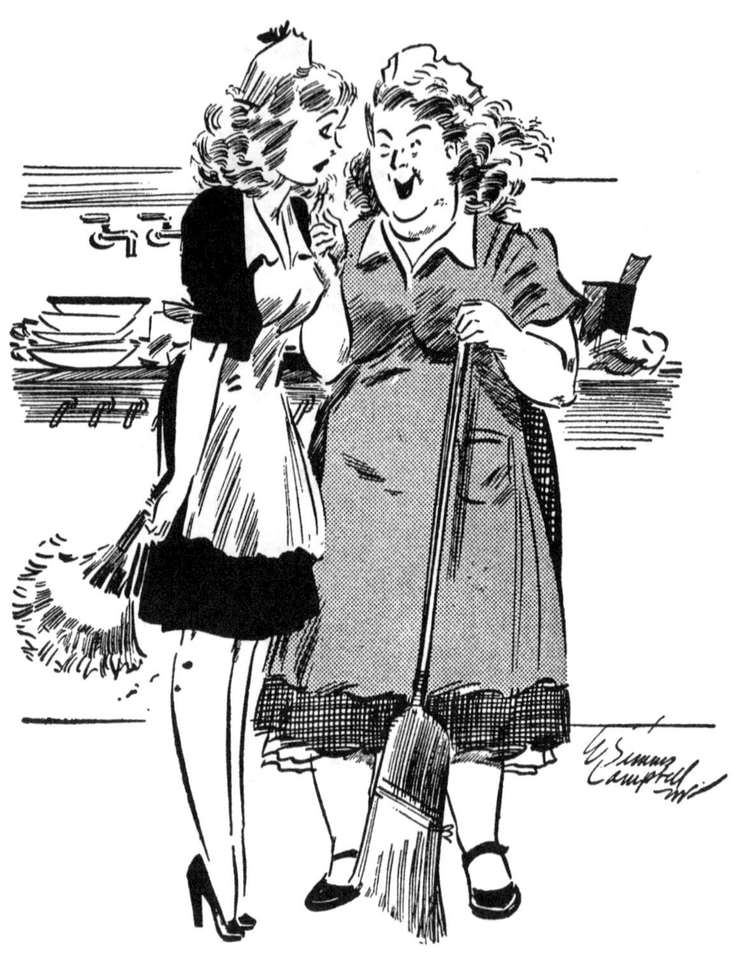

"All the men folks in this house admire you, Marie. Just between us girls, what's the secret, honey-bunch?"

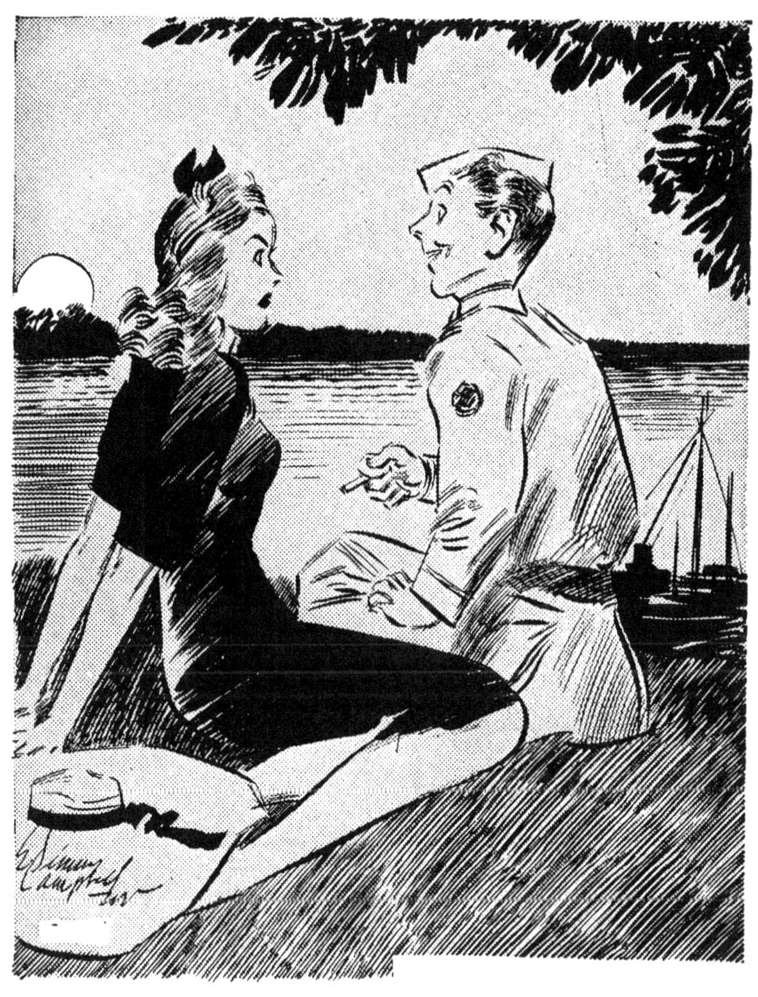

"Gee! The moon's up. What a night for night flying!"

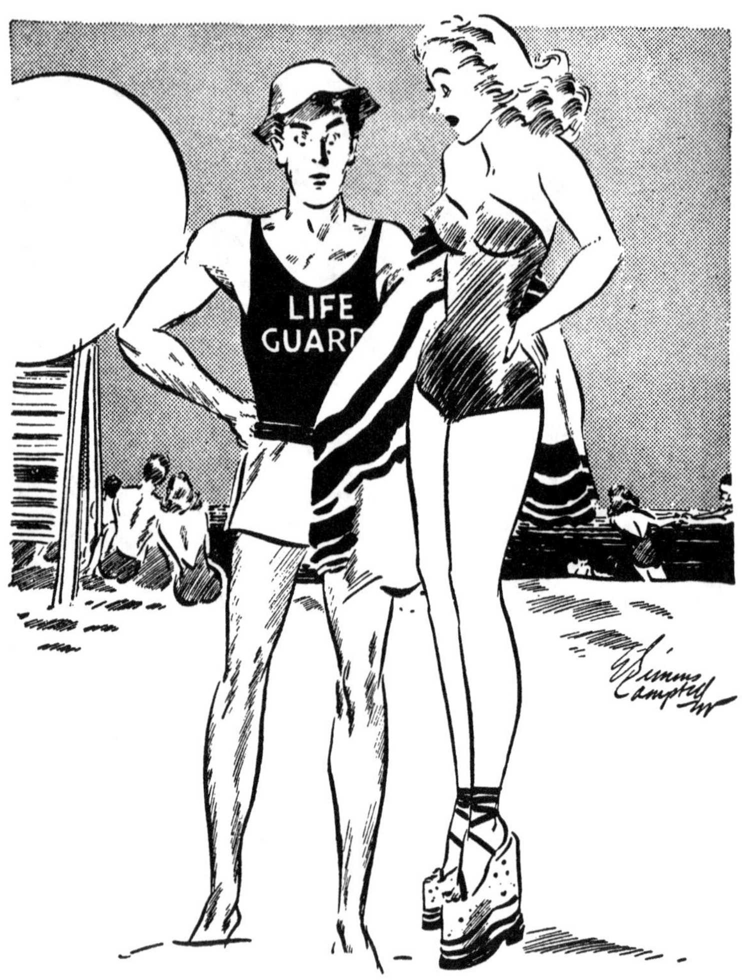

"We can't keep you from wearing 'em, Miss, but we're not responsible, if you fall off 'em and hurt yourself."

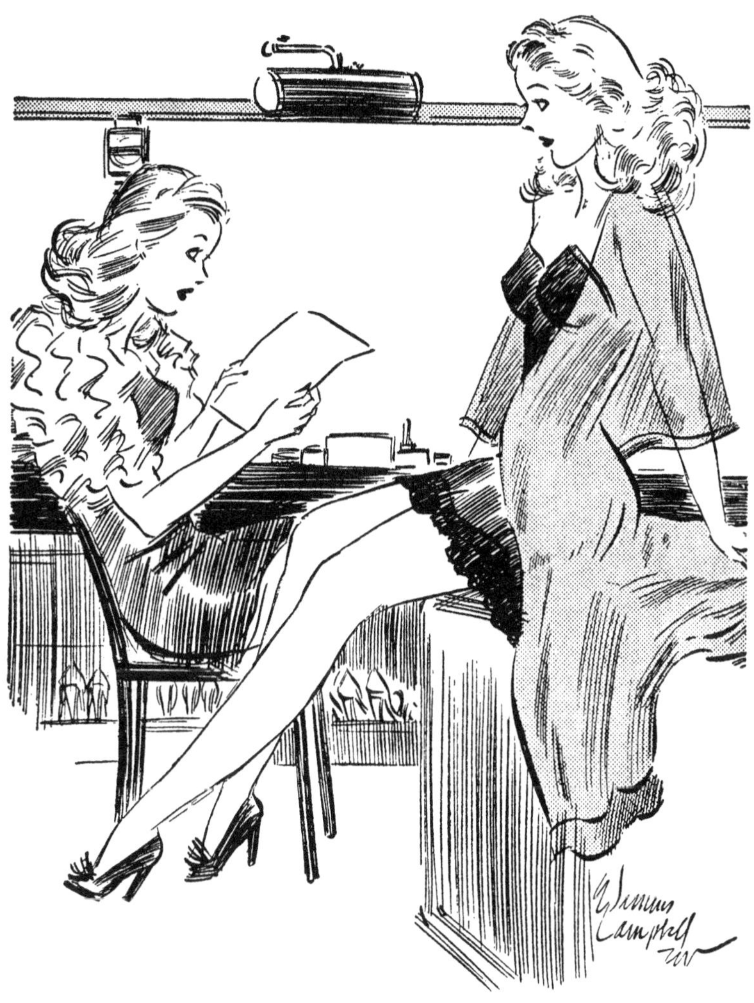

"It's from Harry. He says twenty-one dollars a month isn't much, but it's surprising what it can do in a poker game!"

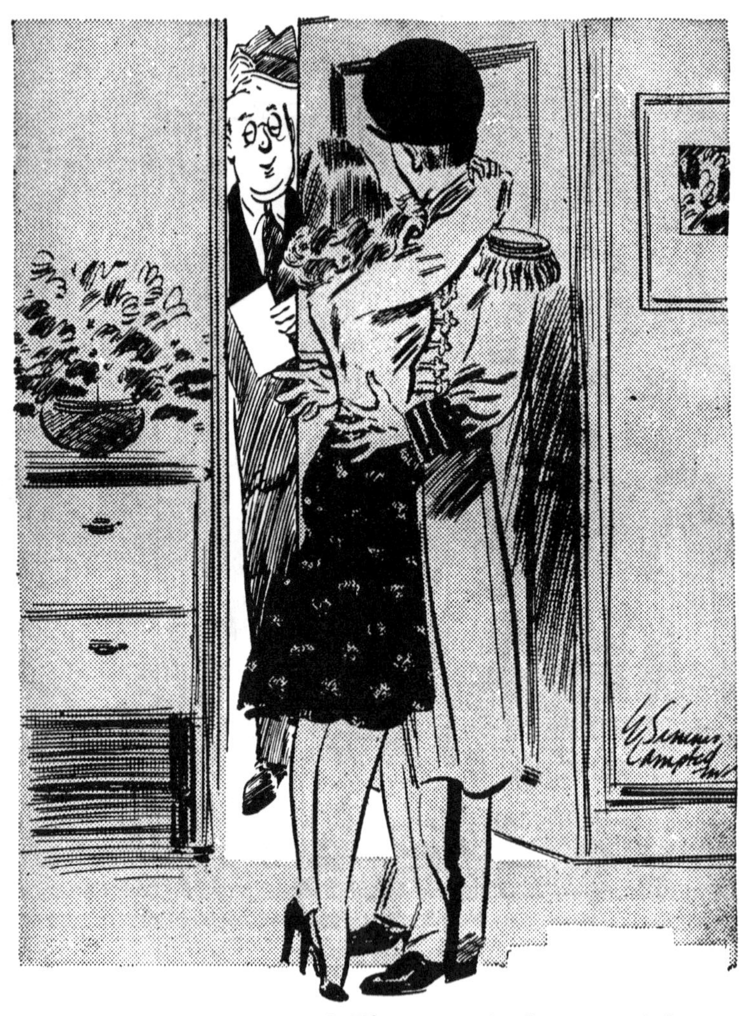

"Pardon me, but we'd like to get the tenants' reaction to the new doorman we've put on!"

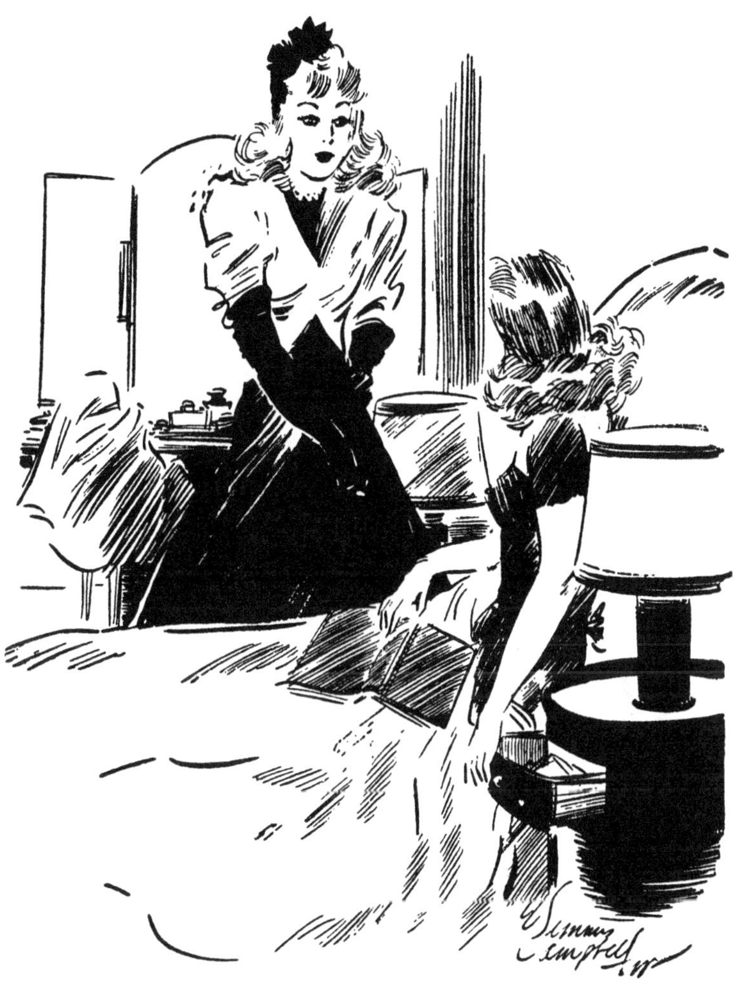

"By the way, lend me your air raid warden's police whistle. I'm going out with a new fellow tonight!"

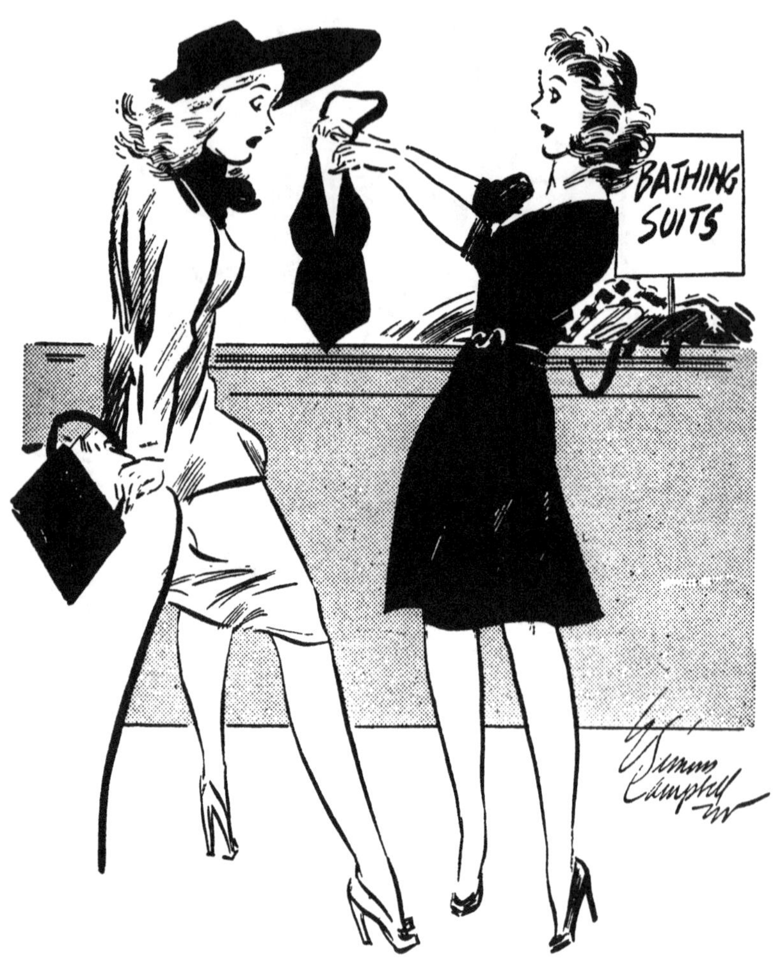

"— of course, that's the chance you take . . . either WINNING the bathing beauty contest or going to jail!"

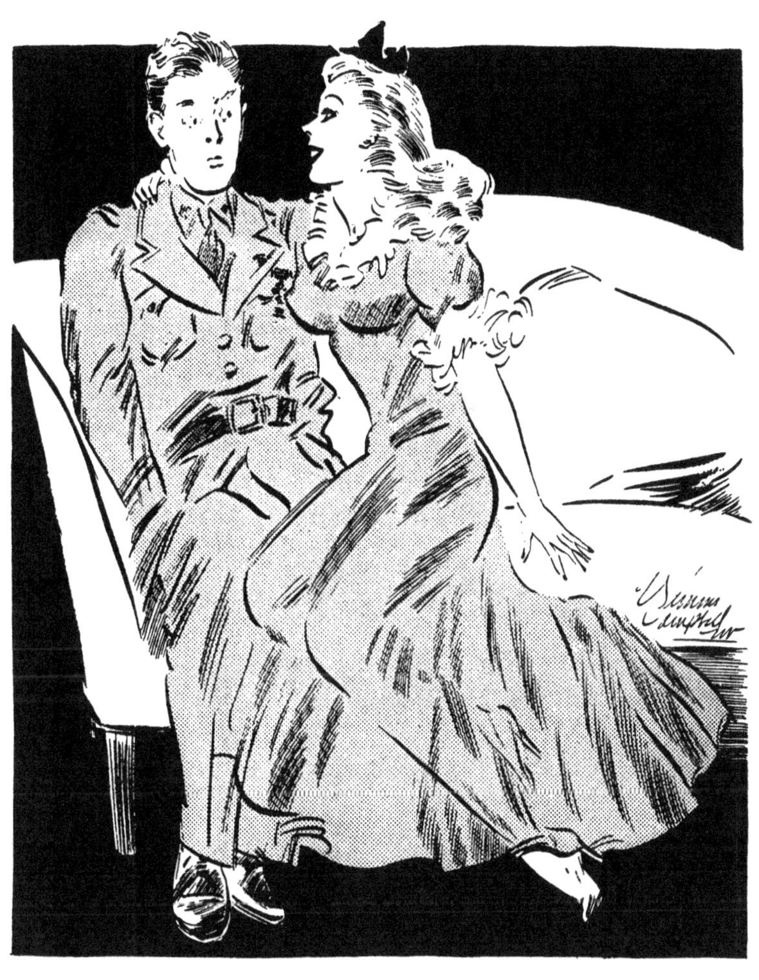

"You DO love me? Oh, this is so sudden! When do we get married, this week or next?"

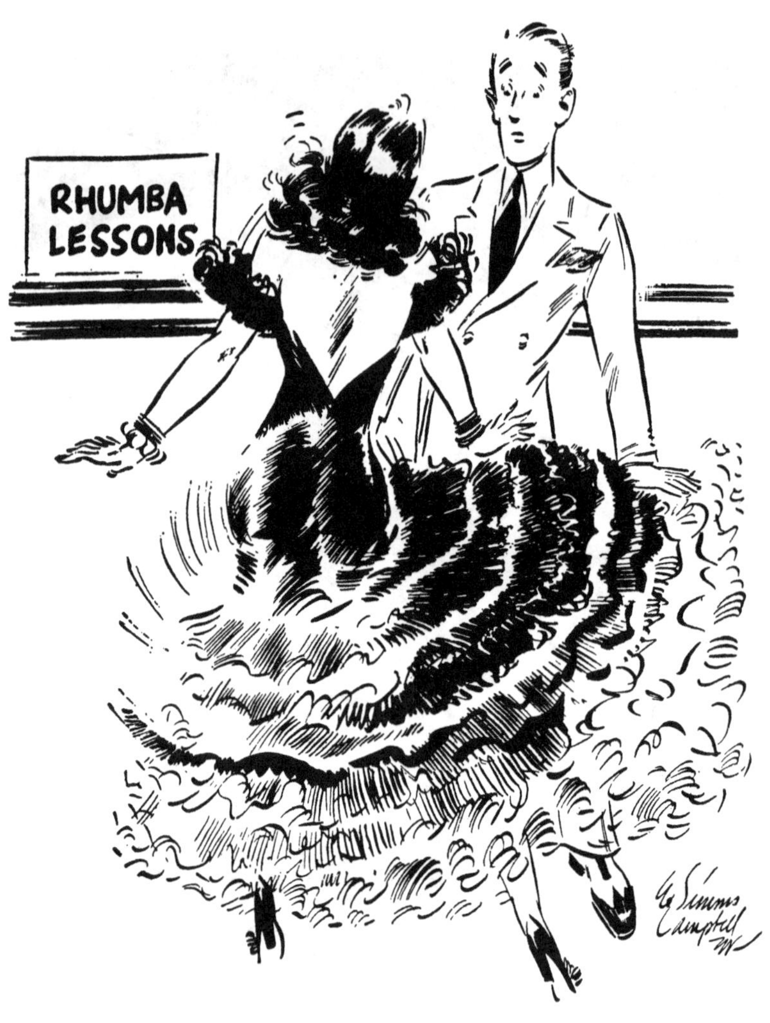

"Look! Like thees. Put more SOUL in eet!"

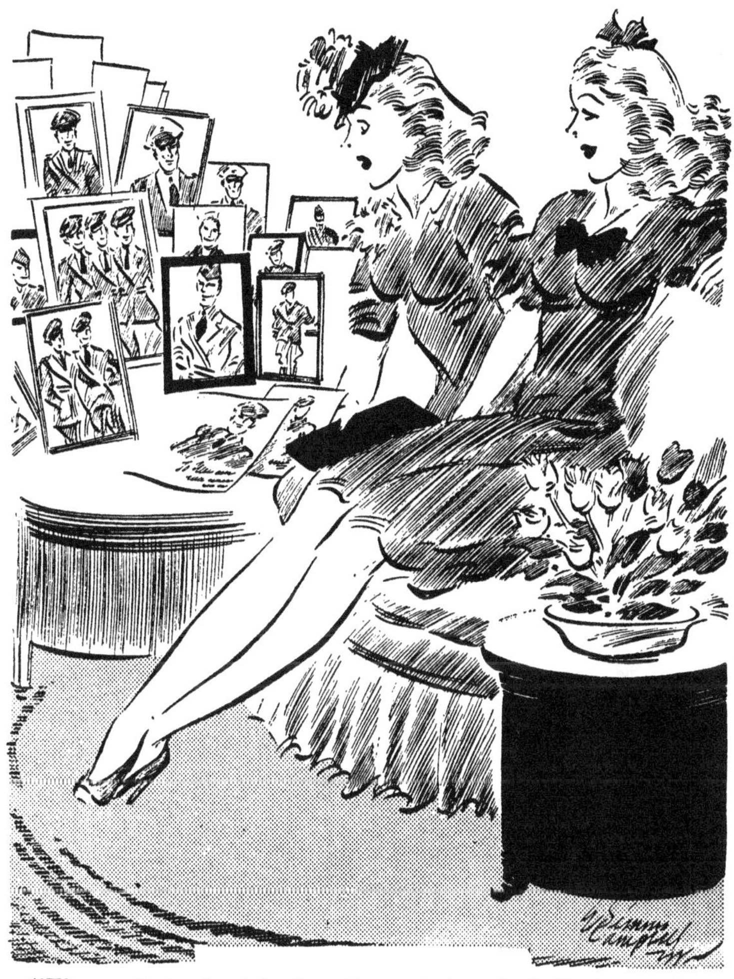

"They all had girls in other states, but that was before I sold kisses at the war relief ball."

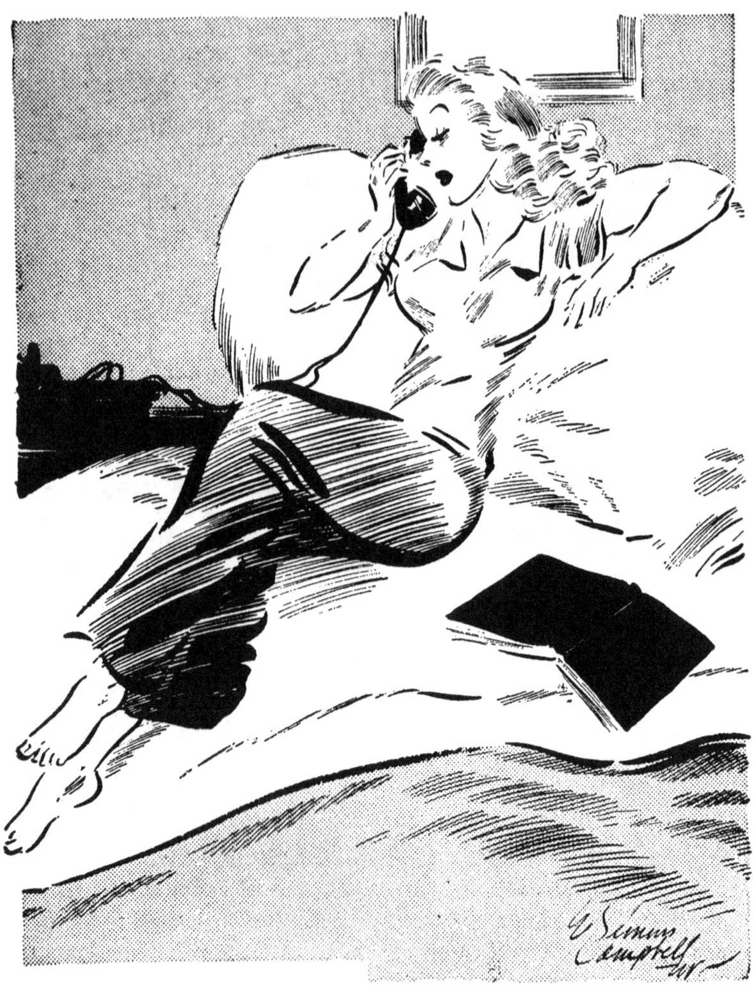

"Oh, married life's O. K., Mabel. It's just the going out with one guy that gets monotonous!"

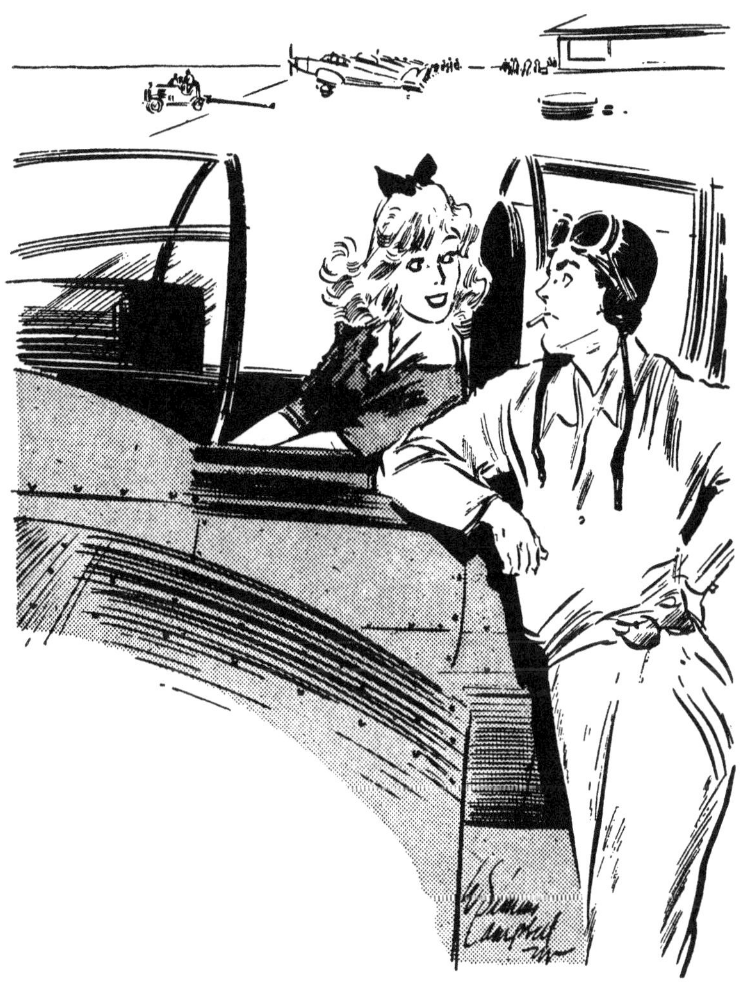

"— and if the fuselage is riddled and the engine shot off AND the the parachute won't open, what gadget do I push?"

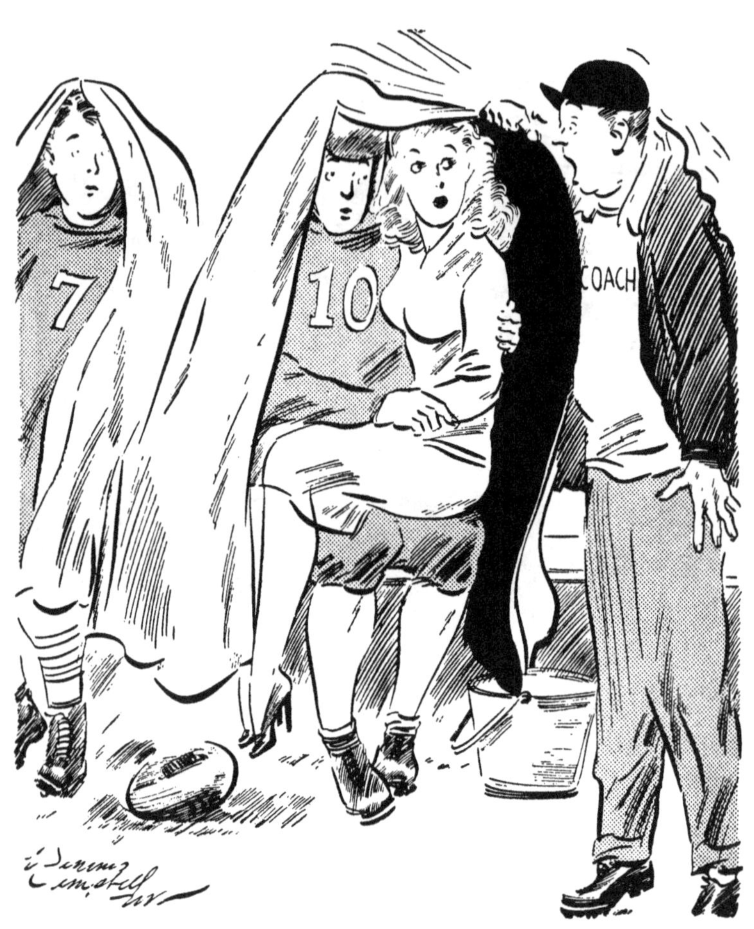

"Why, Jablonsky!"

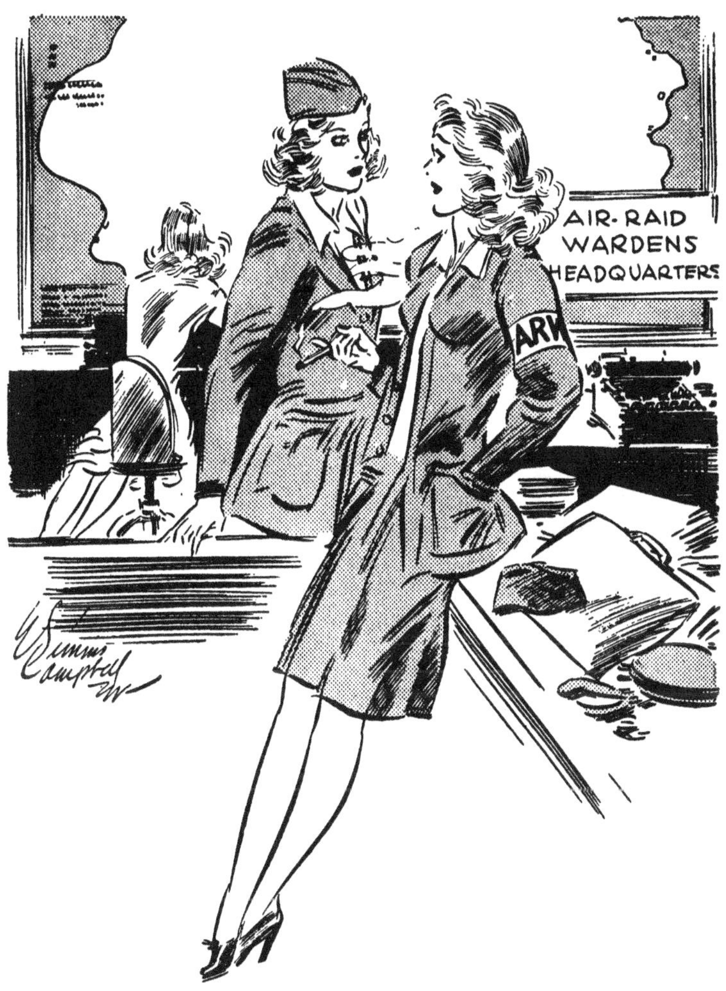

"The men follow me the moment I beckon. It's the women I have trouble with!"

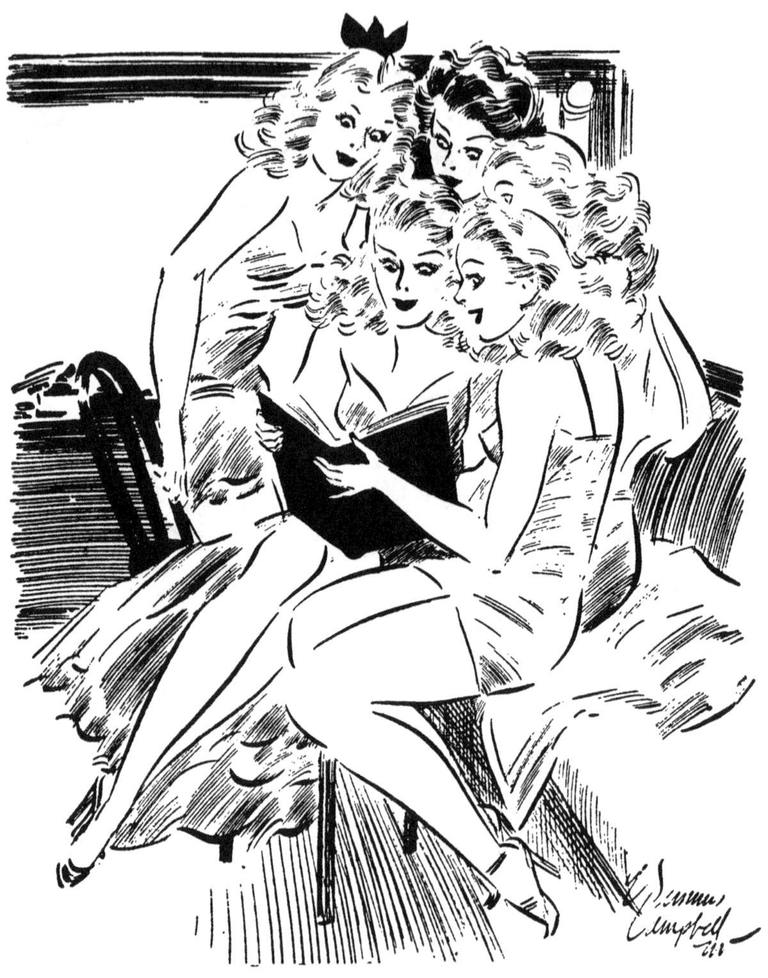

"Here's the part that's censored in the movies!"

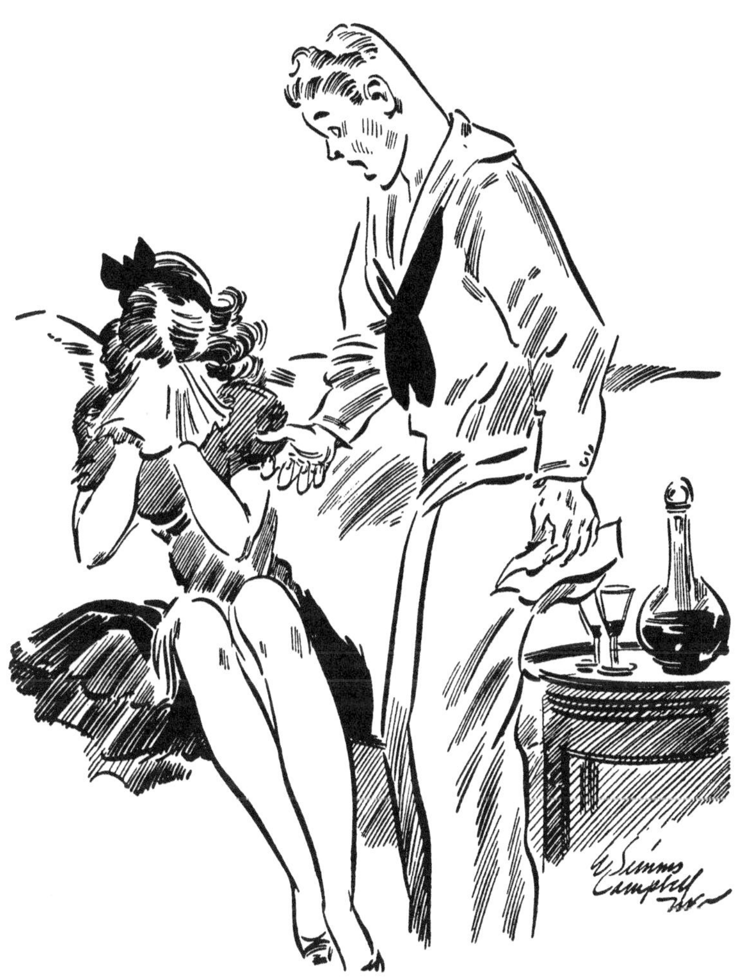

"But, honey, I haven't got a girl in every port. I ain't BEEN in every port!"

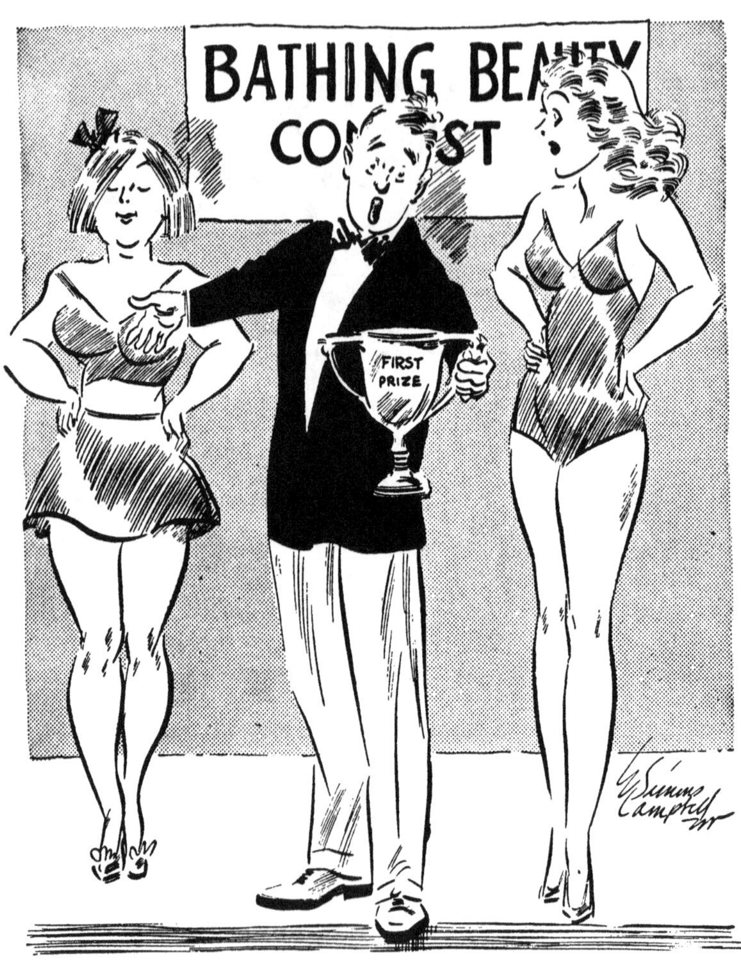

"Ladies and gentlemen, there's been a change! Miss Tootsie Donovan, sister of Muggsy Donovan, of the Third ward!"

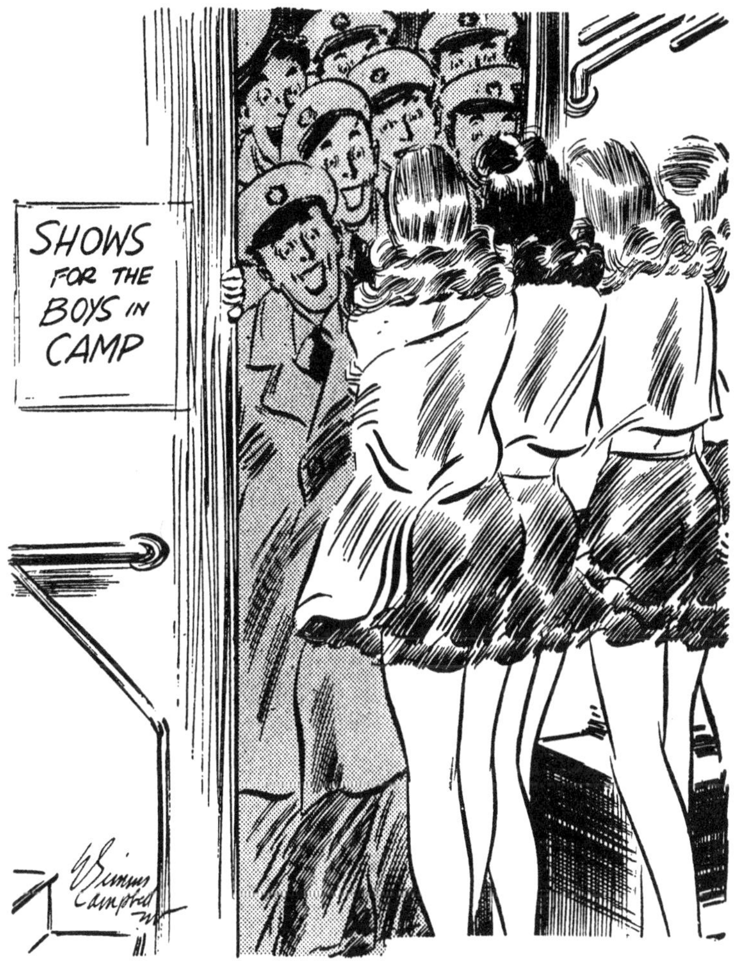

"Do we MIND coming backstage!"

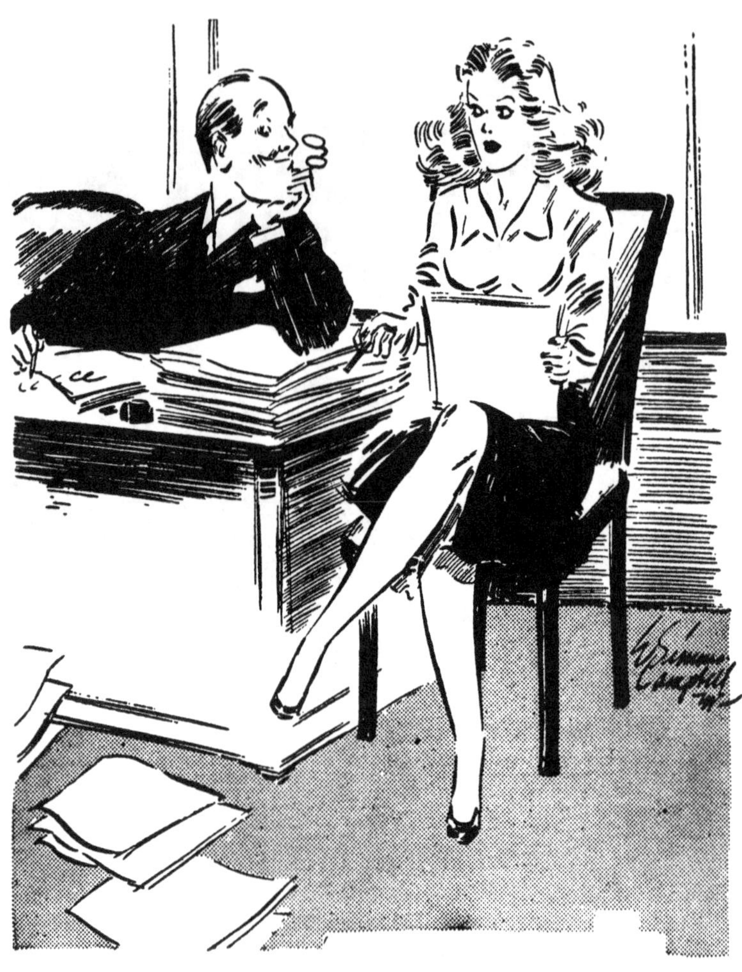

"If you're REALLY busy, Mr. Burton, I'll take the day off, so we can get some work done!"

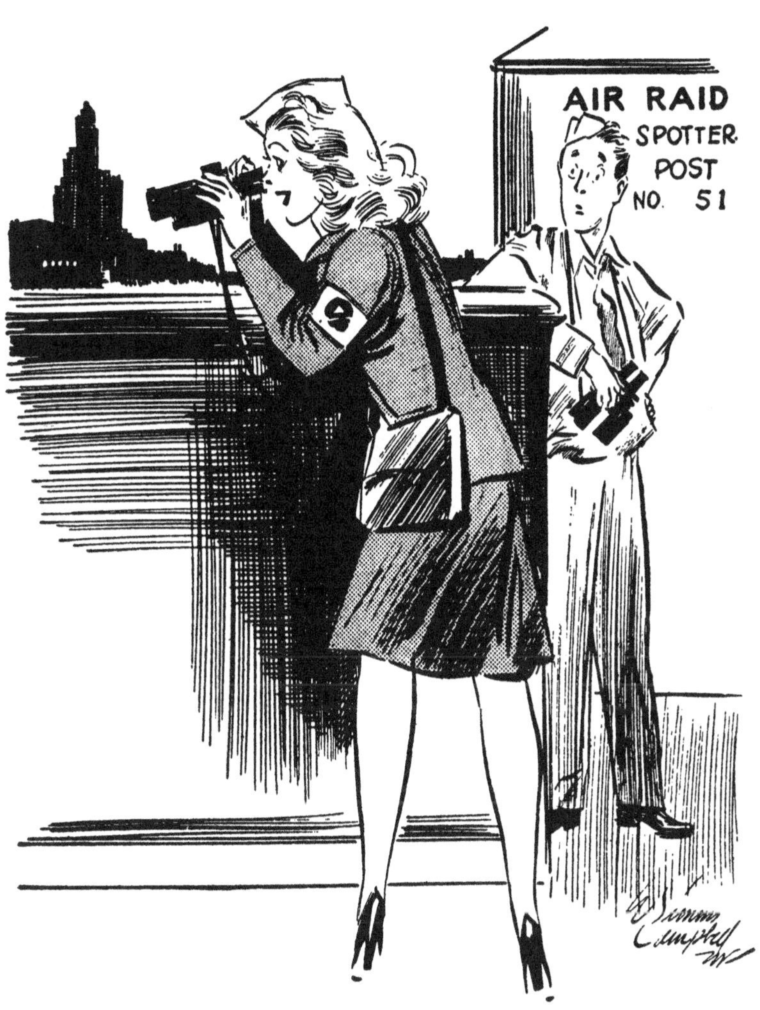

"Oh, look, dear! It's been reduced to nine, ninety-five—that DIVINE rayon print dress!"

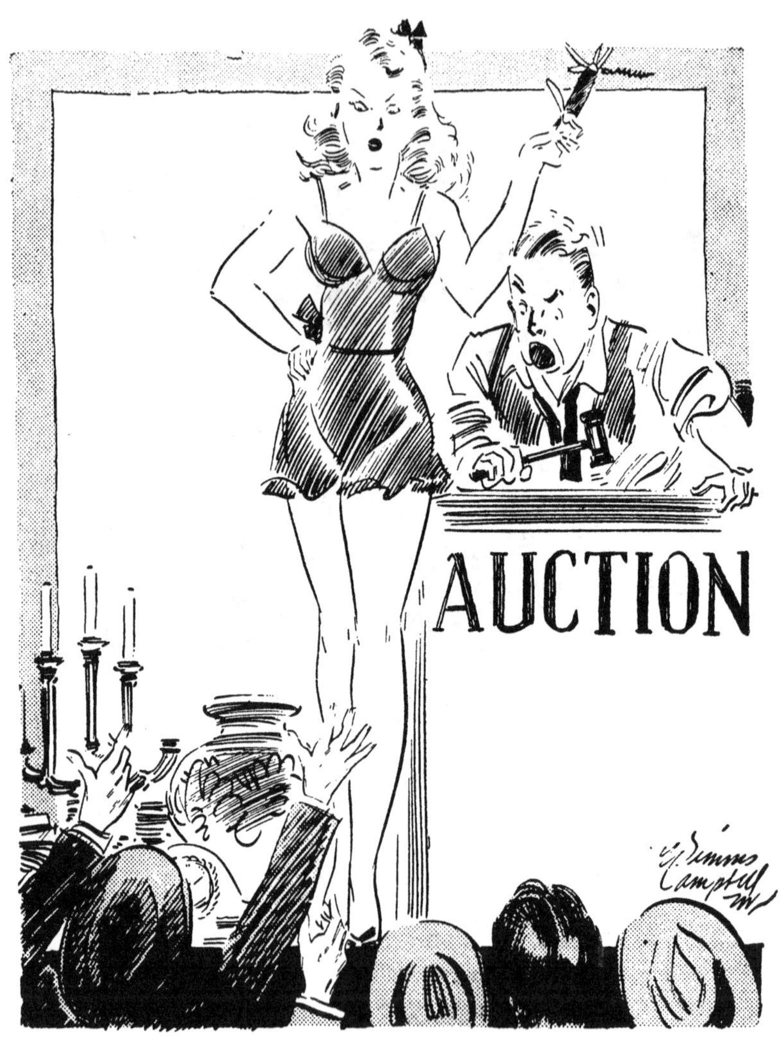

"Five hundred dollars! GENTLEMEN! Remember, Miss Kelly does NOT go with the scout knife!"

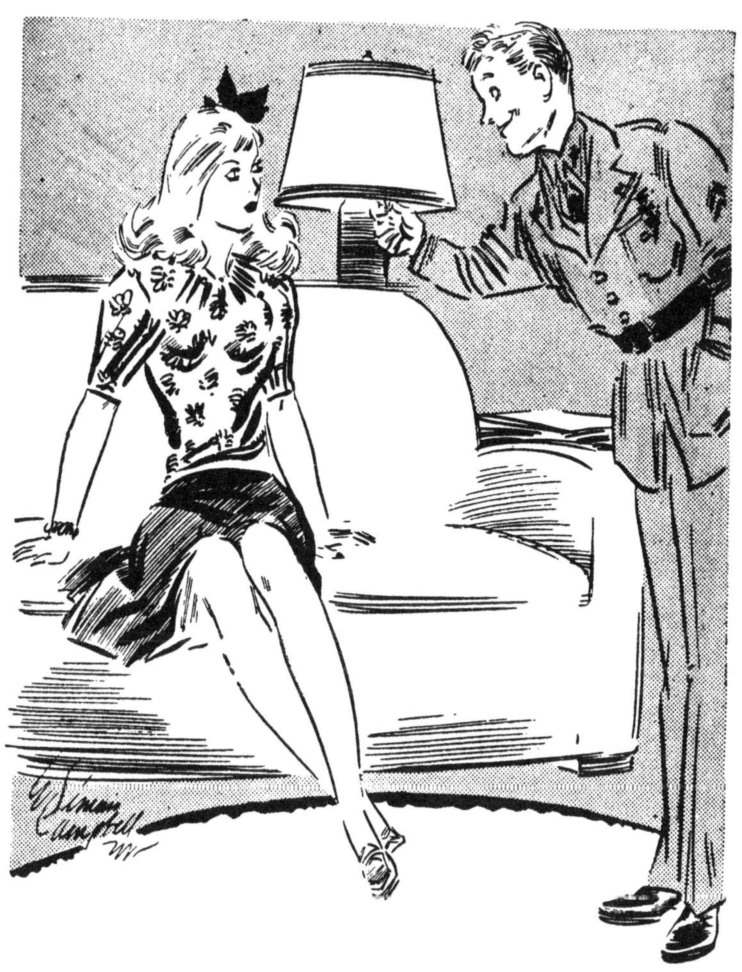

"By the way, d'j'ever play air raid?"

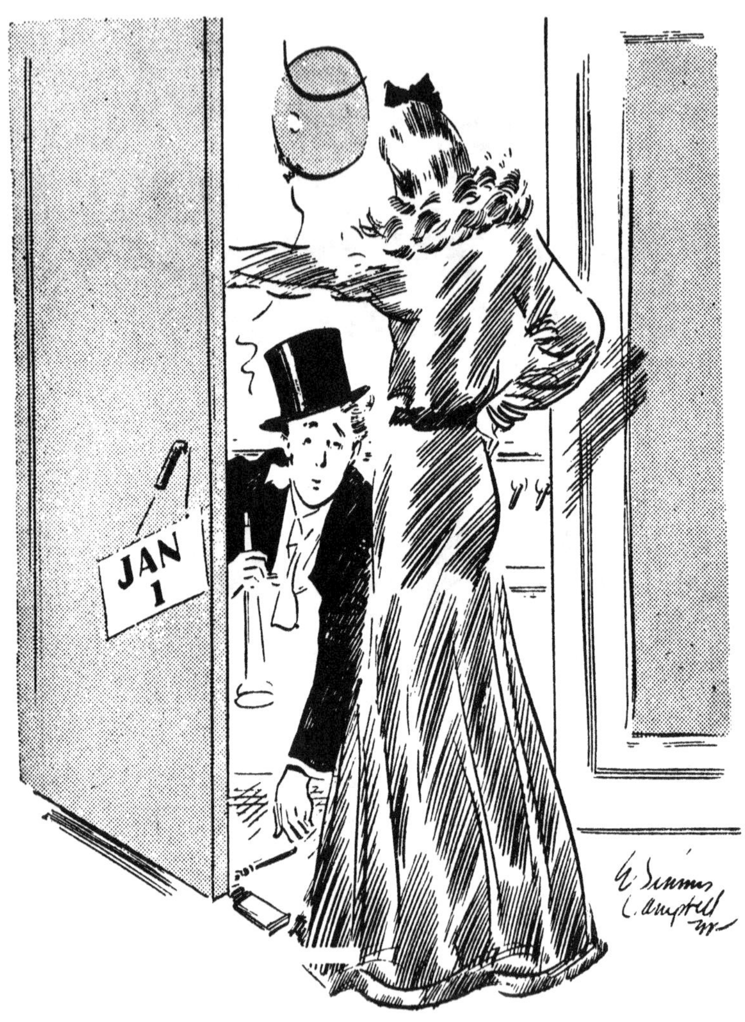

"Of course, I wanted you to have a good time, but did you just HAVE to sleep in the tub?"

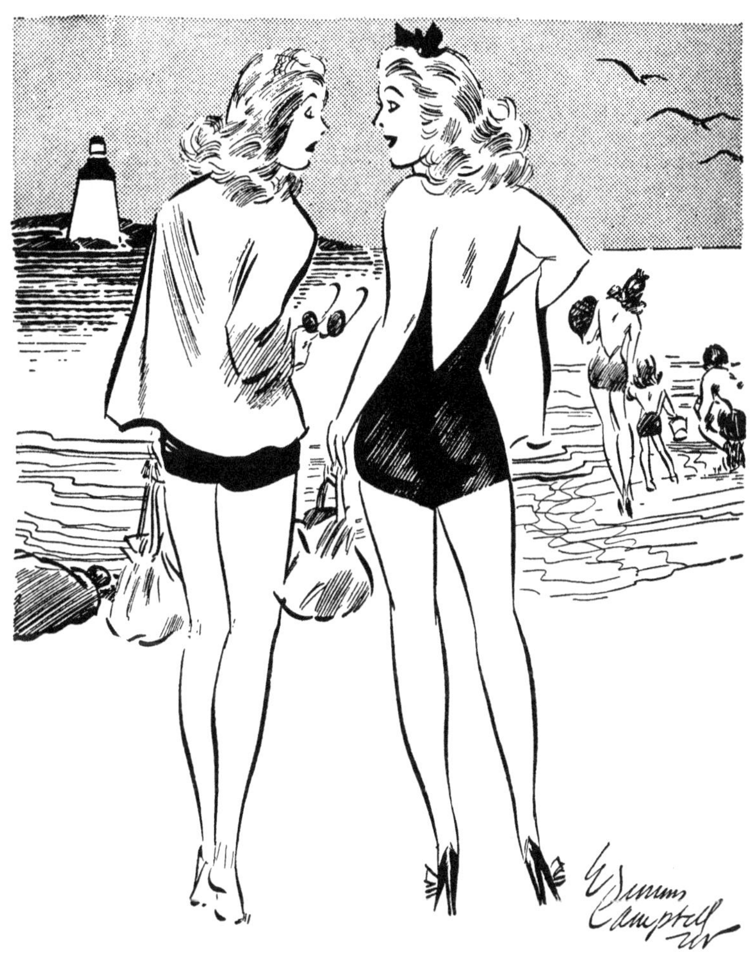

"Since there are so few men on the beaches now, I ACTUALLY come down here to swim."

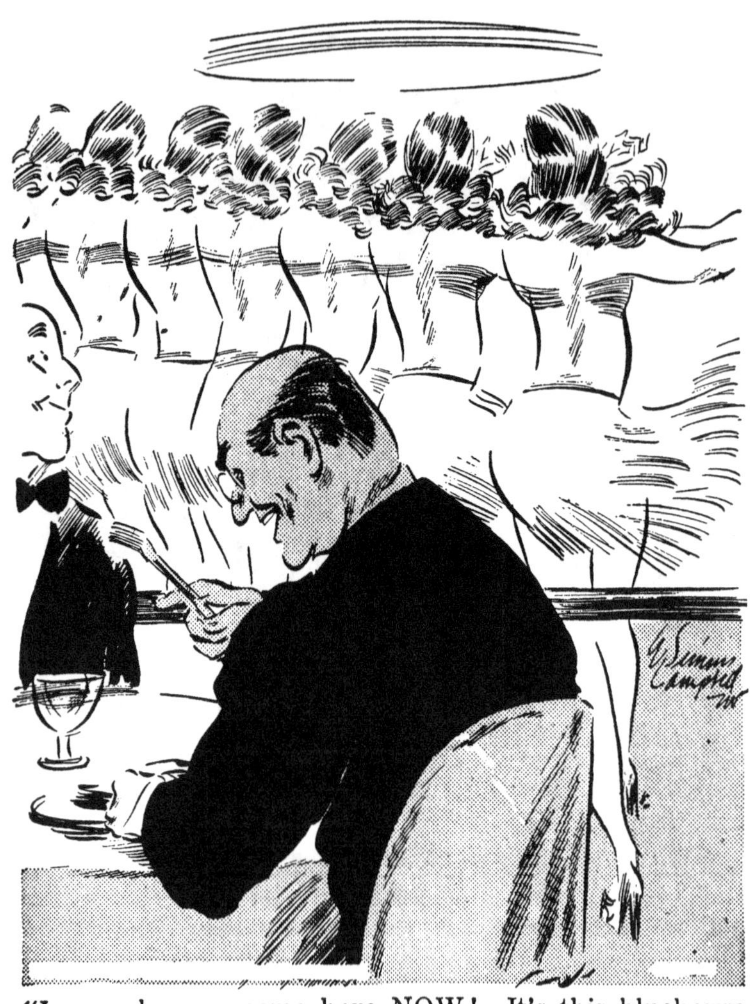

"I see why you come here NOW! It's this blueberry pie!"

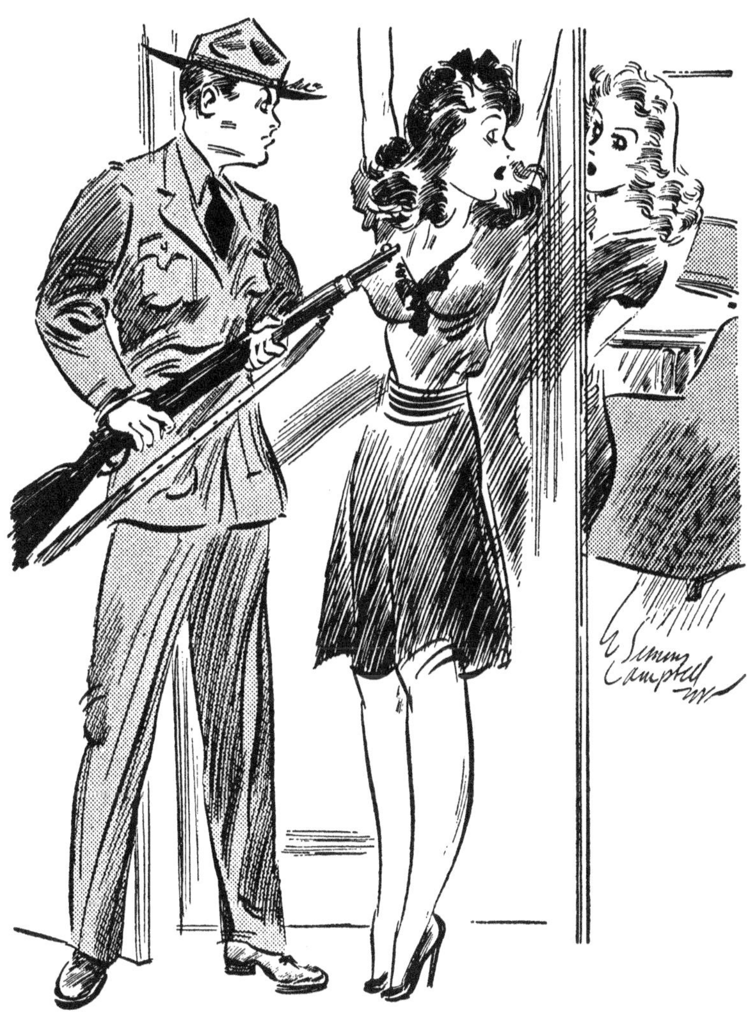

"Ralph heard all about me while he was away, so now he wants his ring back!"

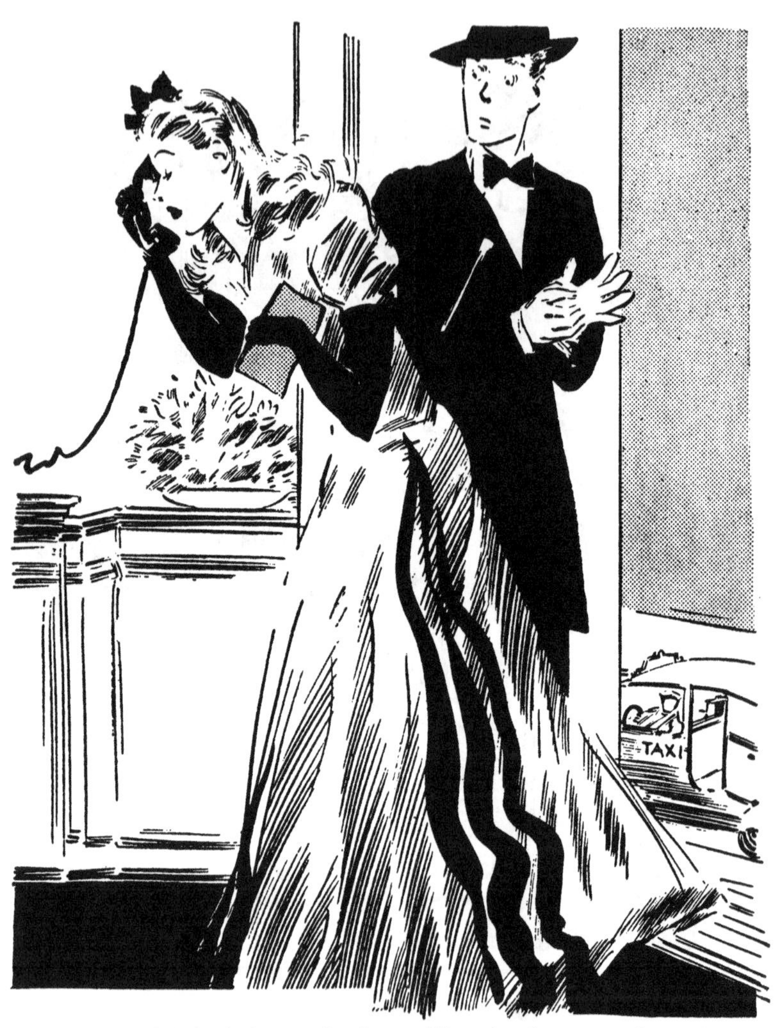

"Yes, a frightful headache. No, don't come by, I'm going right to bed. Thanks for calling. Goodbye, darling!"

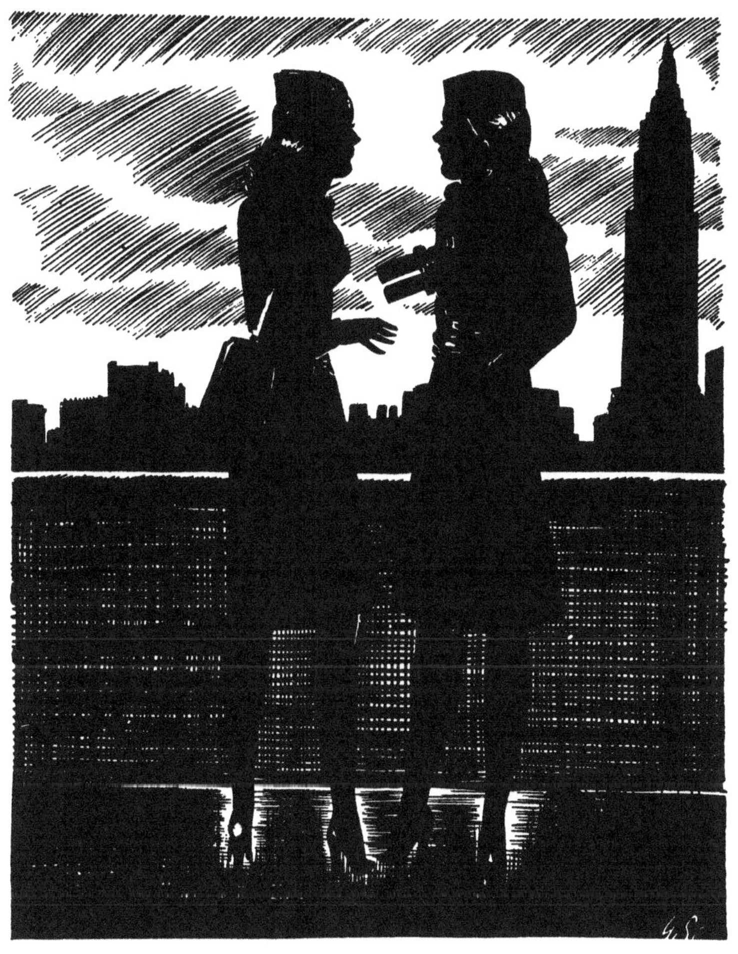

"He's not very handsome, but he's the type you'd like to be with in a black-out."

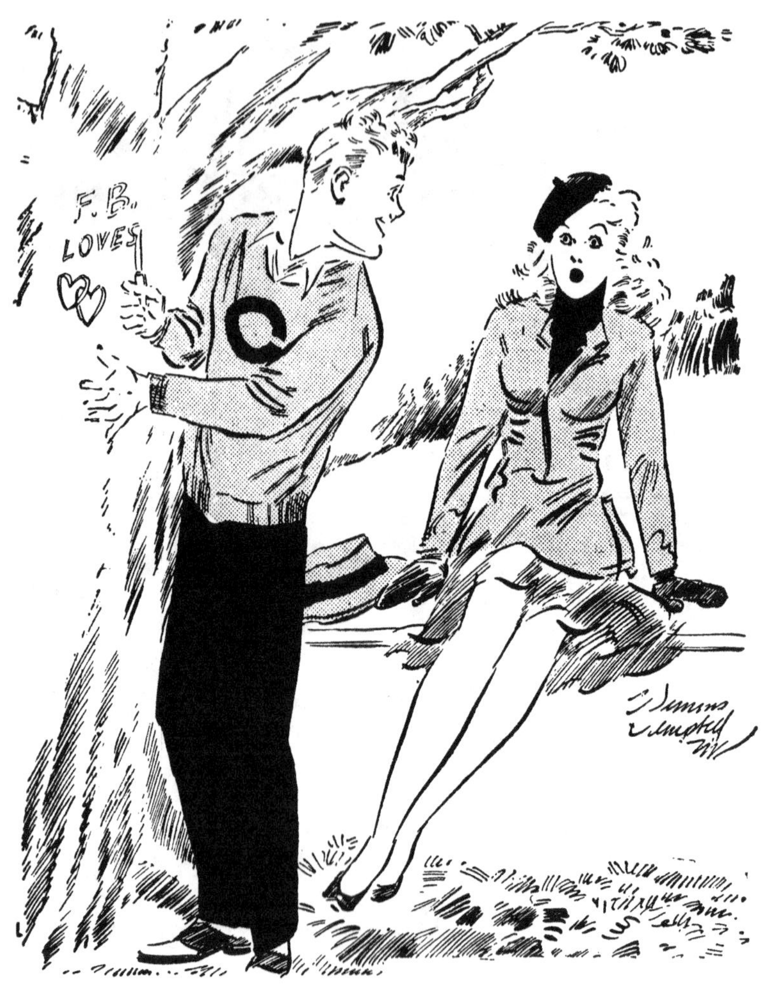

"—er-r—What did you say your name was again?"

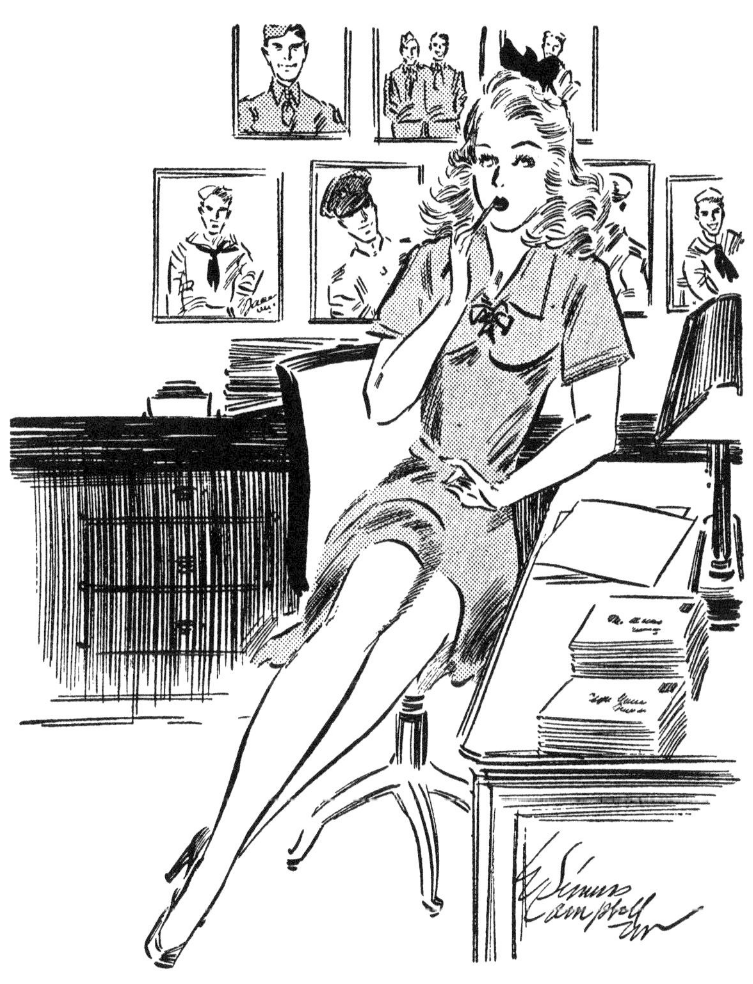

"M-M-M-M, let's see. . . . Have I forgotten any of the boys I promised to be true to?"

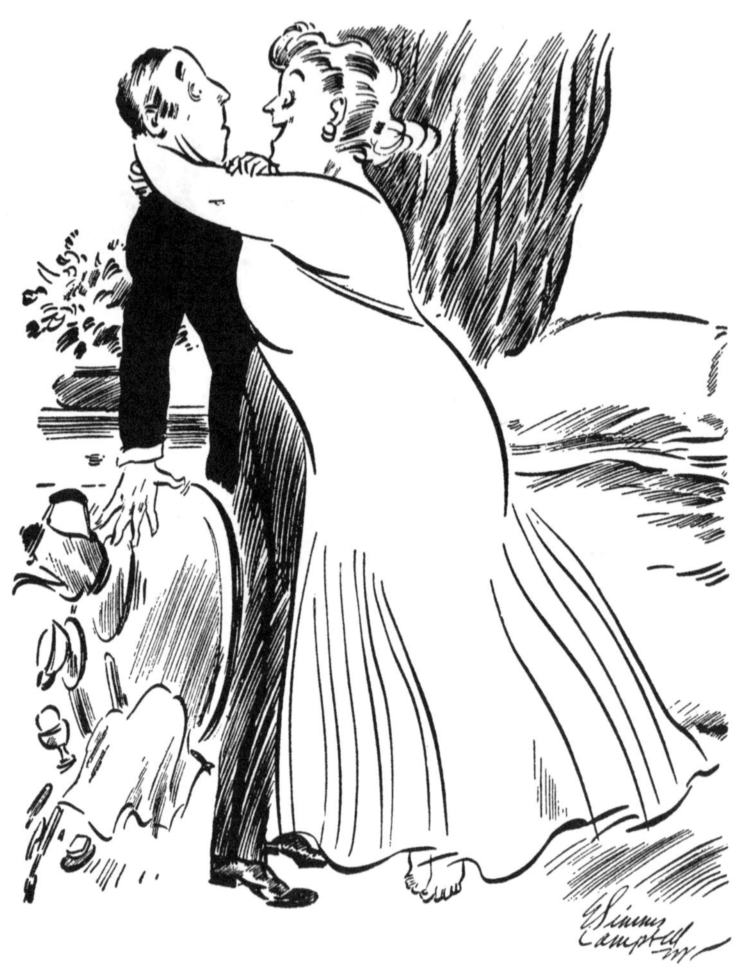

"The heck with my breakfast, Hawkins! I dreamt about YOU last night!"

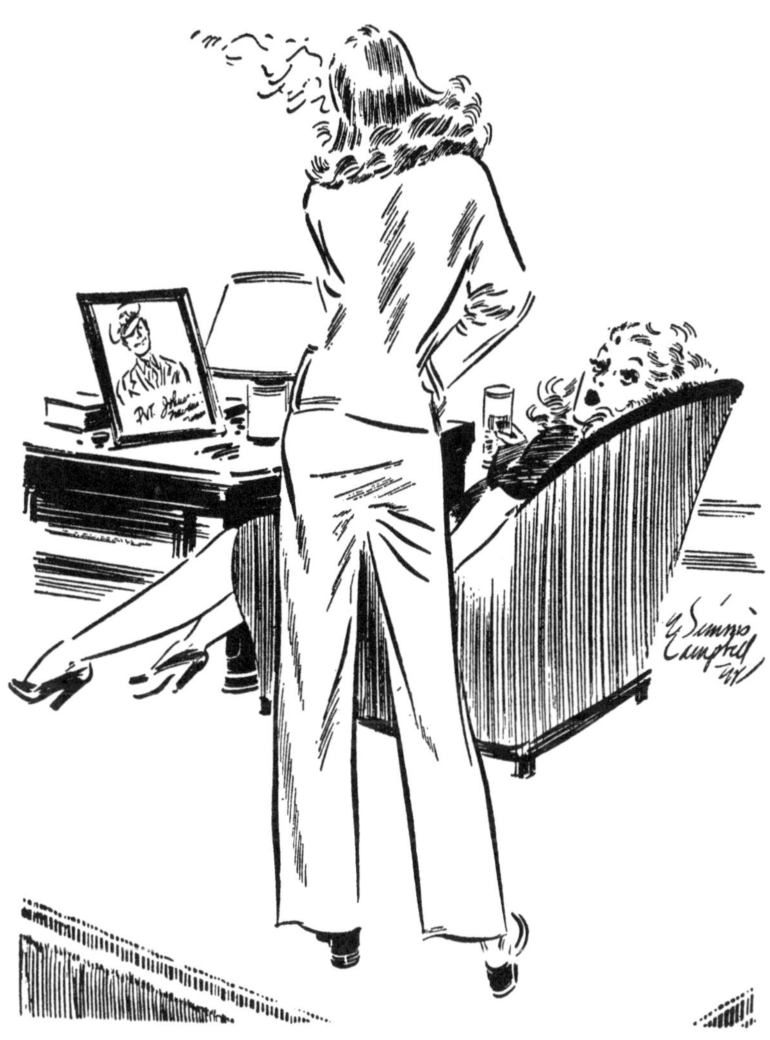

"We're getting married just as soon as he's made a General. They get ten grand a year, you know!"

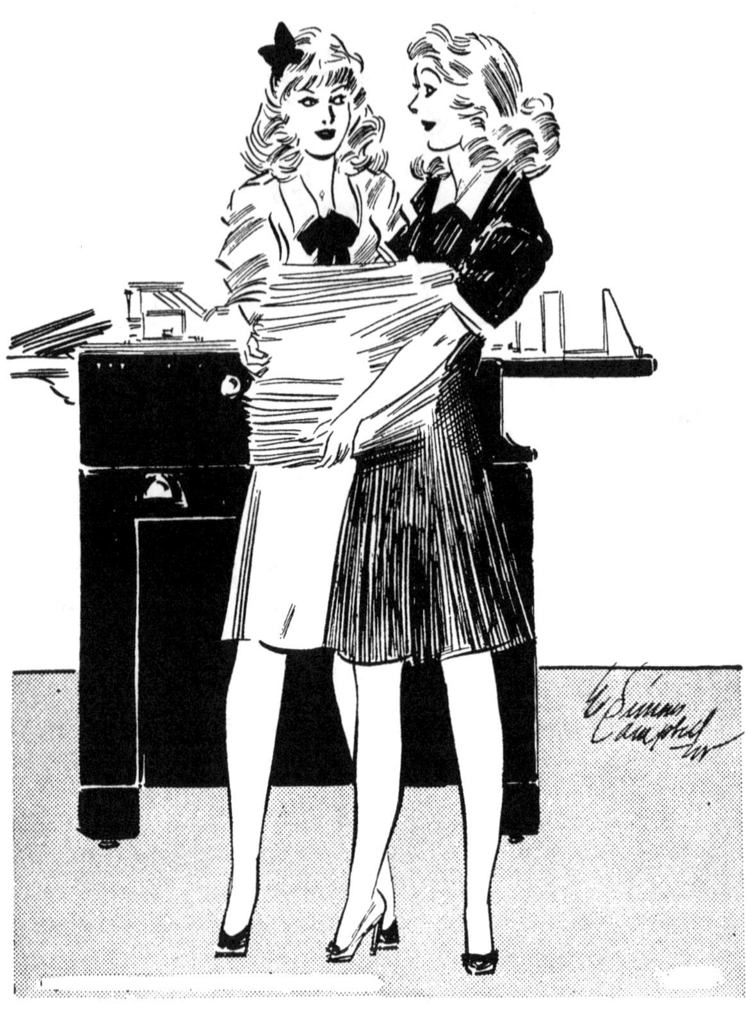

"It's working out beautifully. My boy friend's an air-raid warden and he only comes to see me on black-out nights."

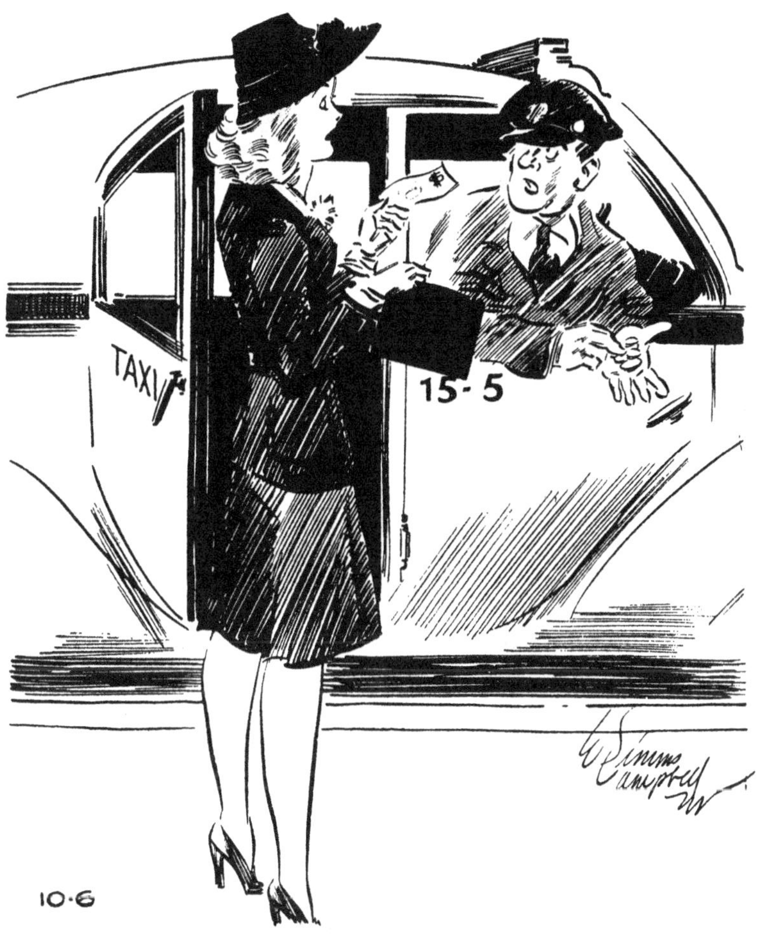

"You women! If you didn't always want change, I wouldn't always be havin' none!"

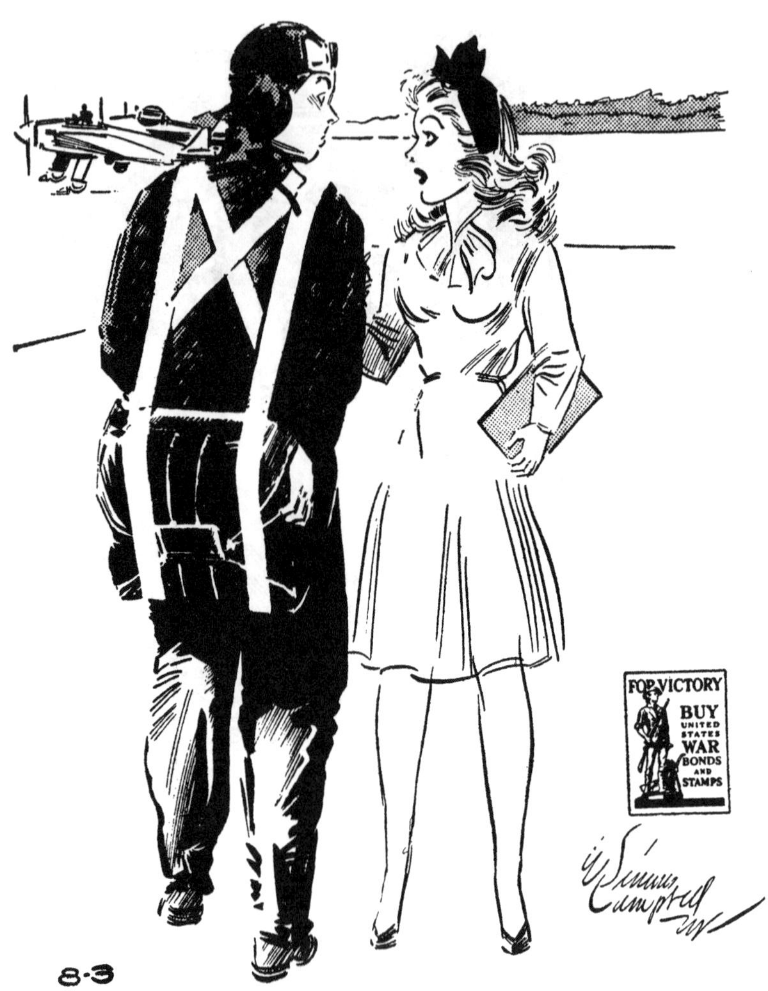

"You mean to tell me you actually FIGHT in all those clothes!"

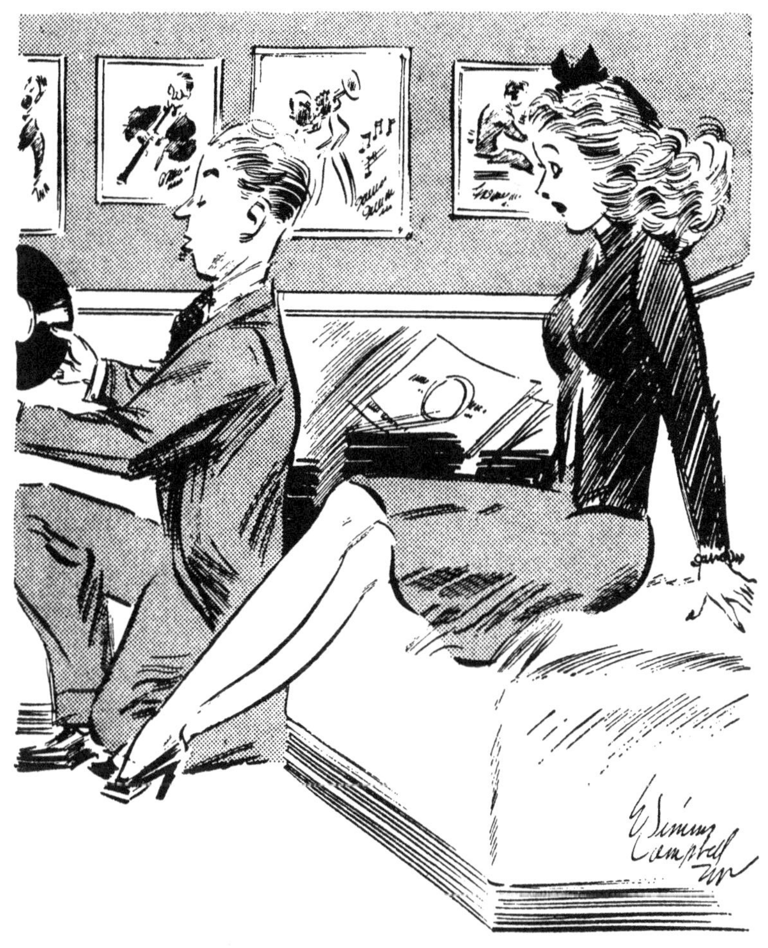

"Oh, I don't believe in heredity. My Mother was crazy about collecting phonograph records, but it never—but it never—but it never—but it never affected me!"

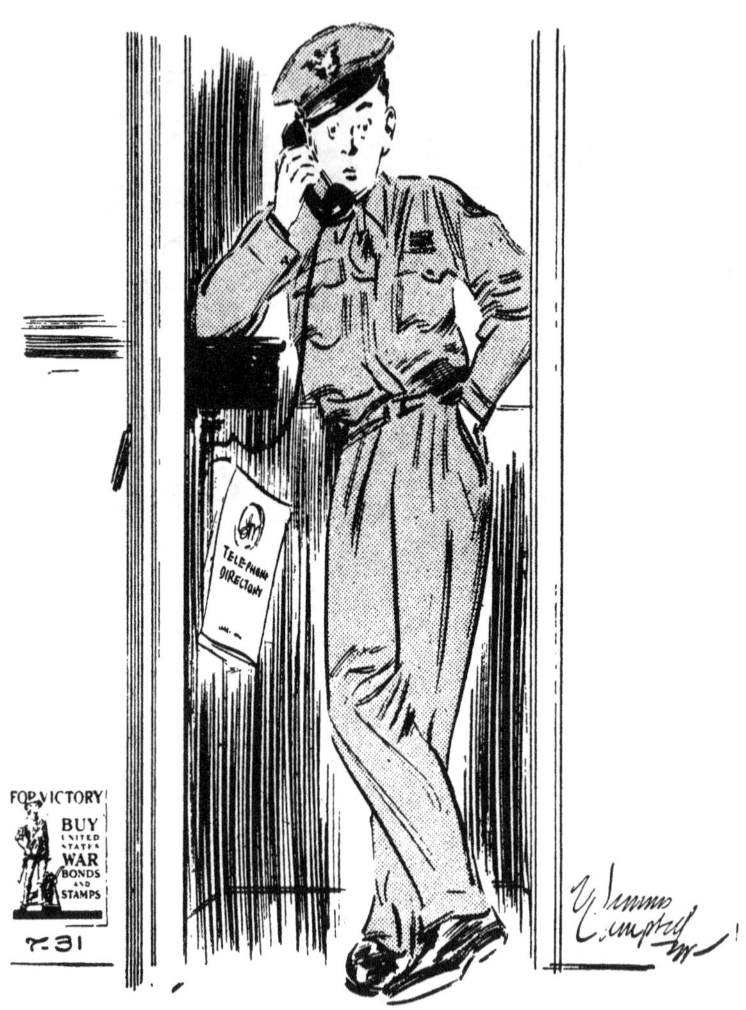

"—And have you got your nice, new raise of fifty - dollars WITH you, darling?"

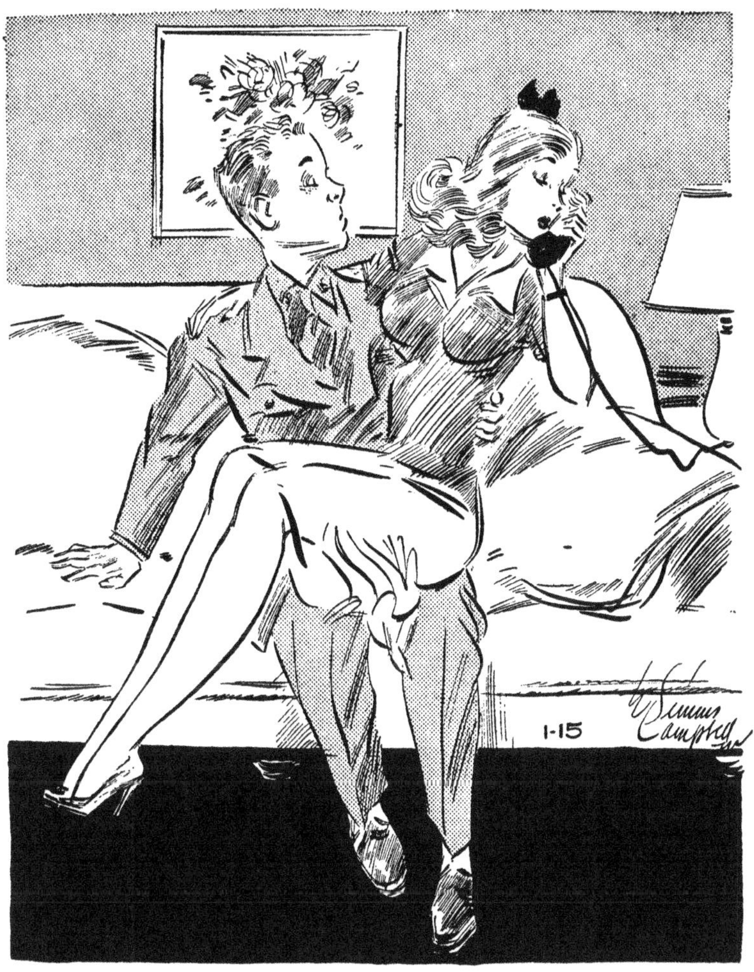

"Well, no, I'm not exactly busy, Jane, but I AM engaged in a little war work at the present time!"

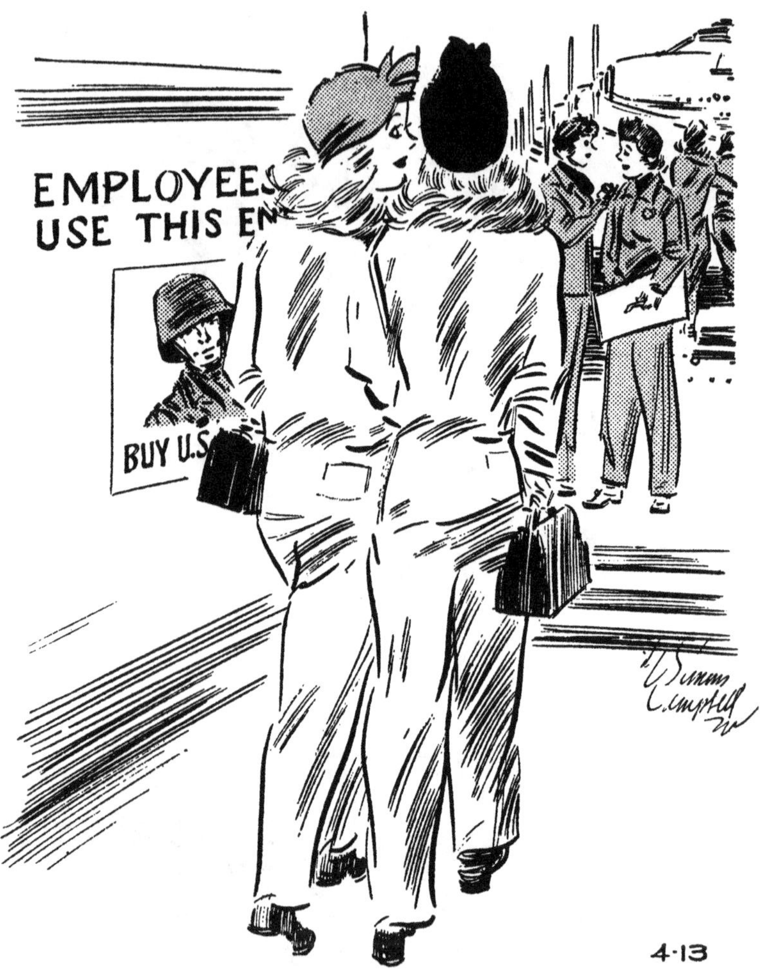

"He's not much company, but he's full of tattoo marks and makes interesting reading!"

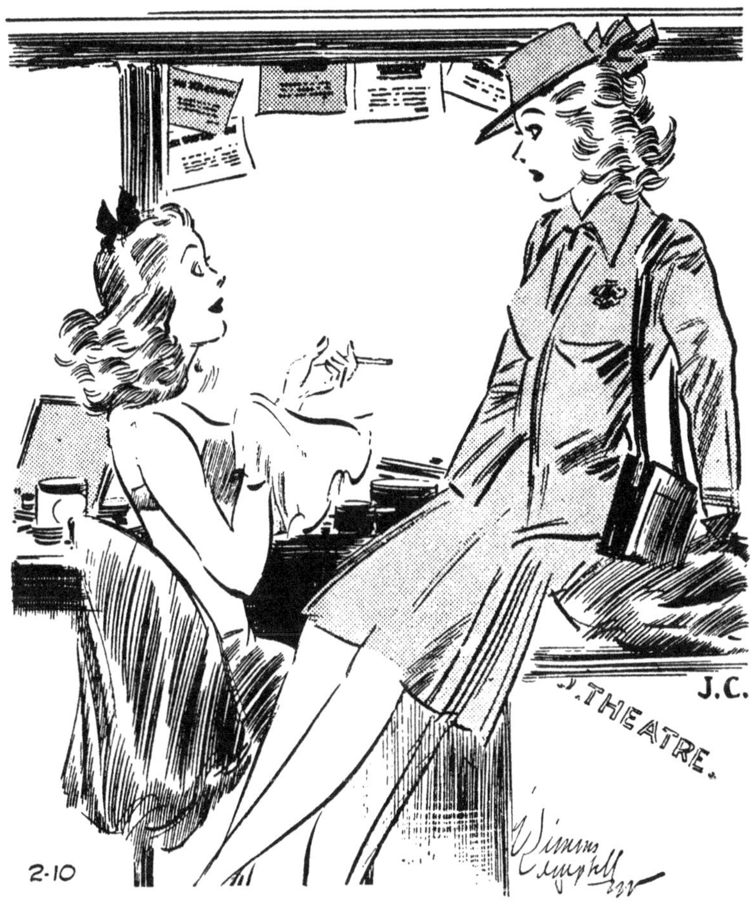

"You remember that psychiatrist she went to when she thought she was losing her mind? He's lost his, over her!"

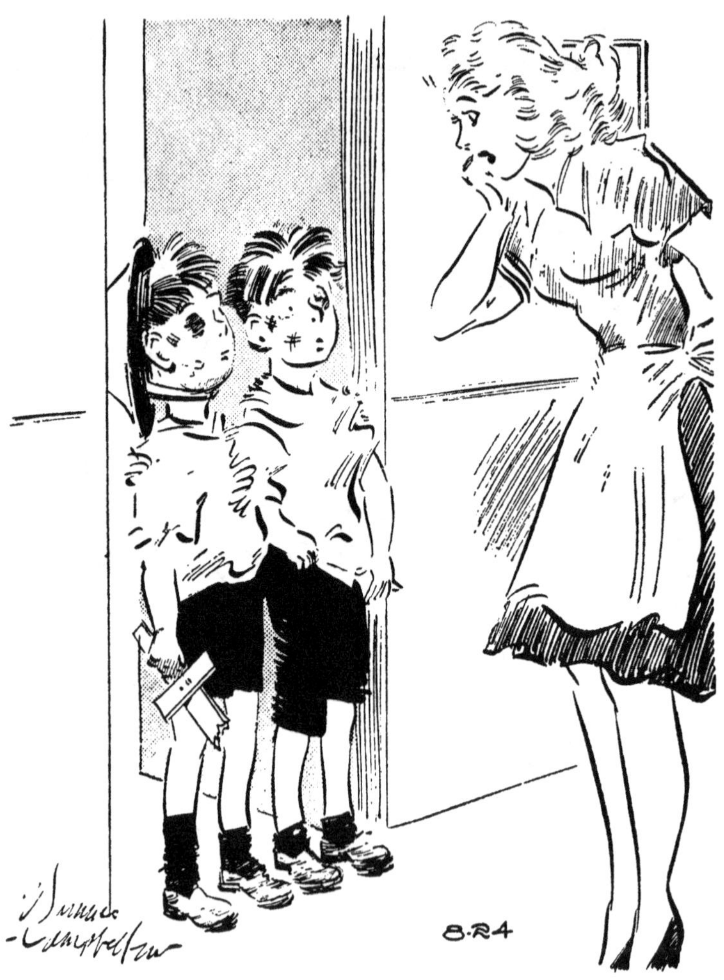

"—T-T-T-Then it became OUR turn to be the Japs!"

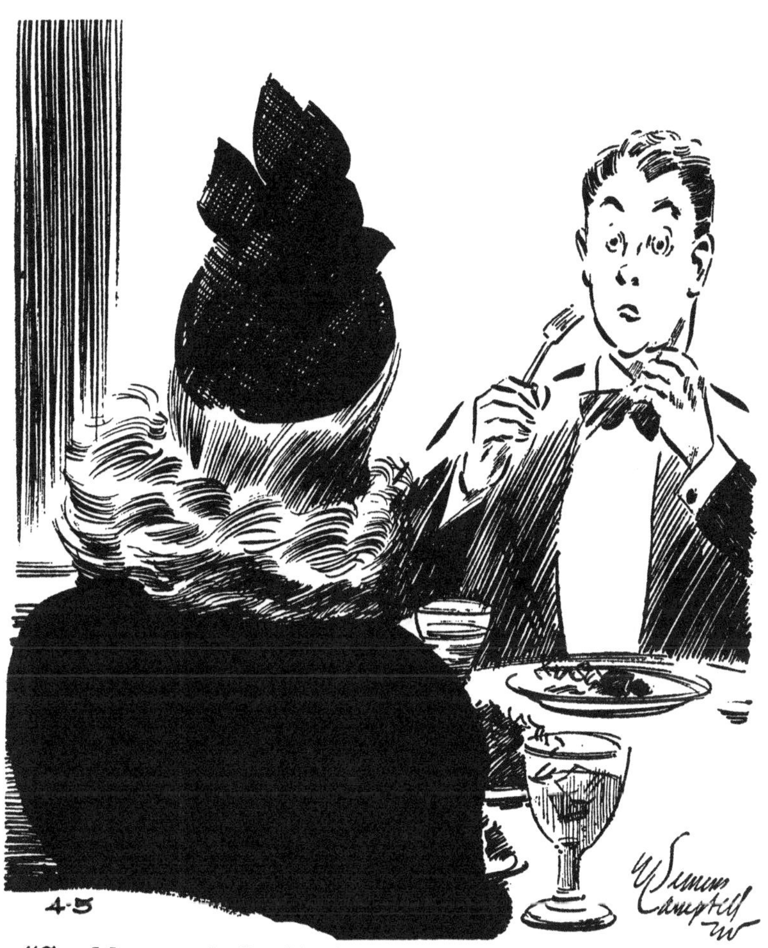

"Good heavens! I said, "Whoa," and this meat stuck in my throat!"

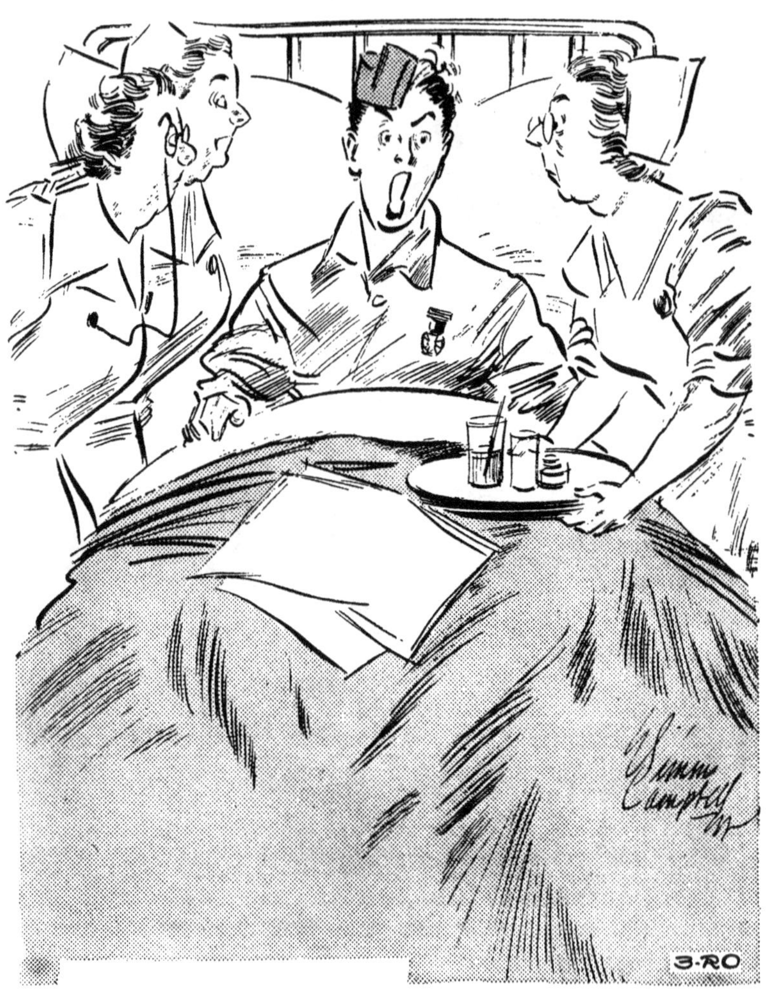

"Well, gimme a young, **INEFFICIENT** nurse, **then!**"

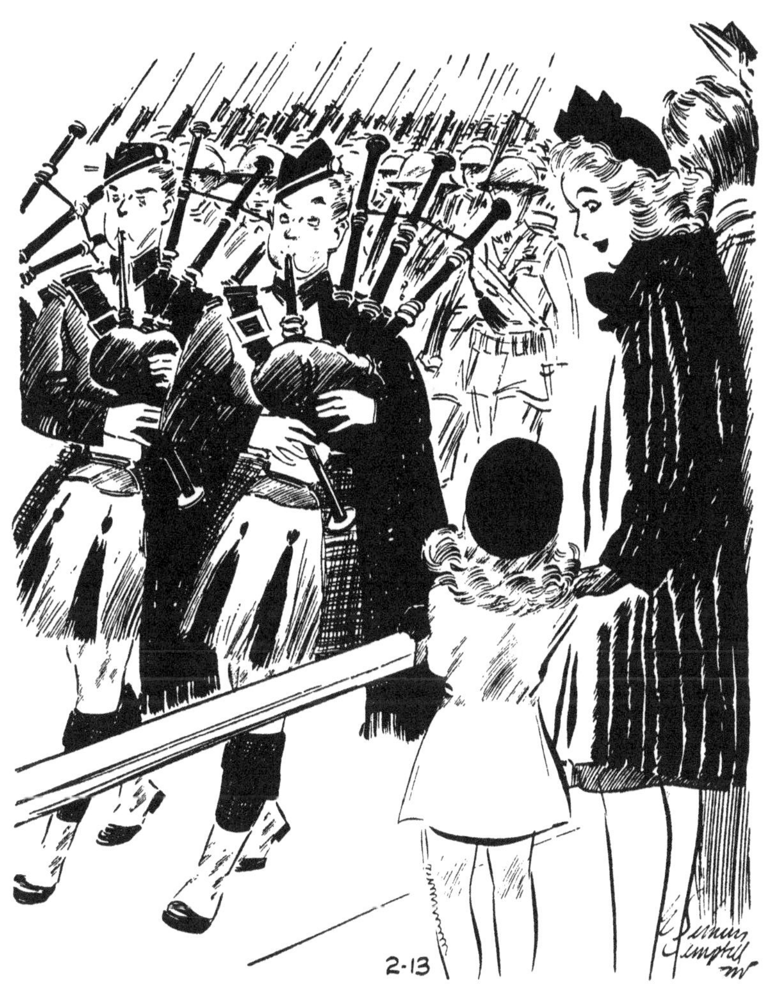

"What's that they're squeezing under their arms and hurting so, mama?"

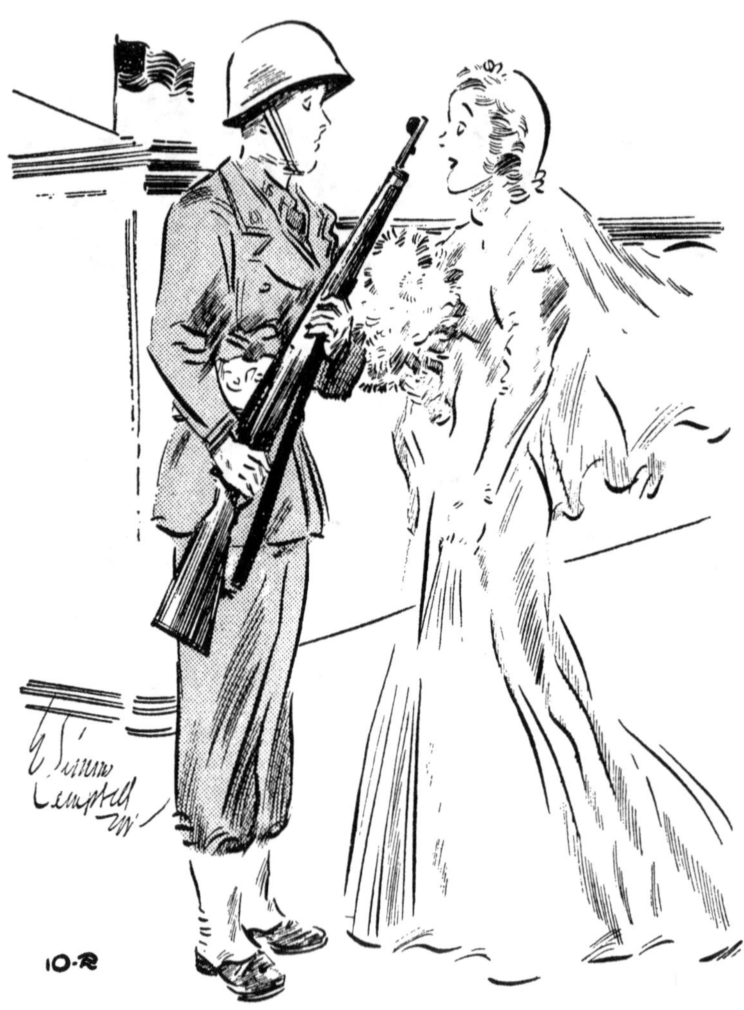

"Corporal John B. Jones of this regiment gets **his** leave in five minutes! Tell him I'm ready!"

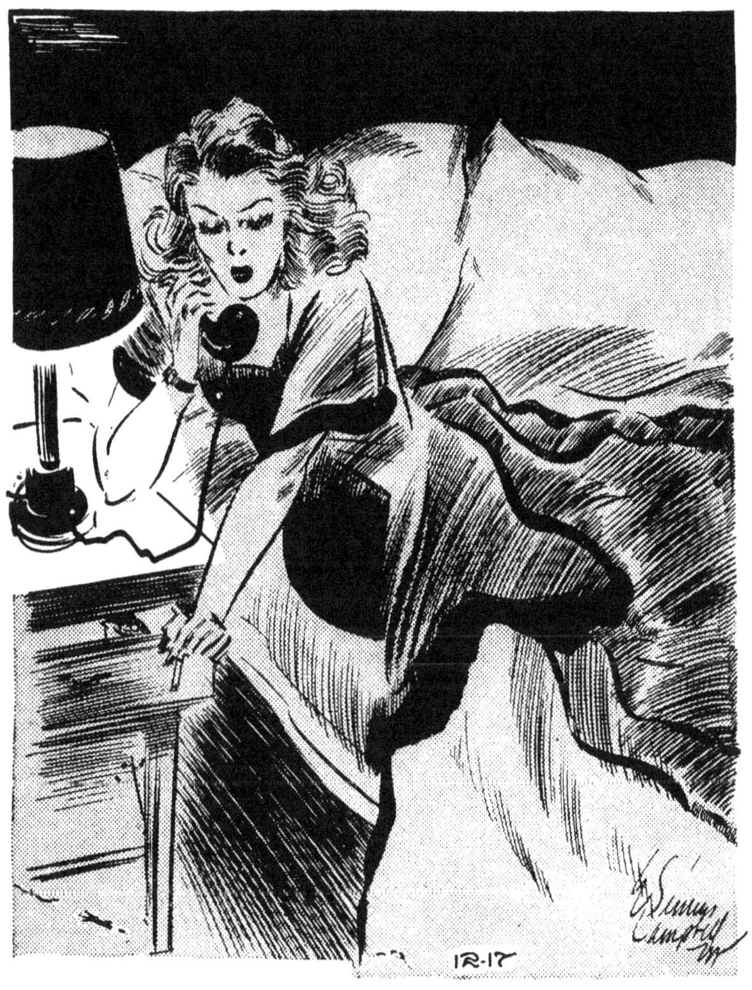

"Well, since you're working all night, dear, isn't it difficult working with that ORCHESTRA in your office?"

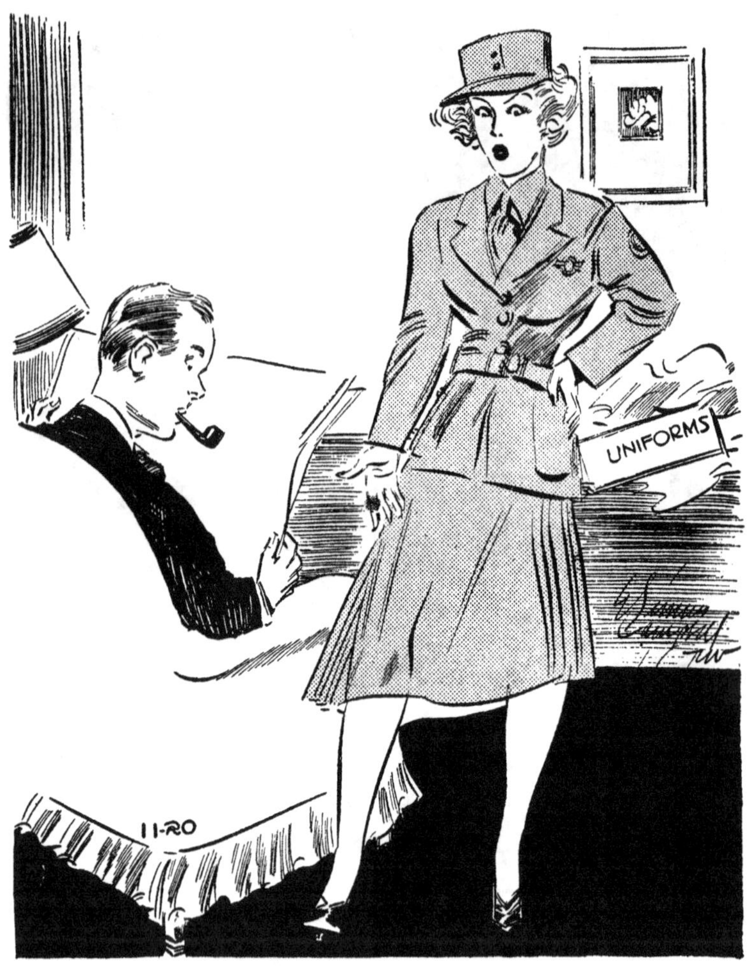

"Of course, I'm sending it back! Imagine me, trying to do war work in a dress THIS long!"

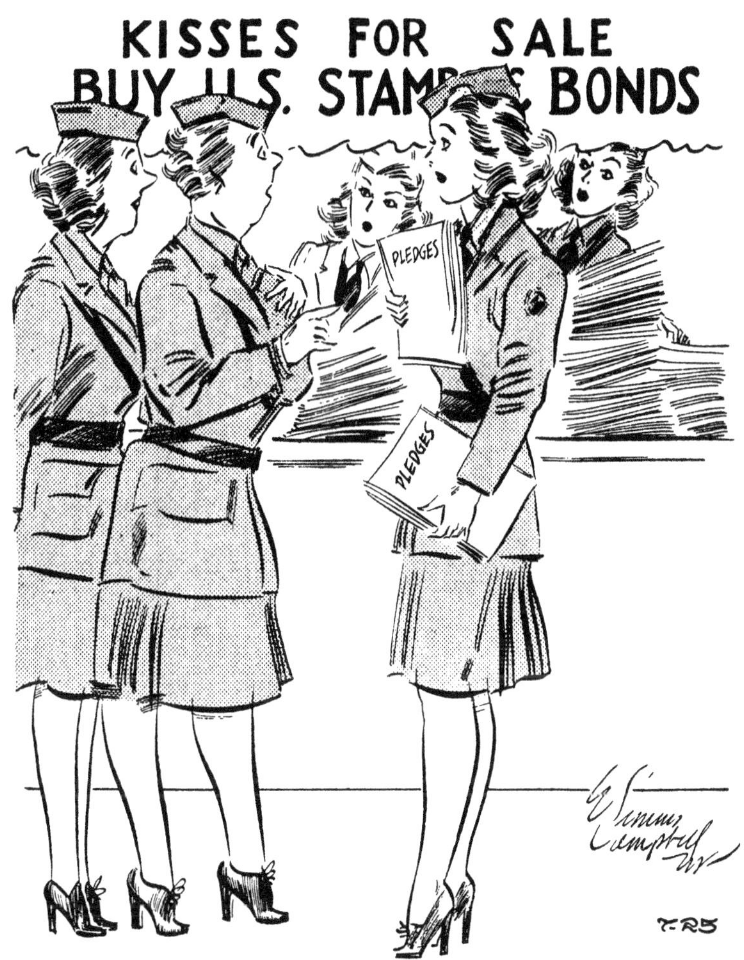

"You girls have a better location than ours. Would you believe it, we haven't even sold ONE stamp?"

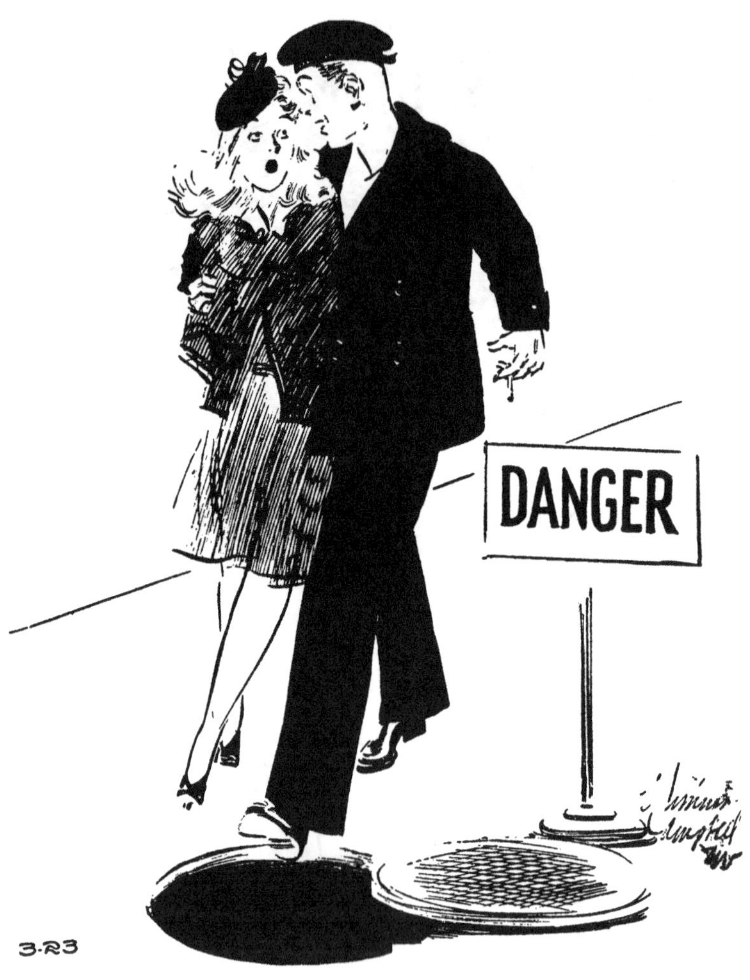

"Why, Darling, if I ever THOUGHT about another girl, I'd wish the earth would swallow me up!"

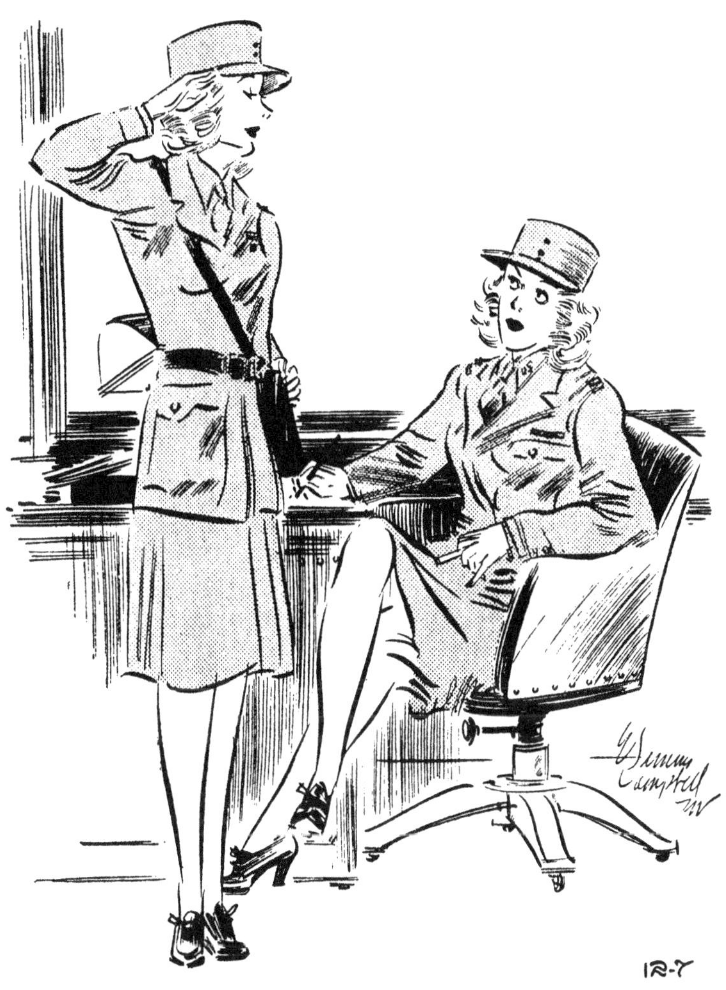

"Lieutenant Wilson reporting. There are no eligible men in Company C, but Company F has infinite possibilities!"

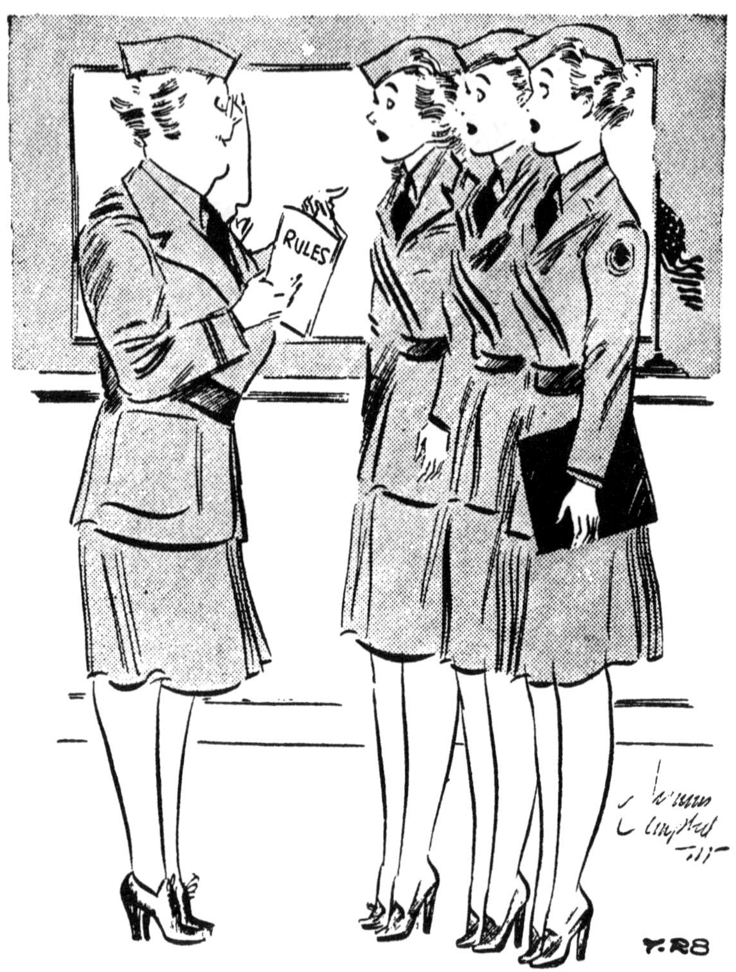

"—Now I'll show you what to do, if a man gets fresh. By the way, do any of you girls KNOW any fresh men?"

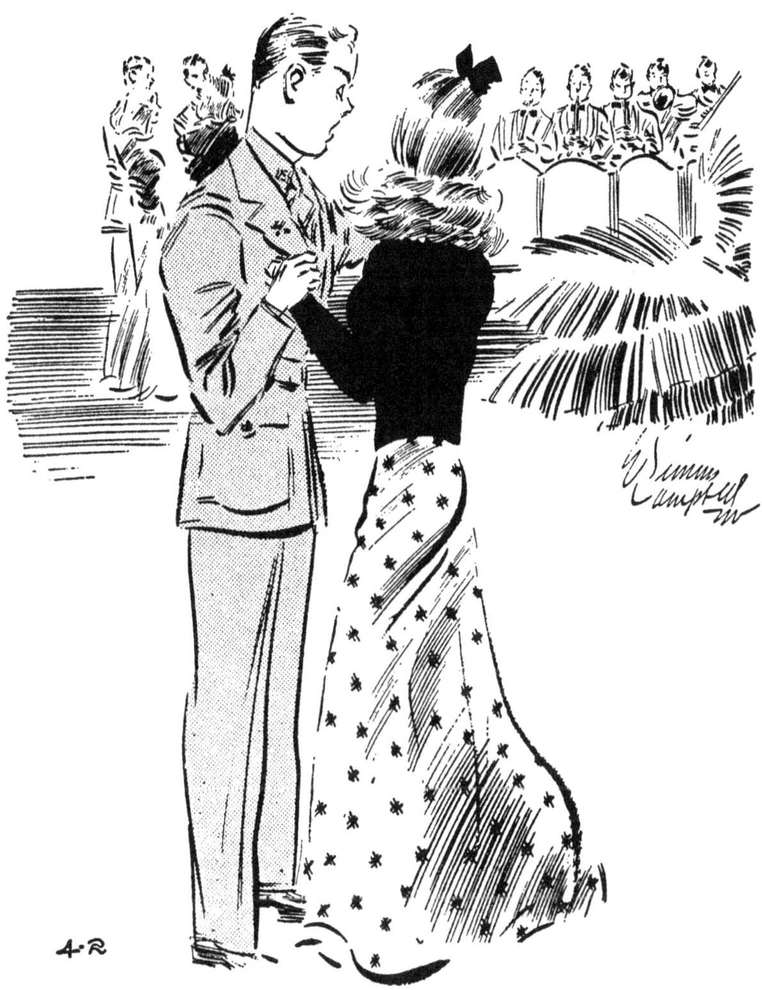

"What an orchestra! I asked them to play a swing number and they're playing 'Swing Low, Sweet Chariot!'"

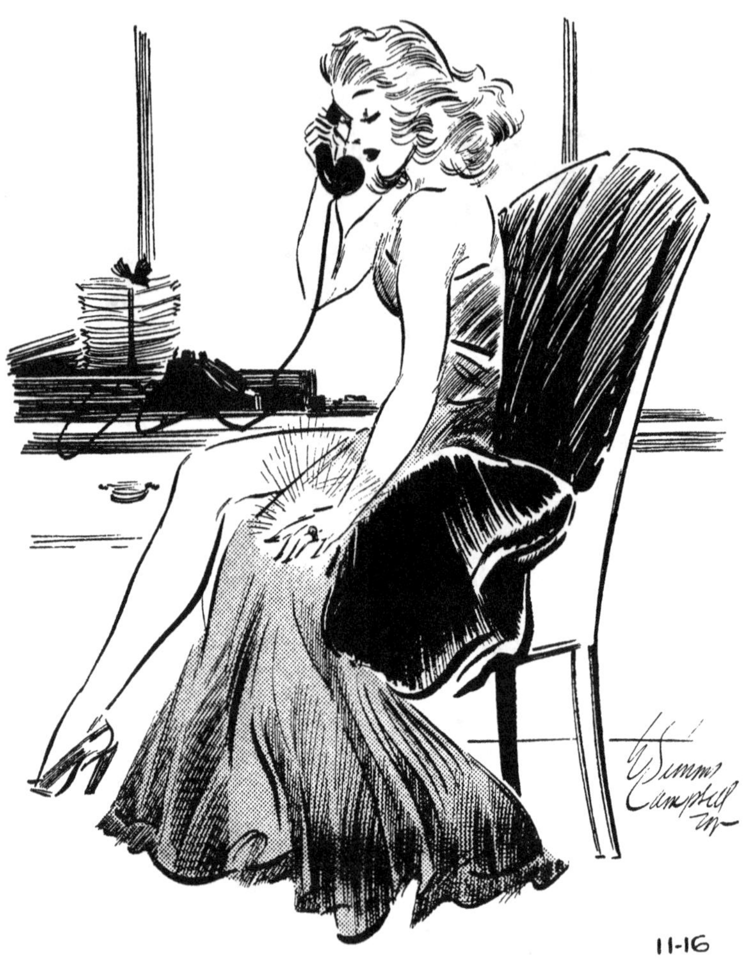

"It's no use! I'm sending you back your letters and everything.
I'll just keep the ring for sentiment!"

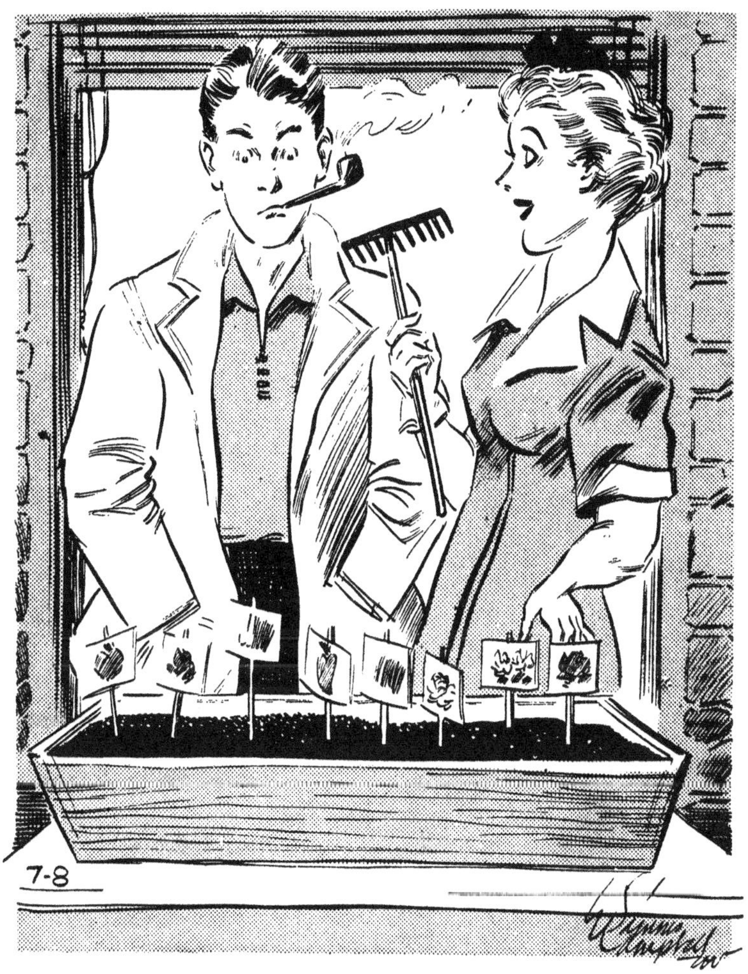

"Aren't you proud of me? I planted beans, tomatoes. corn, peas, carrots, radishes and even flowers!"

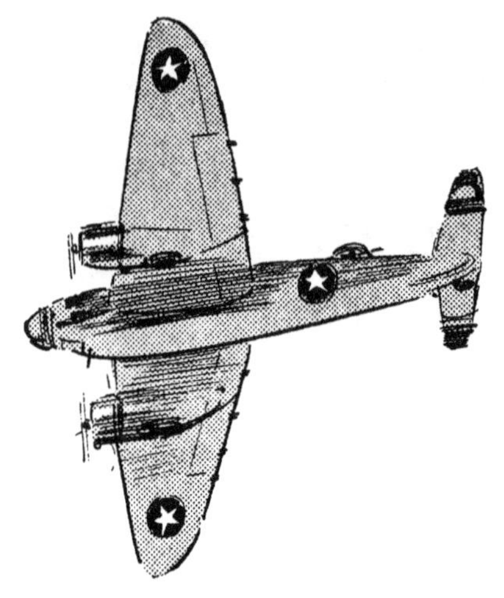

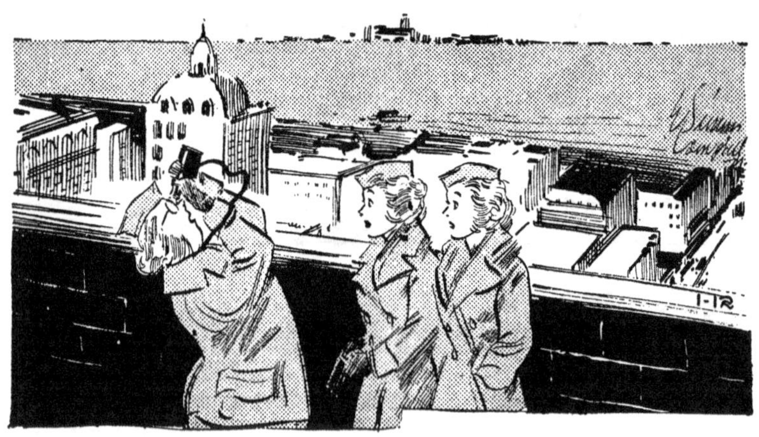

"Off-hand, I'd say it was one of ours!"

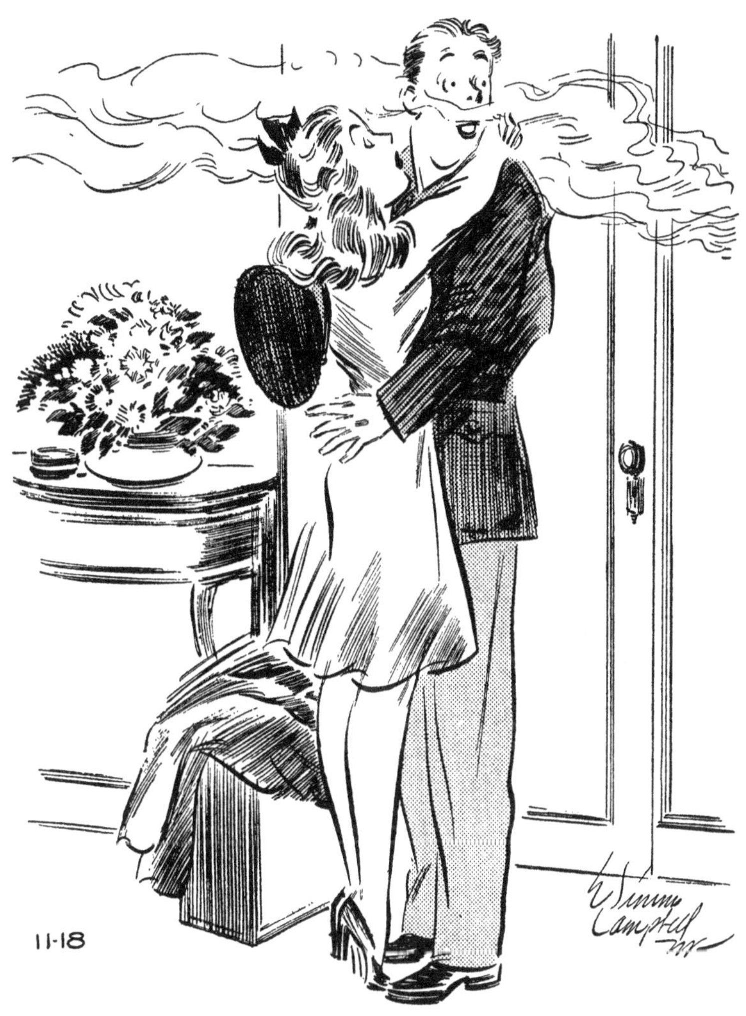

"—And I'll miss you, too, darling! SAY, is that **CHICKEN** your mother's cooking?"

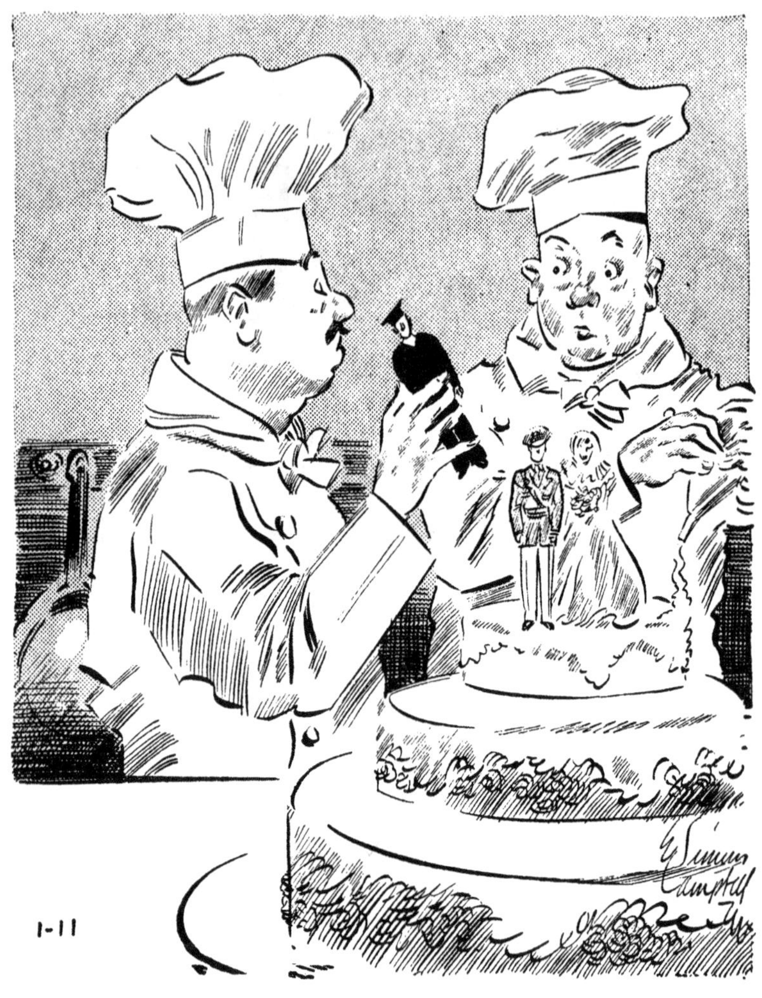

"She told me to keep a sailor handy, just in case she changes her mind!"

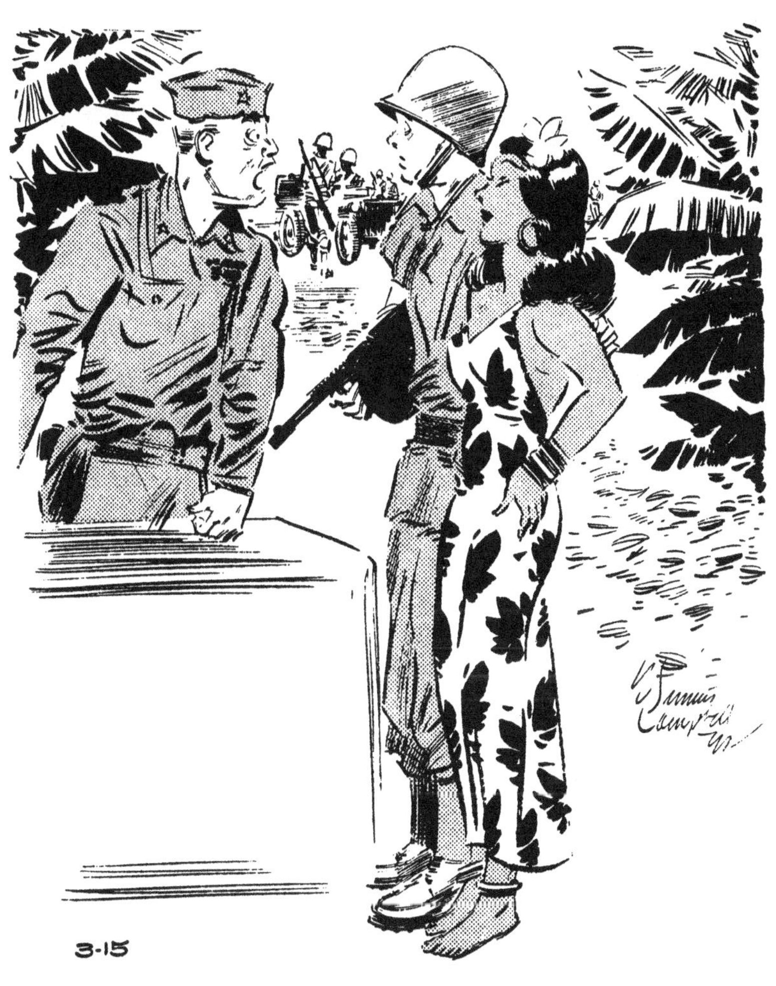

"I don't care WHAT you thought! You can't HAVE any mascot!"

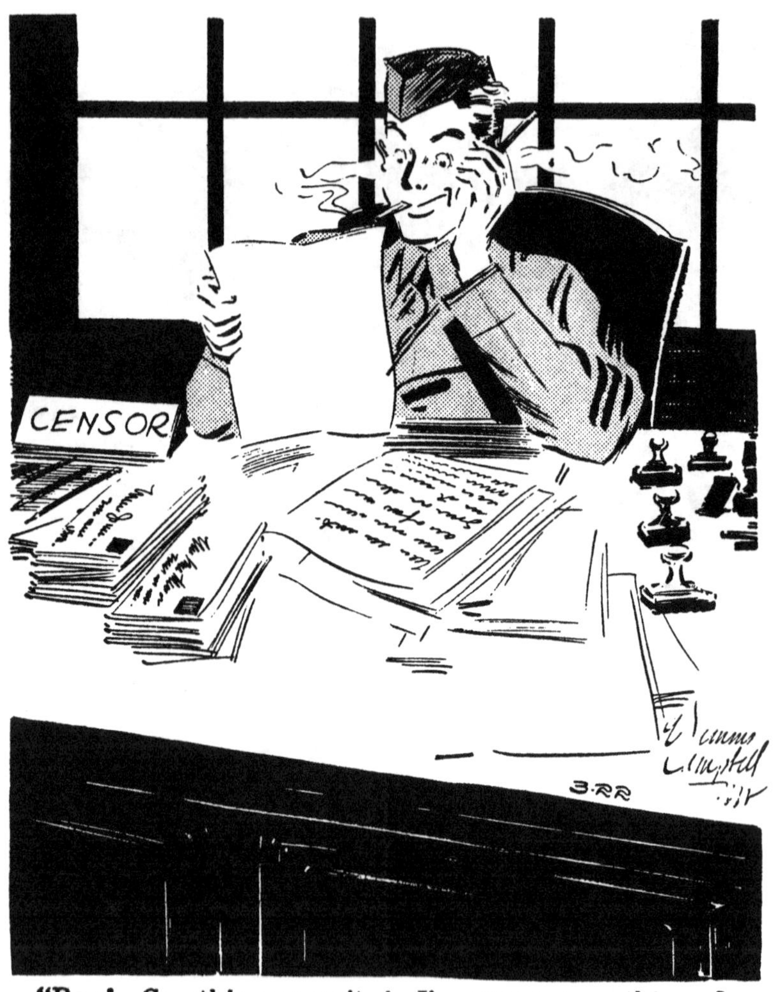

"Boy! Can this guy write! I'm gonna copy this and send it to MY girl!"

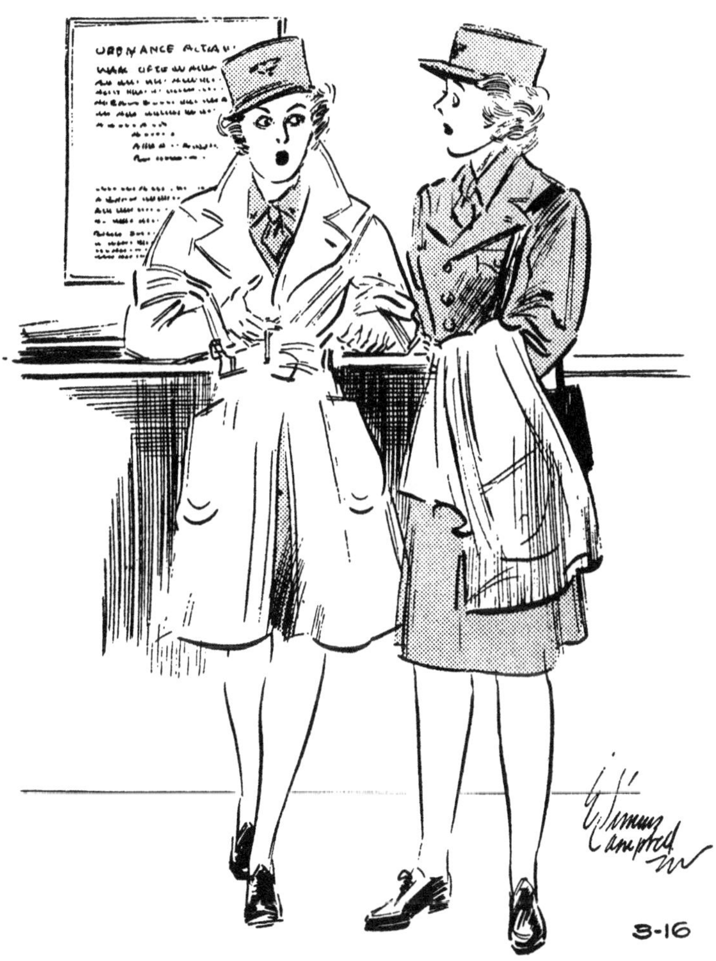

"They used to say, 'hello, Babe.' Now all they do is salute!"

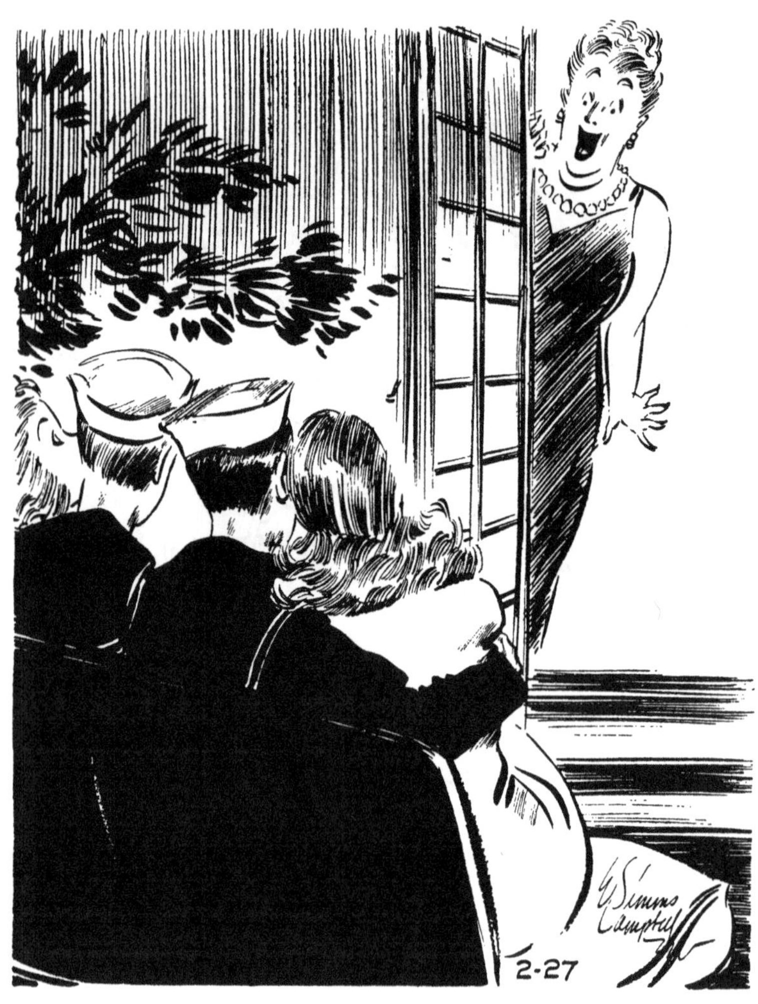

"Boys! We're serving ice cream now!"

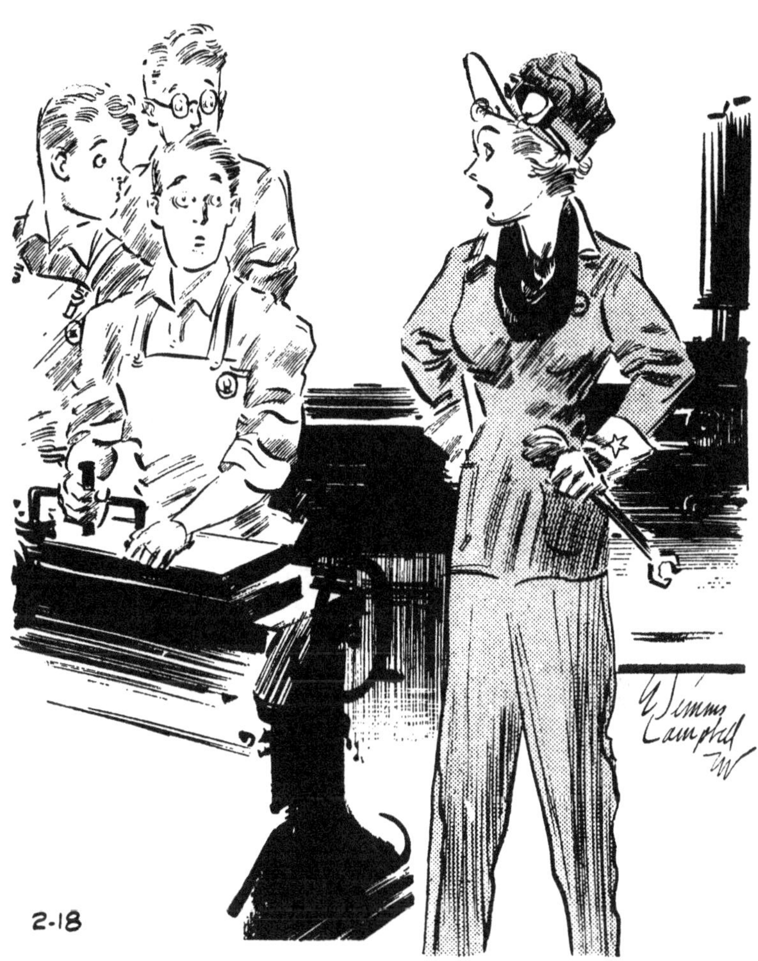

"You're the dumbest bunch of guys I've ever had to break in. I'd rather work with women any day!"

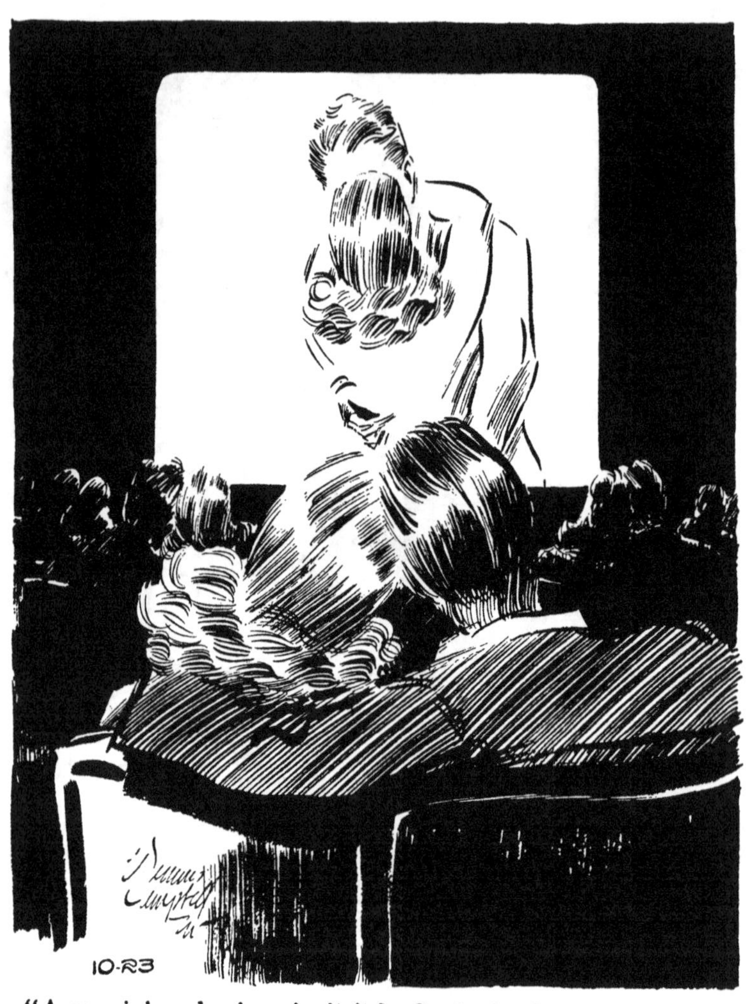

"A movie's relaxing, isn't it? Sort of takes your mind off things!"

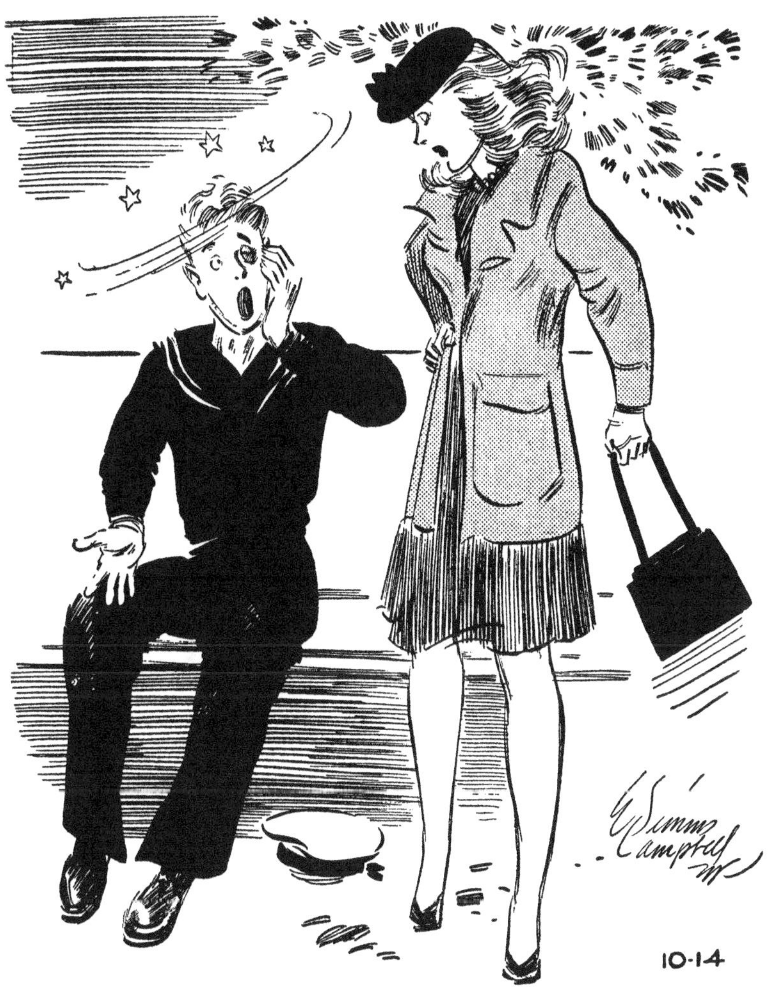

"All I can say is—actin' like that don't help our MORALE!"

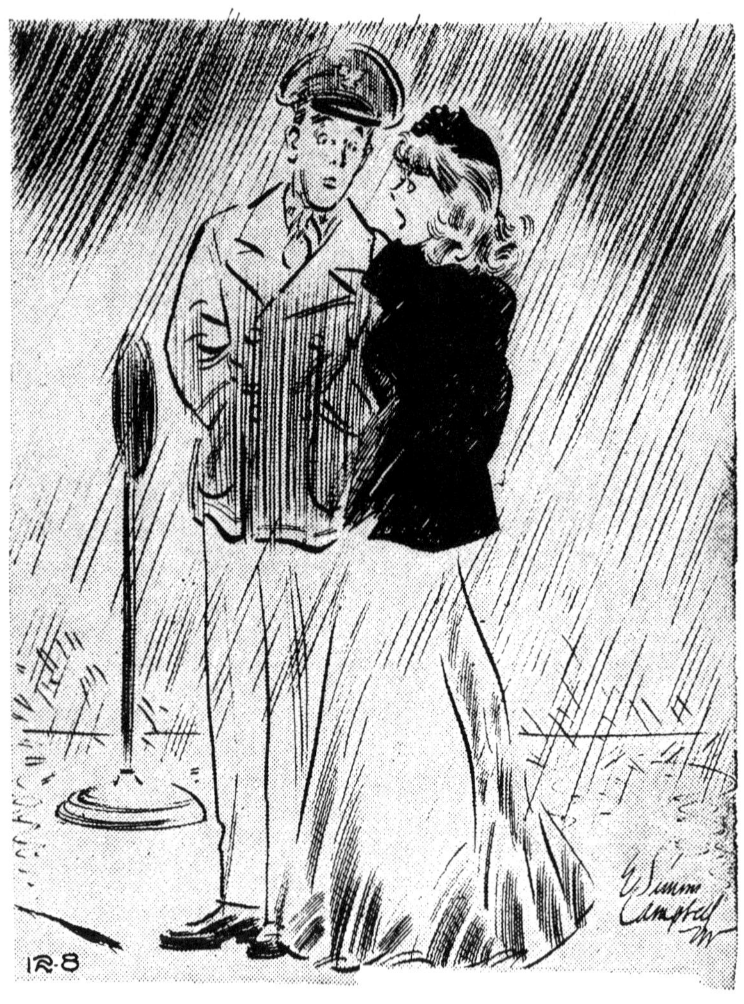

"Quit telling me how proud you are to be seen **on** the street with me and call a CAB!"

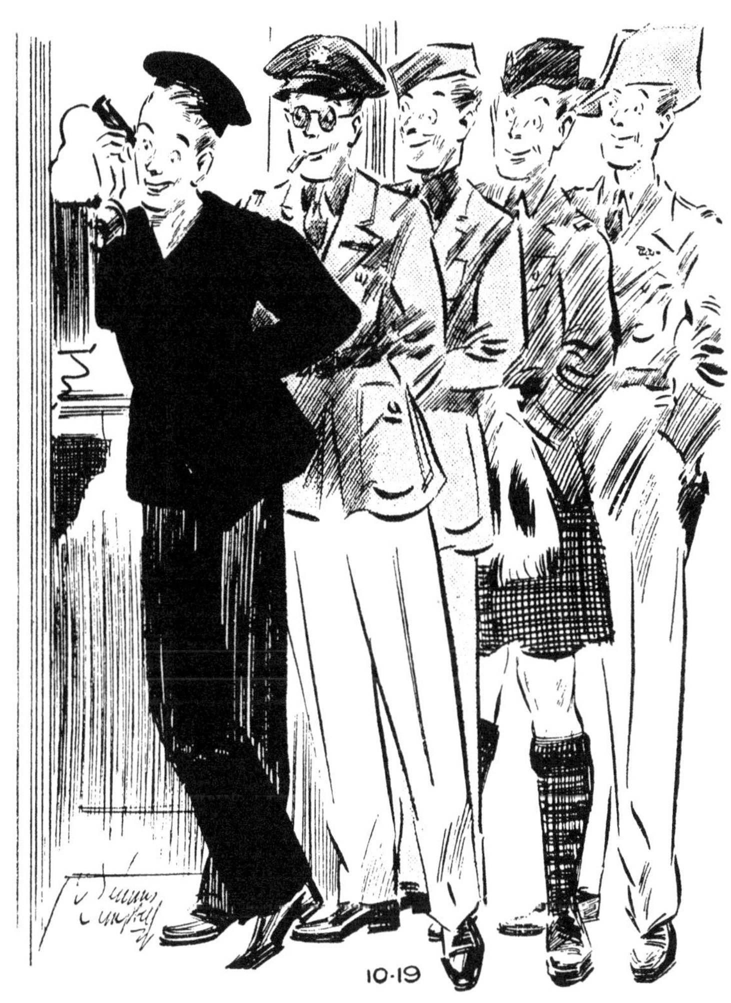

"Well, see if you can get a friend. I've got a few Allies with me, darling!"

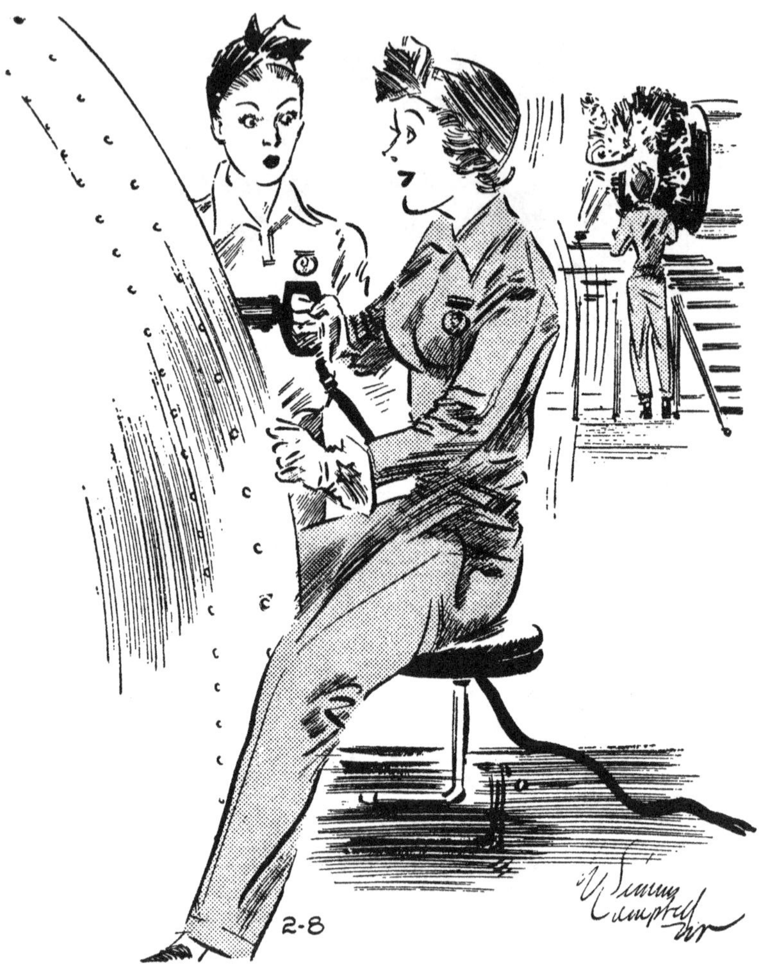

"... And would you believe it, the baby cries like **this**: Bah-R-R-R-R-R-R-R-R-R-R-R-R-R-R-R-R-R-R!"

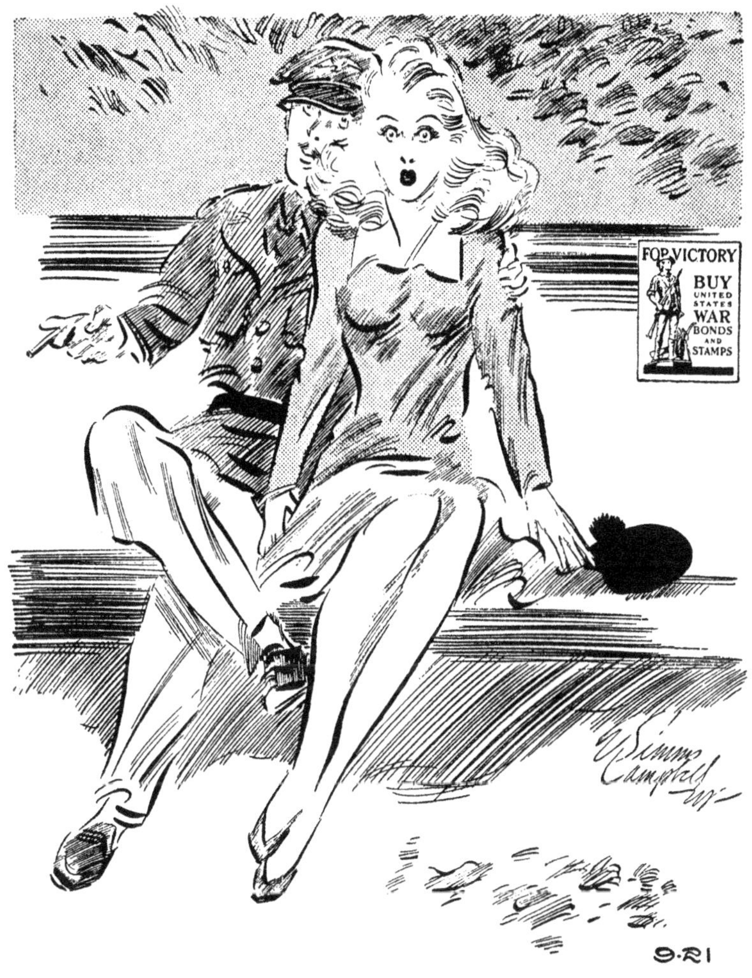

"Listen, Babe, those girls in England and Australia and Hawaii—yes, even in Egypt—haven't got a thing on you!"

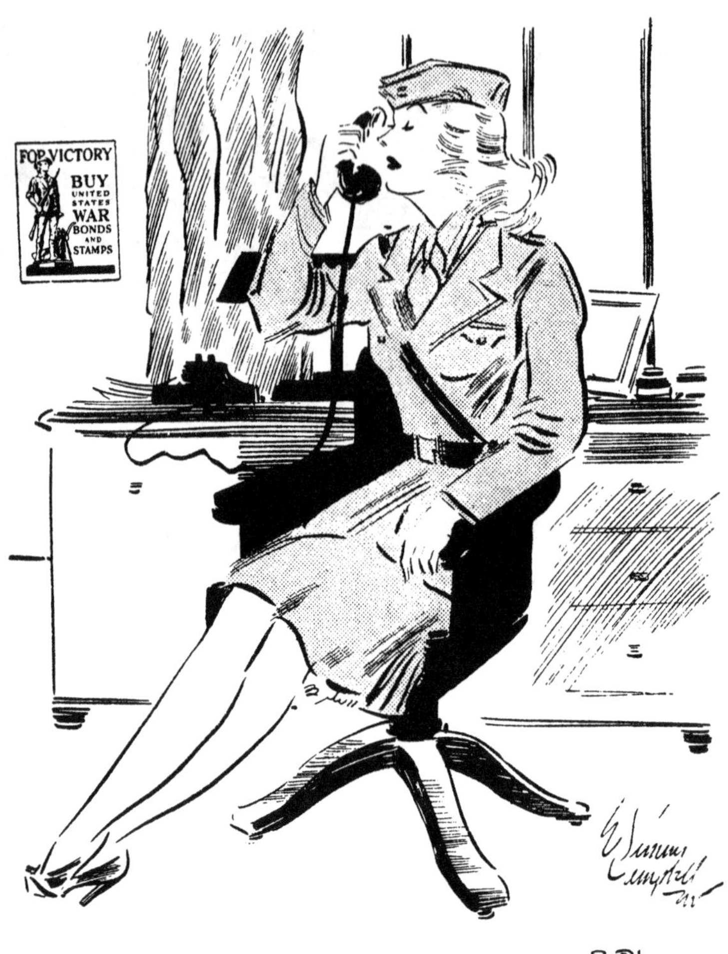

"Lieutenant Murphy speaking. Now just when may I expect those pink princess slips?"

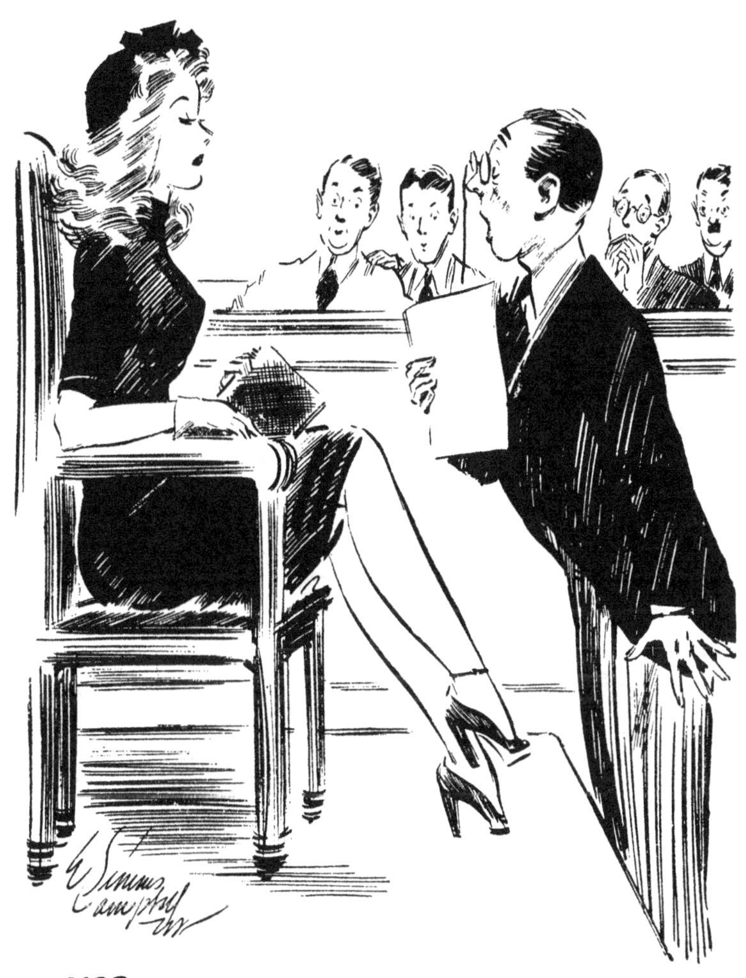

T-RR

"What! He gave you a penthouse and a diamond bracelet, because your typing was so NEAT?"

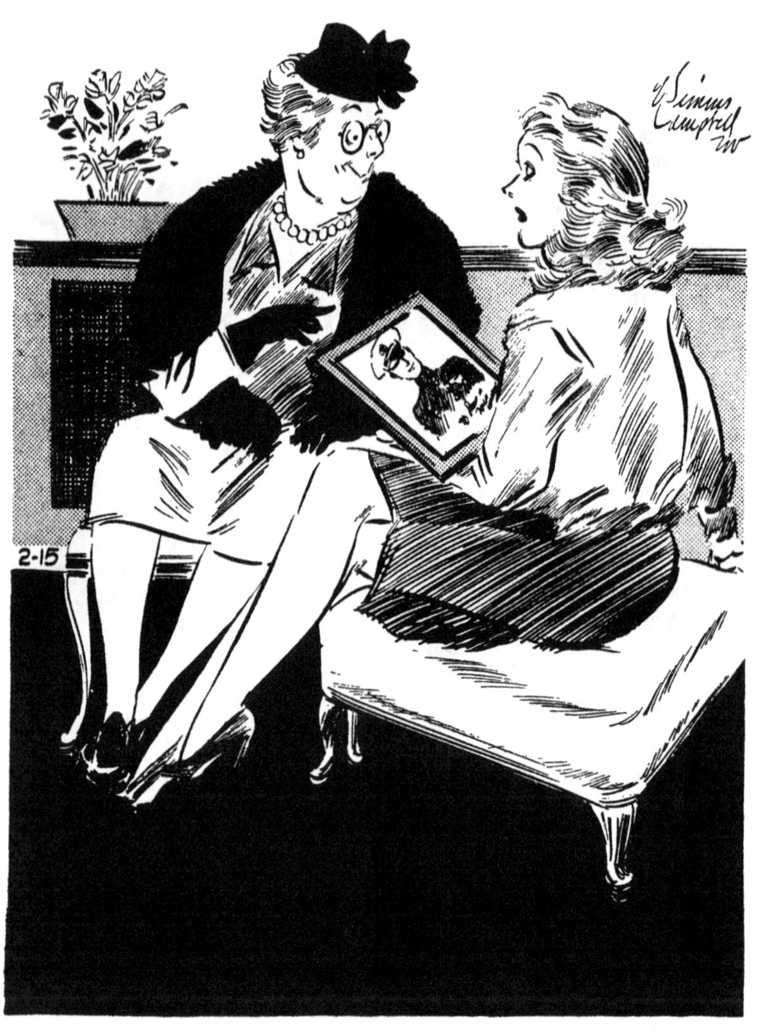

"Listen, Dearie, if I were you, I'd get married before I was old enough to have the sense not to!"

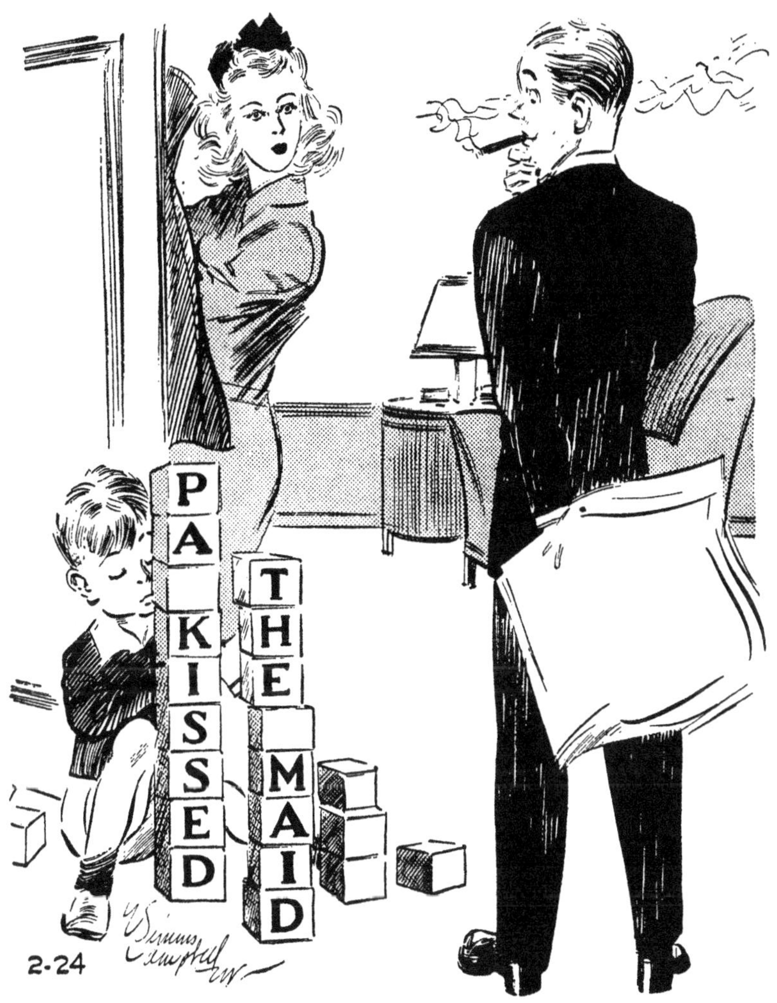

"M-M-MM—I've been thinking it over, dear. Junior's a little too old to play with blocks!"

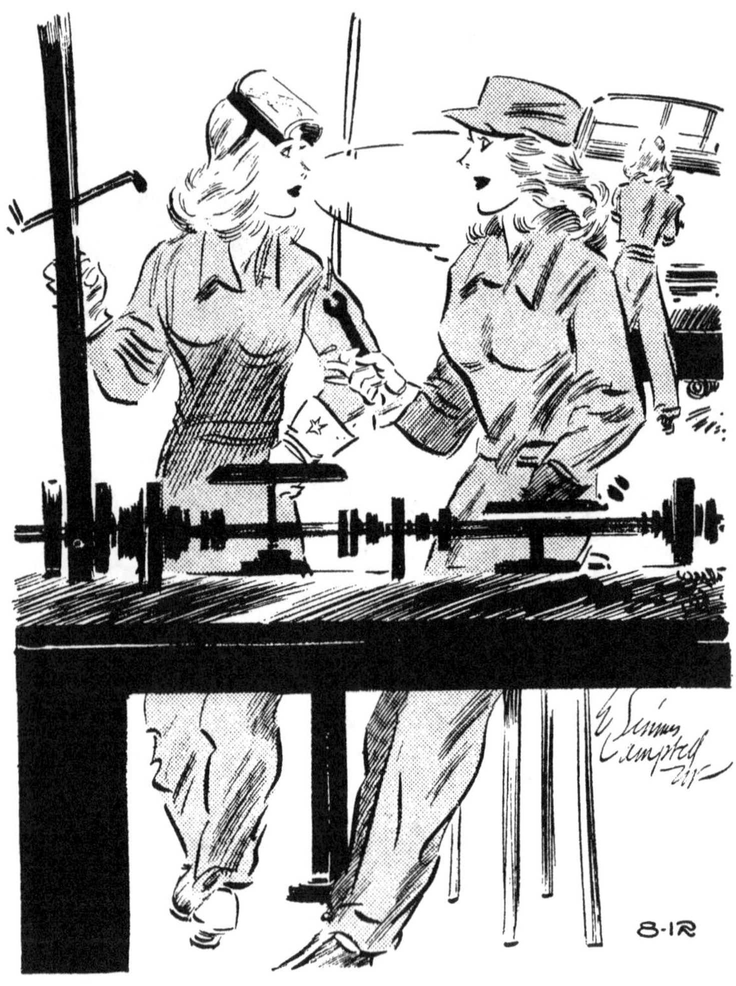

"I think I'm due for a promotion. The foreman wants to take me to dinner!"

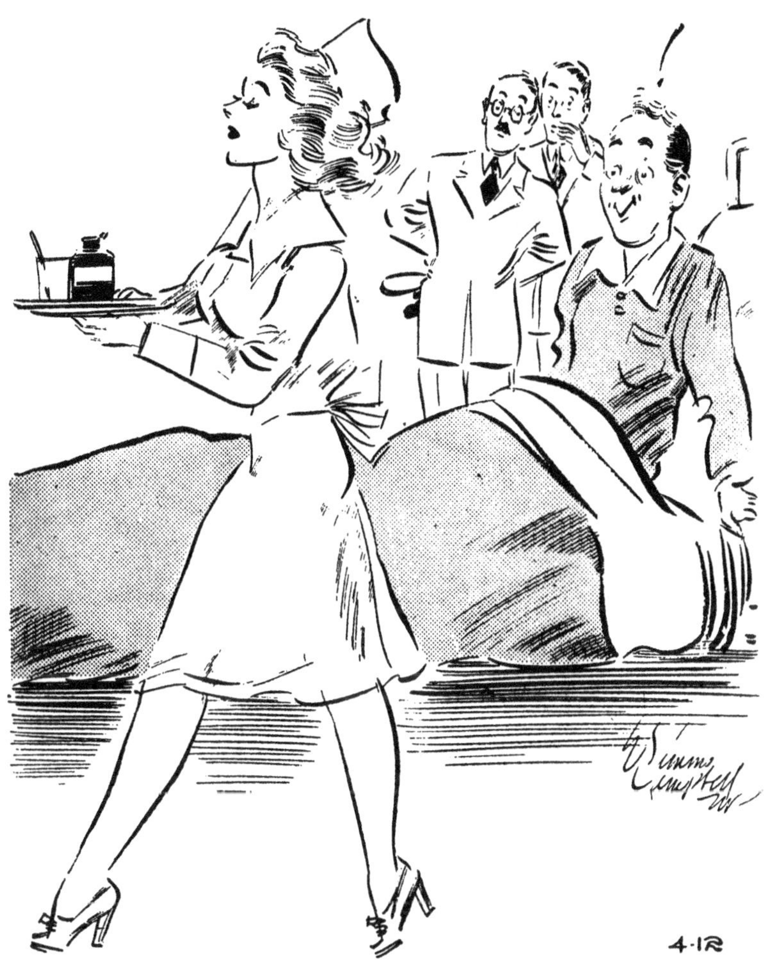

"I think we'd better transfer her from these high blood-pressure cases!"

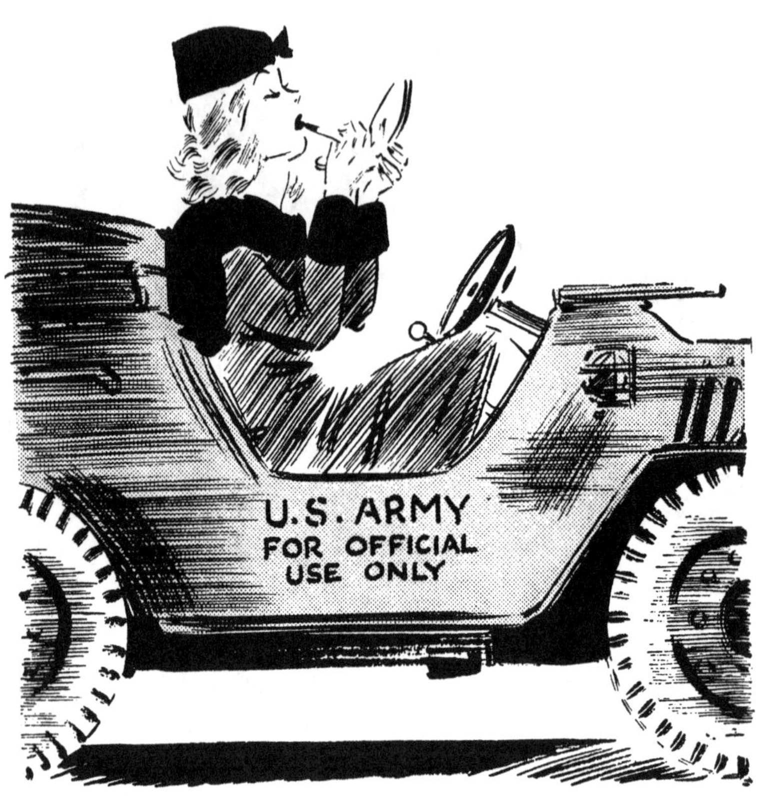

IR.14

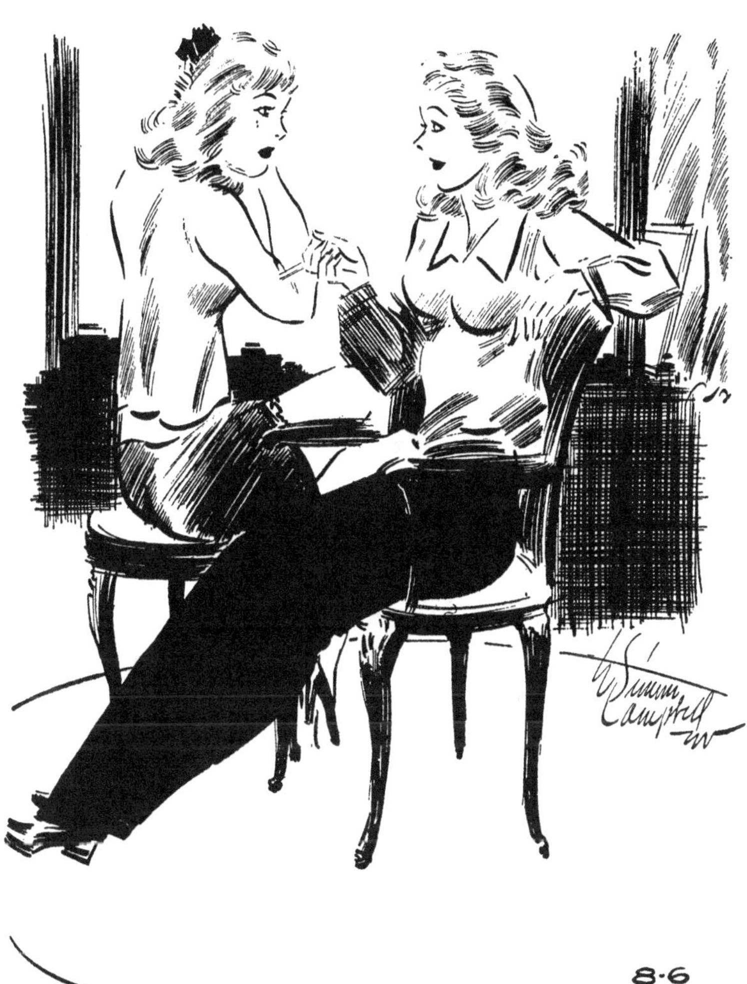

"She's the type who gives shows for the boys in camp and makes plays for the officers!"

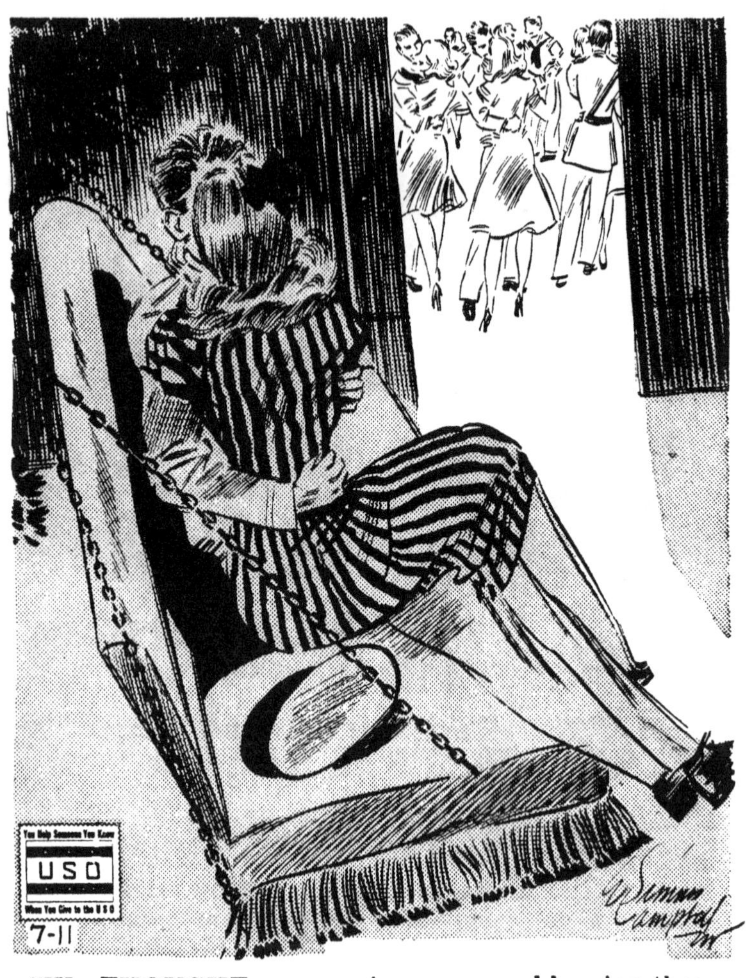

"We THOUGHT you service men would enjoy these dances!"

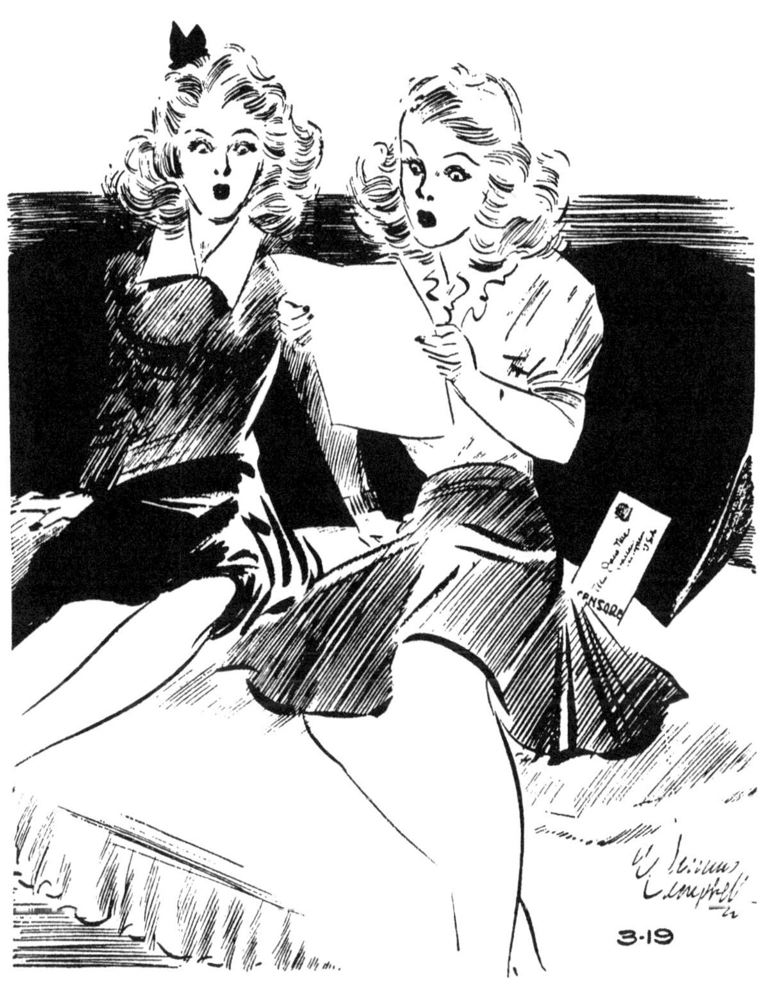

"His letter is all blacked out, but the censor sends love and kisses!"

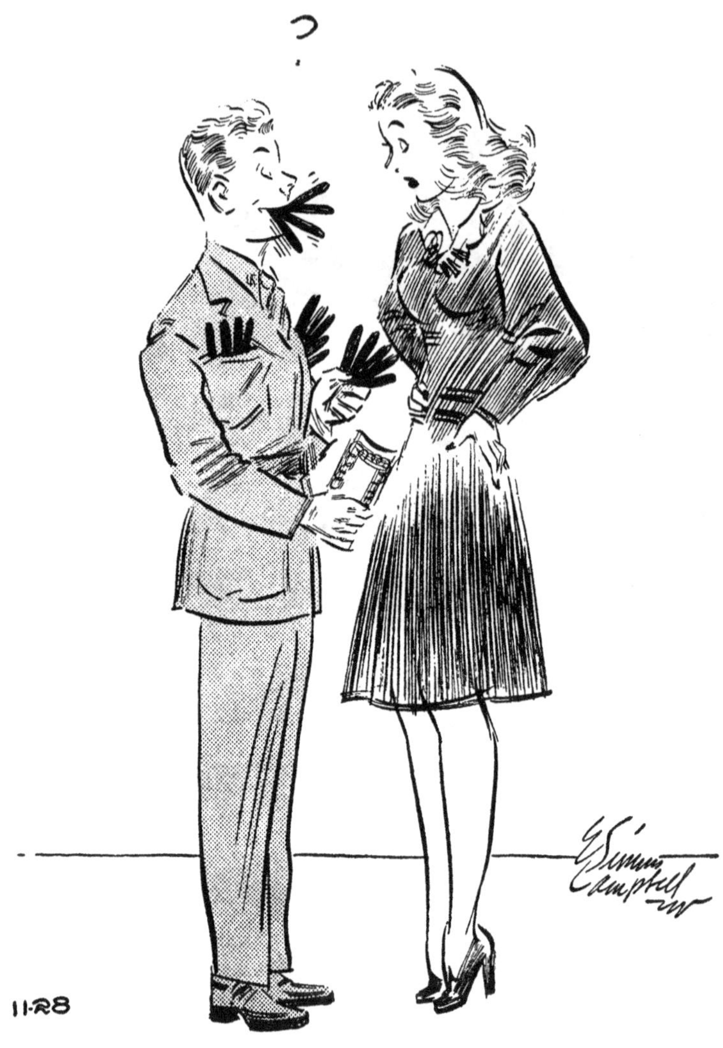

"When I asked your father for your hand, he stuffed me with cigars, gave me a Defense Bond and let out a war whoop!"

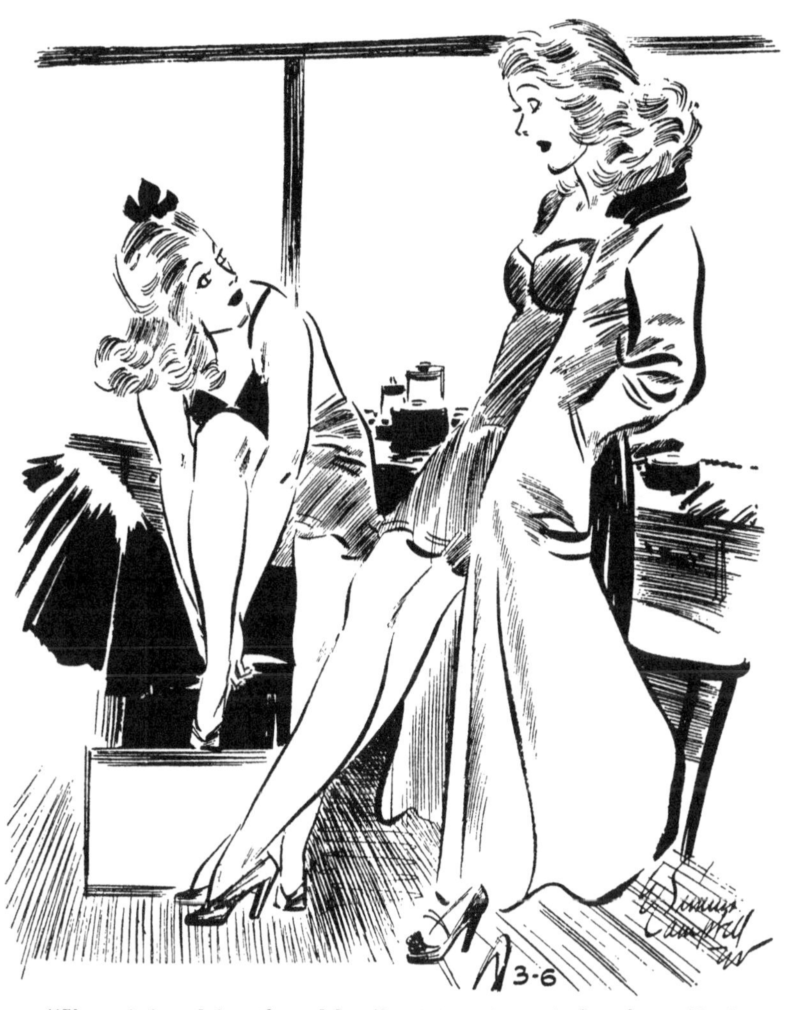

"I'm giving him the old, silent treatment. I only called him twice today on the 'phone!"

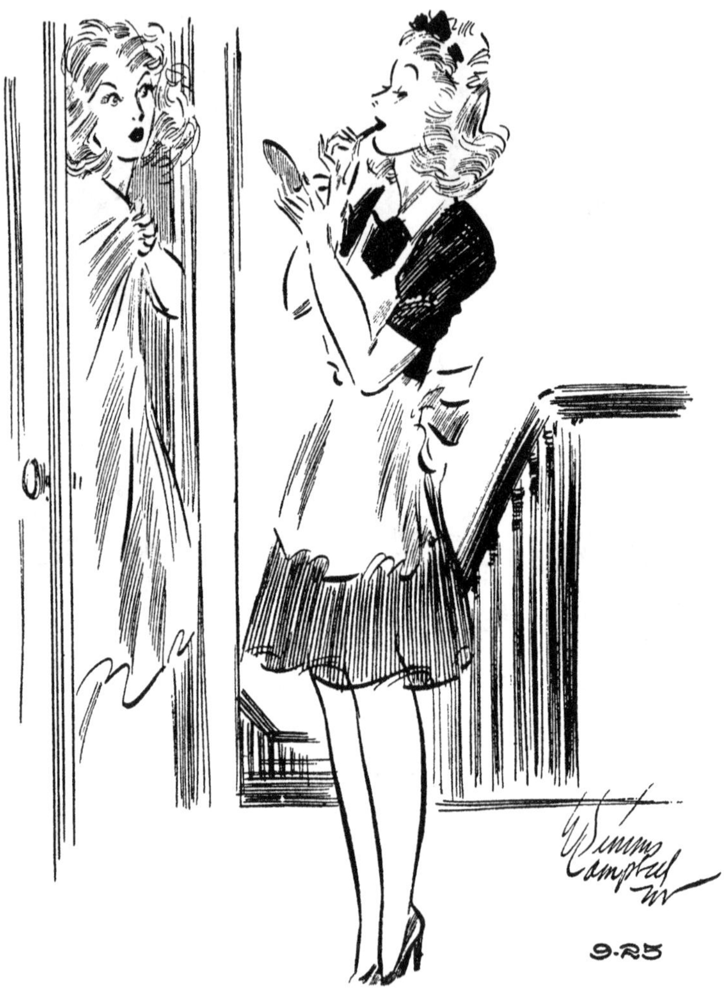

"It's that good-looking Lieutenant Smith downstairs to see you, ma'am!"

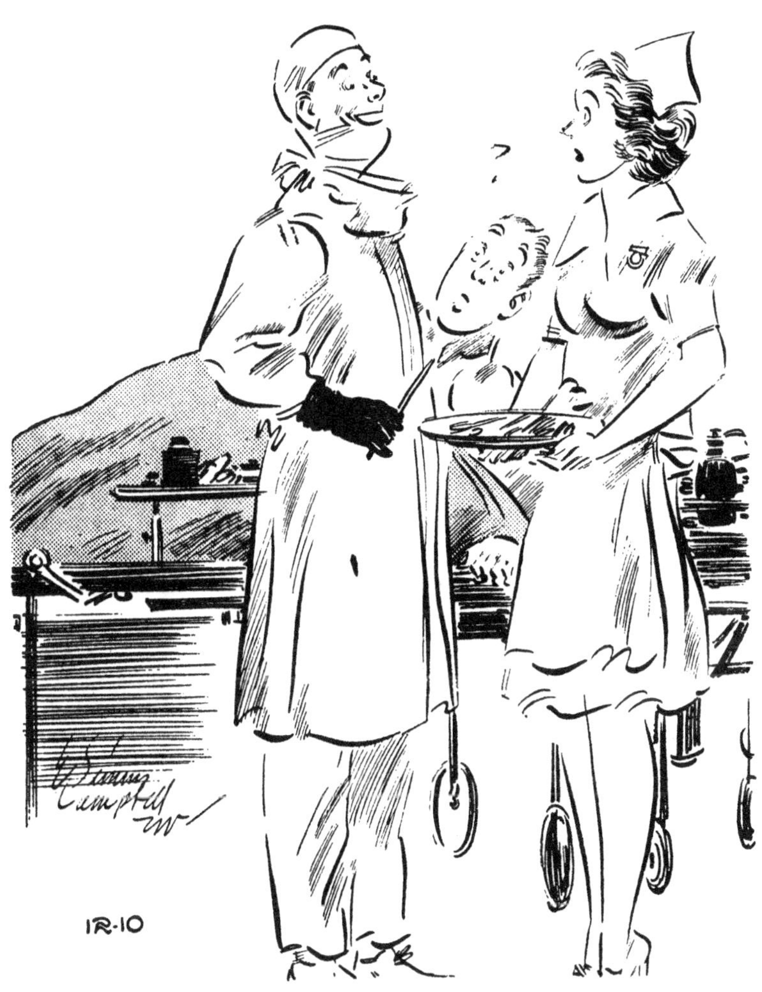

"By the way, Miss Hollis, will you get me that book on appendicitis?"

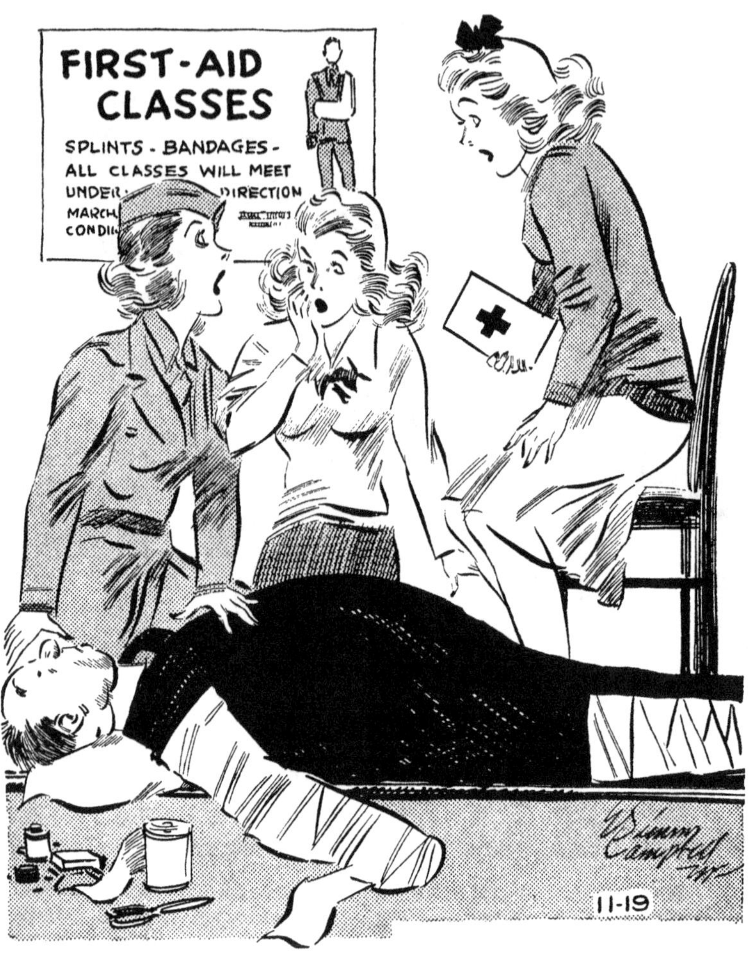

"Quick! Call the doctor! He really HAS fainted!"

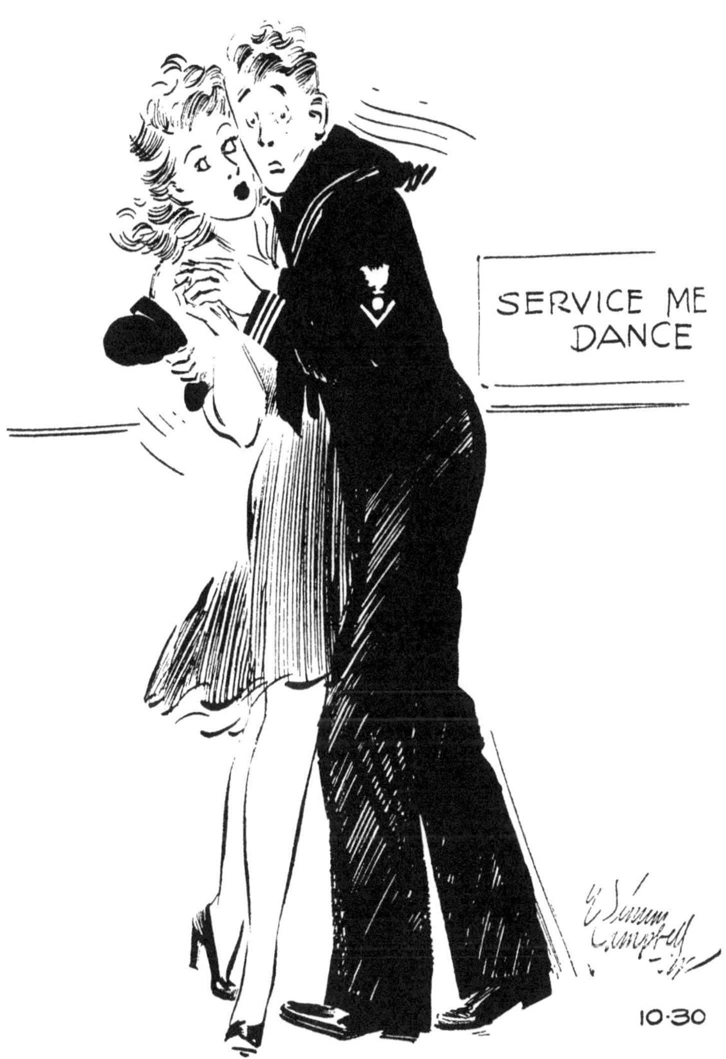

"Gosh! It's been nearly a week since I've seen any dames!"

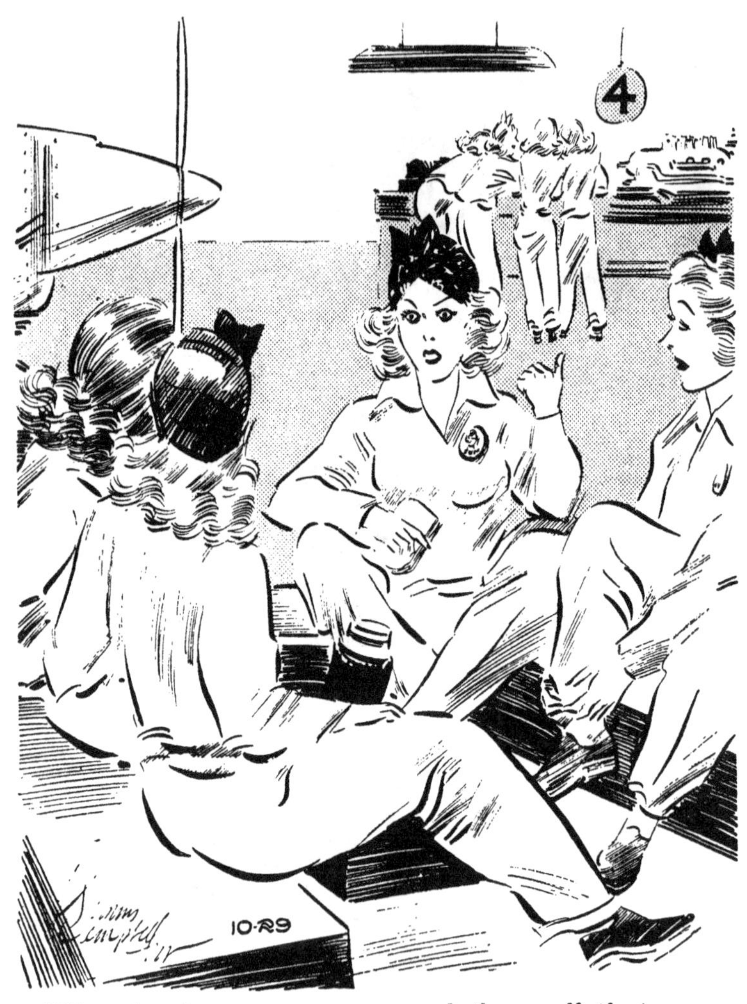

"Marcels, finger-waves, men, clothes—all that gang on job four talks about is shop!"

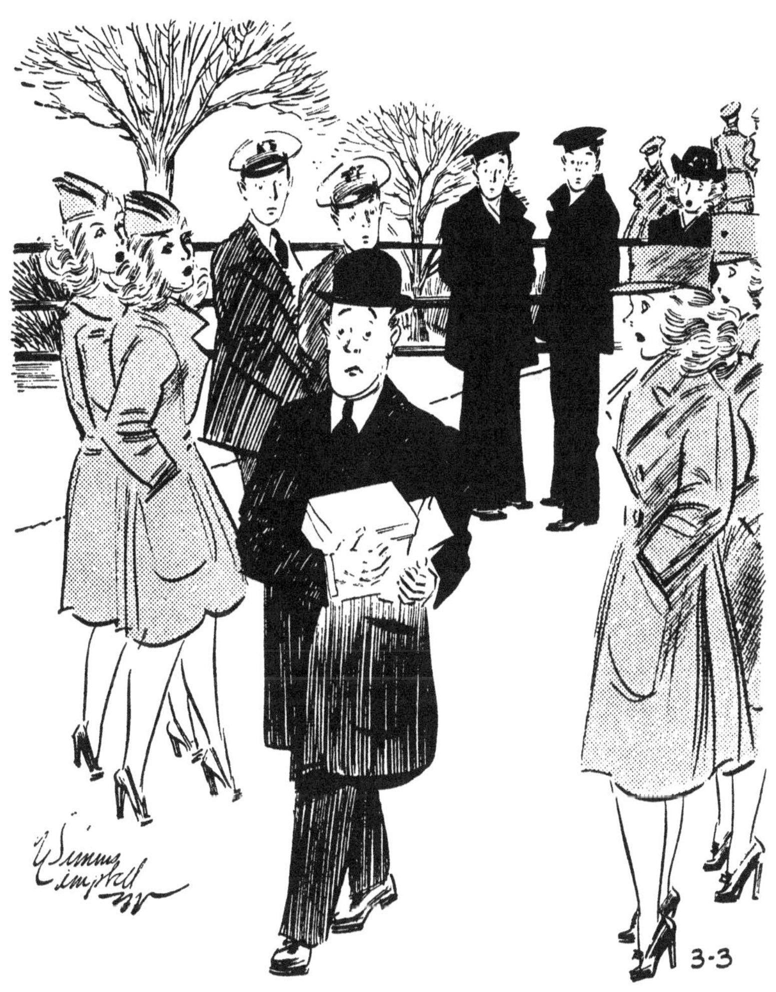

"Look—A Civilian!"

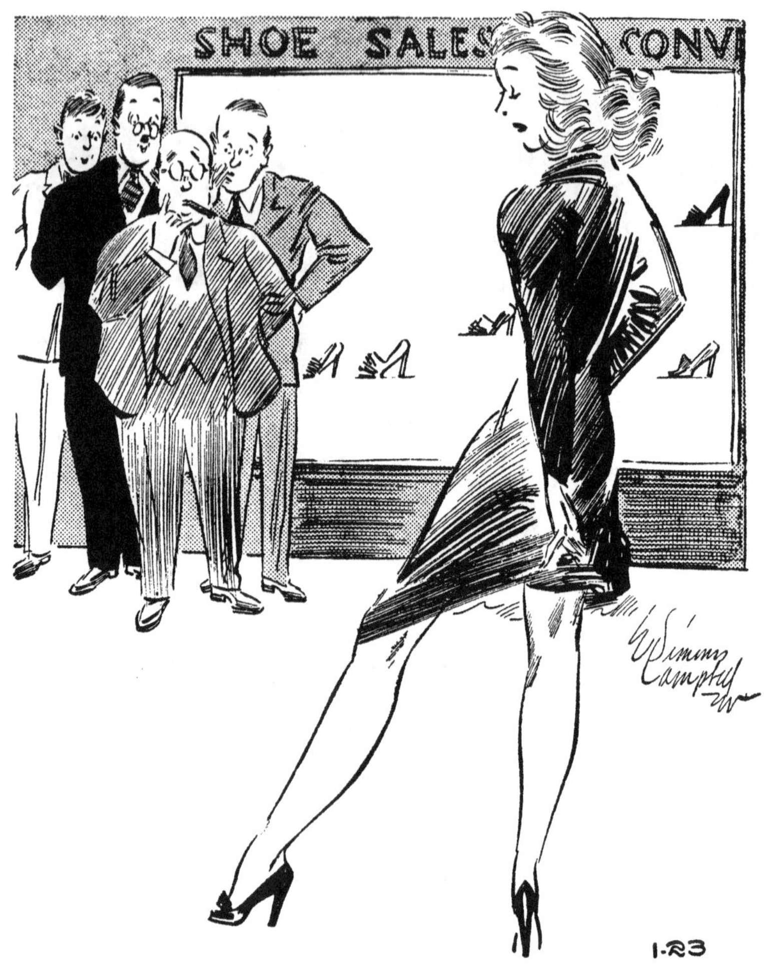

"She's an excellent model, but I'm afraid she'll take the buyers' minds ENTIRELY off our shoes!"

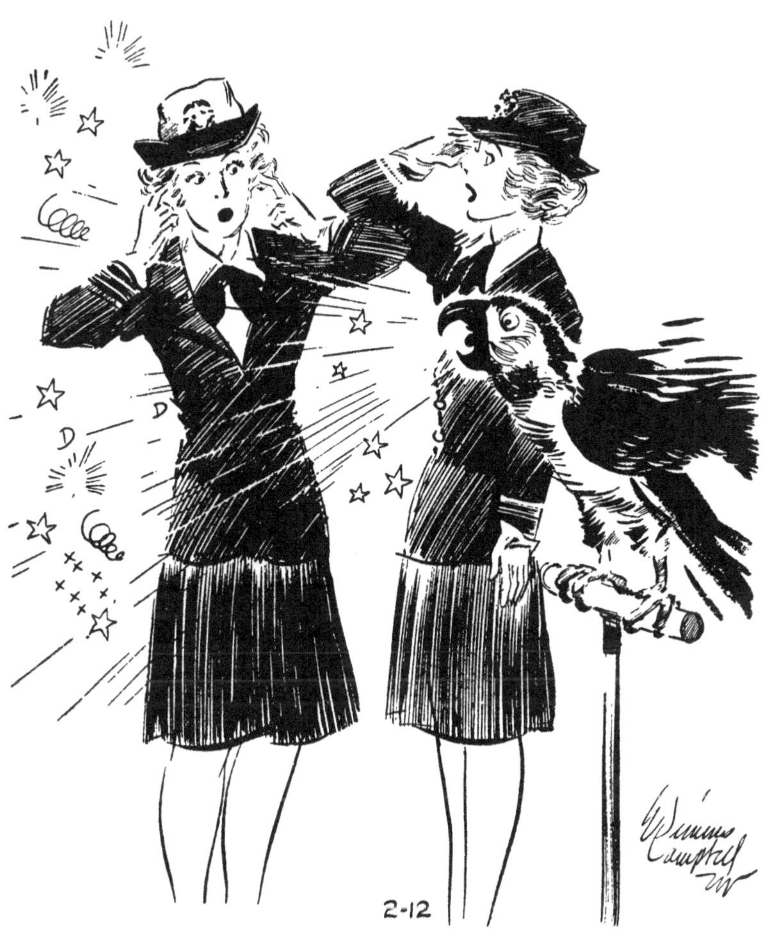

"... But, Lieutenant Wilson, I thought he had belonged to a Captain in the Waves, not a sea captain!"

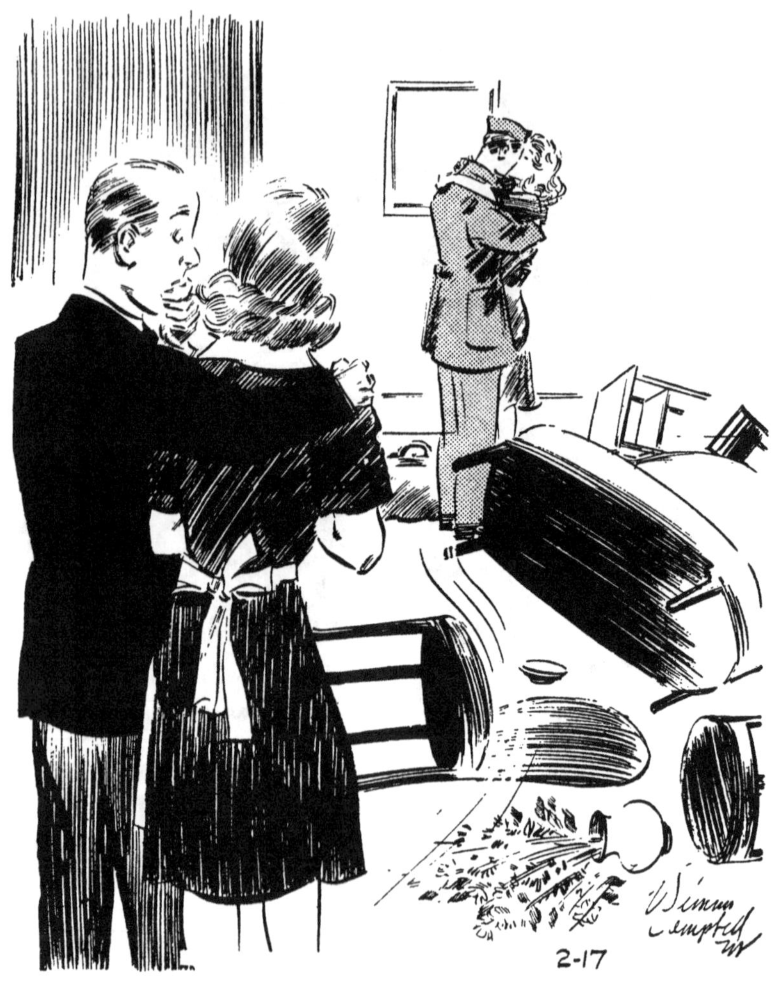

"I'm glad he's back on furlough, but there are times I wish daughter hadn't married a young man in the Tank Corps!"

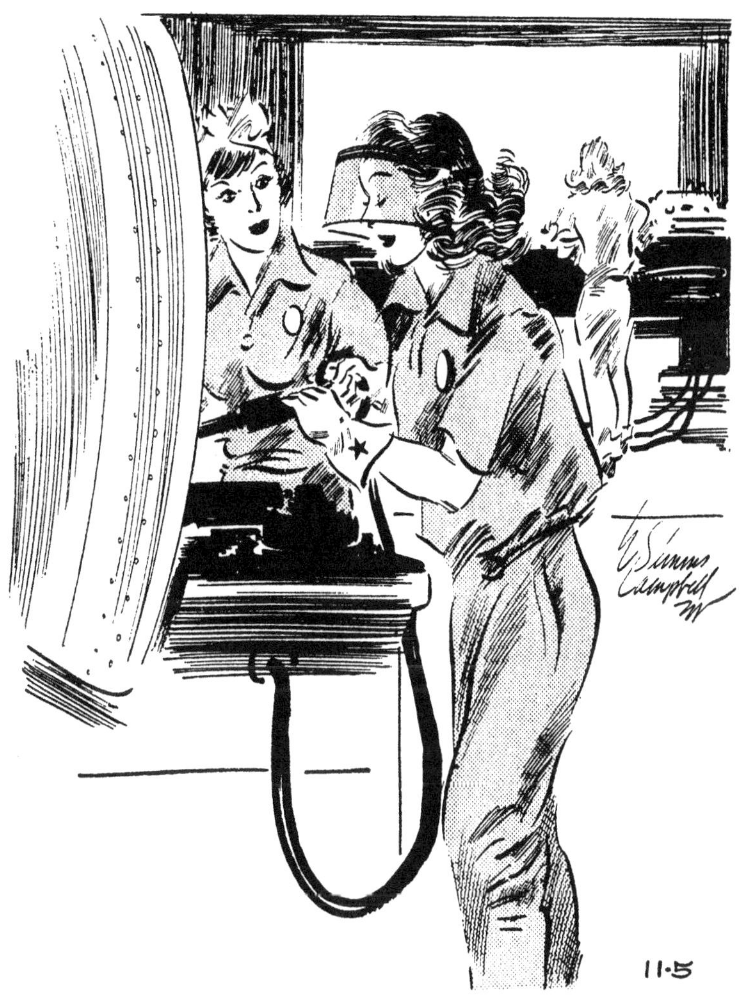

"It must be love. We talked about differentials, combustion and the theory of aerodynamics all evening!"

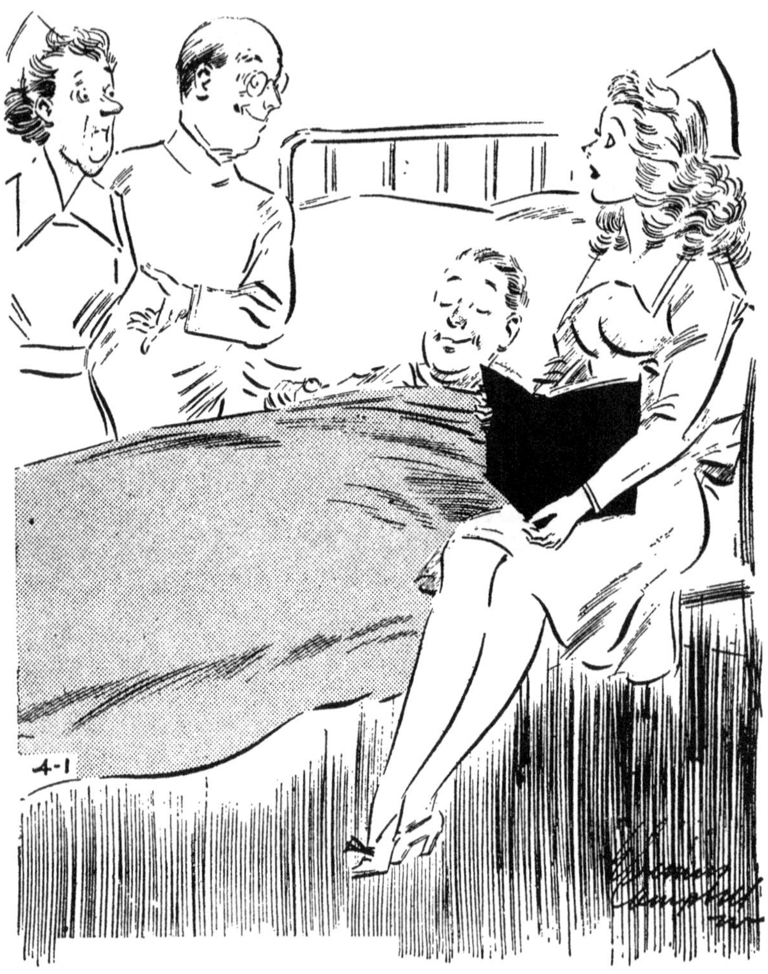

"Since he's unconscious now, you can change places with Miss Jones. I'll be needing you on the other wards!"

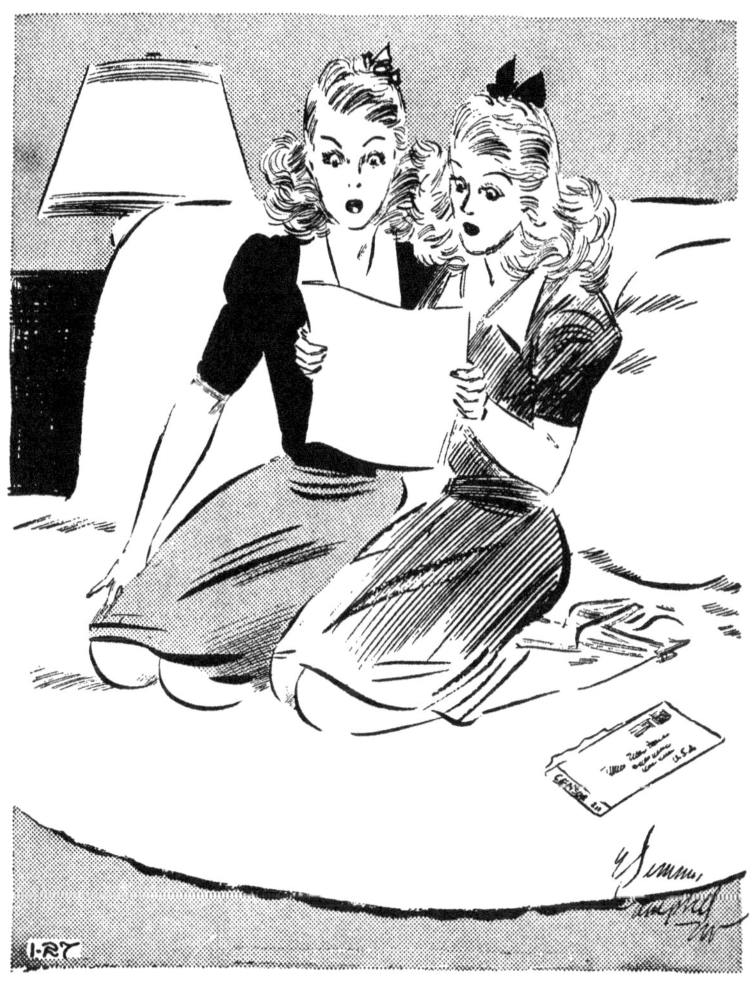

"—And these Australian girls haven't anything on you, except, of course, that they're HERE!"

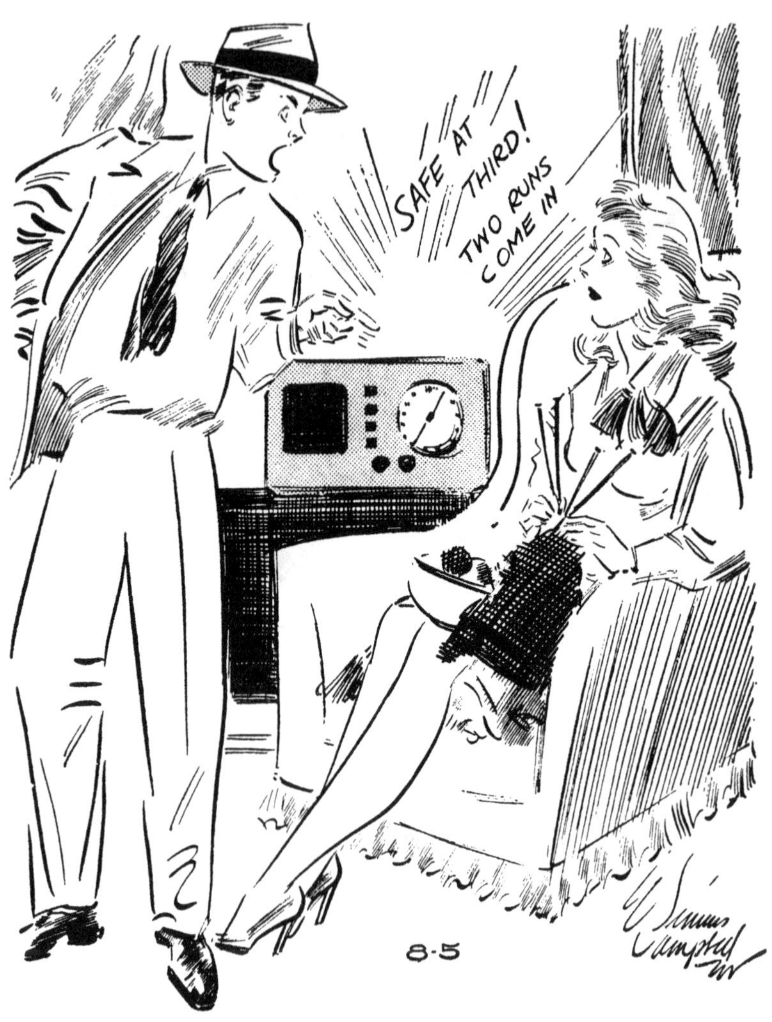

"I'm going out to the ball game. That guy was **out a MILE!**"

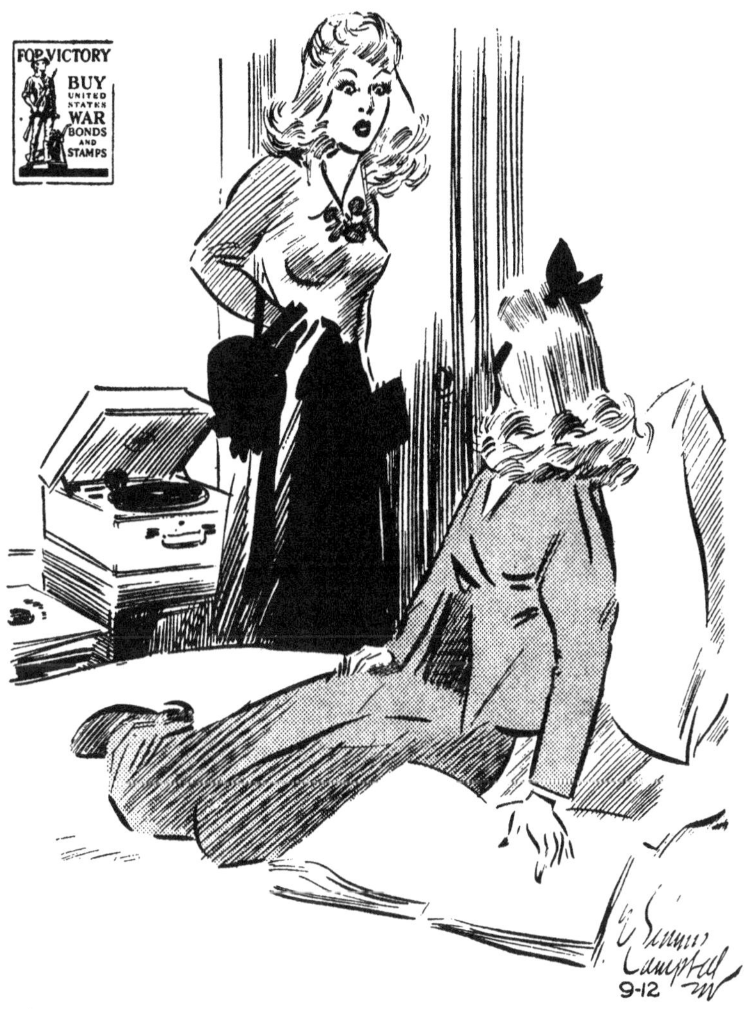

"What an evening I've had! He was a captain all right, but a captain in the FIRST World War!"

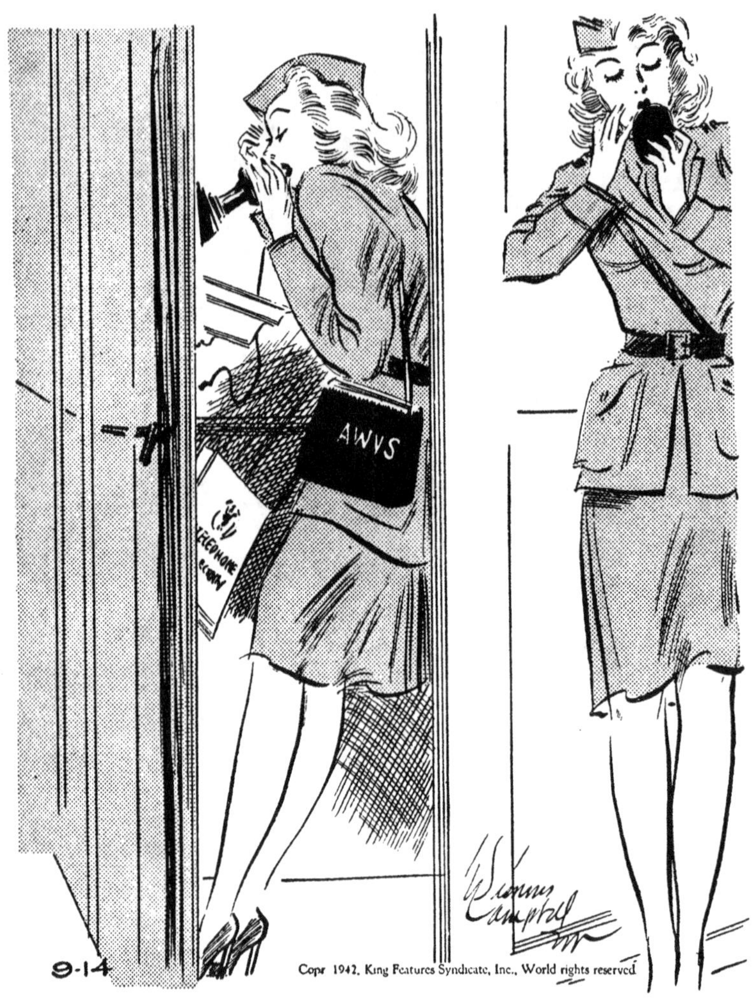

"Well, have dinner on time, dear. I'm bringing an important executive home with me!"

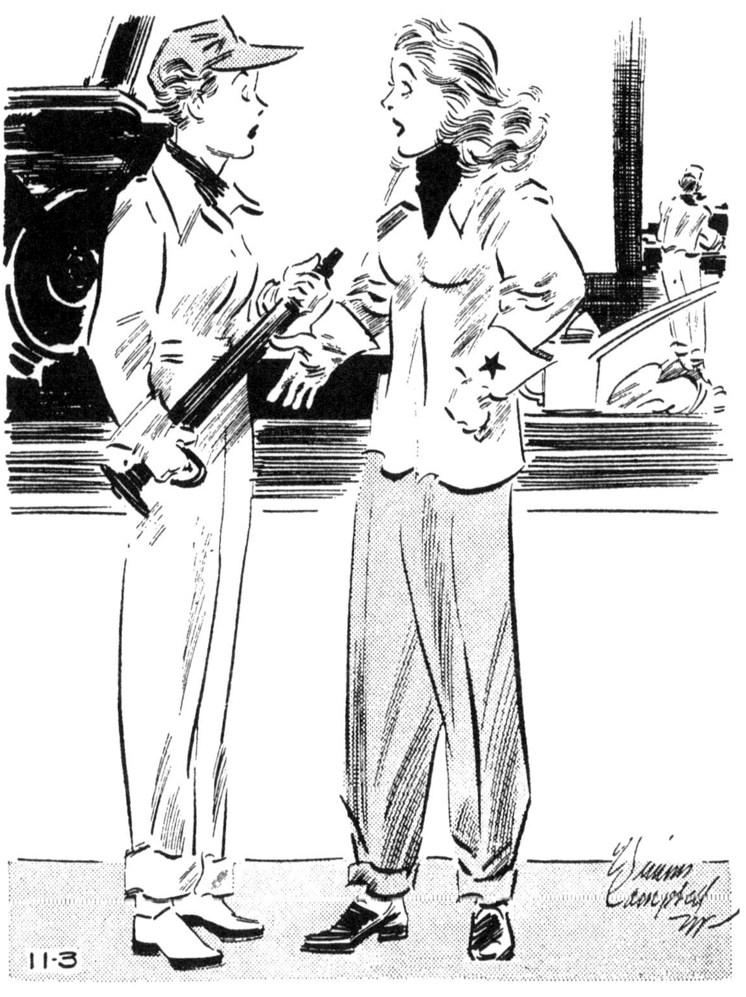

"I'll say times have changed! He now goes in **MY** pants pockets before **I** go to work!"

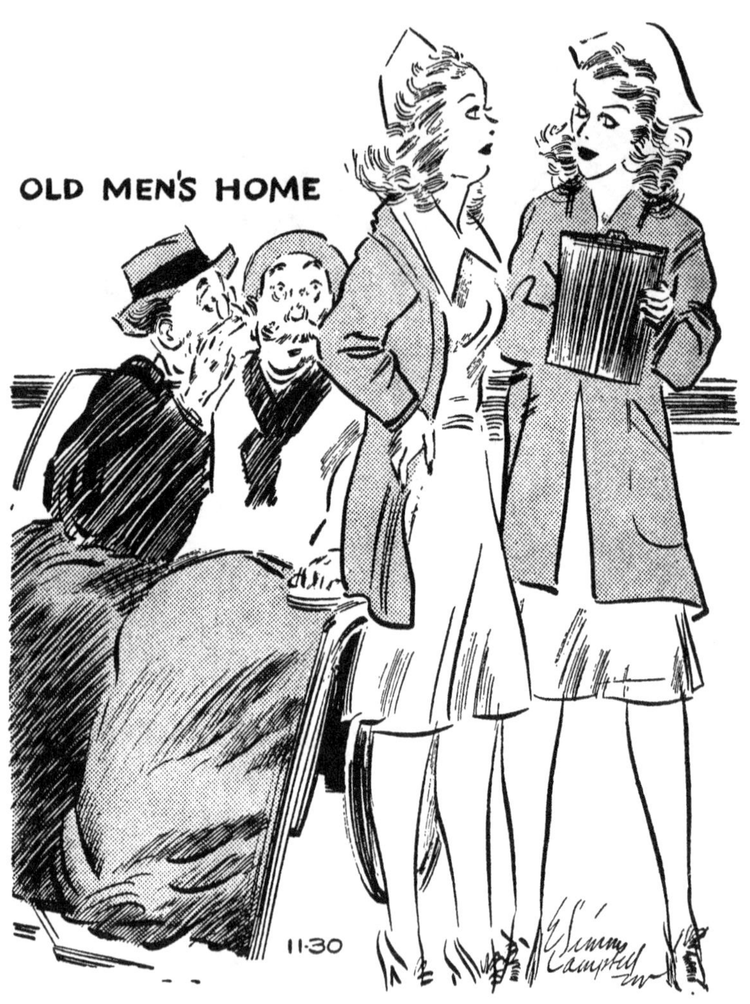

"I wish I'd been sent here forty years ago!"

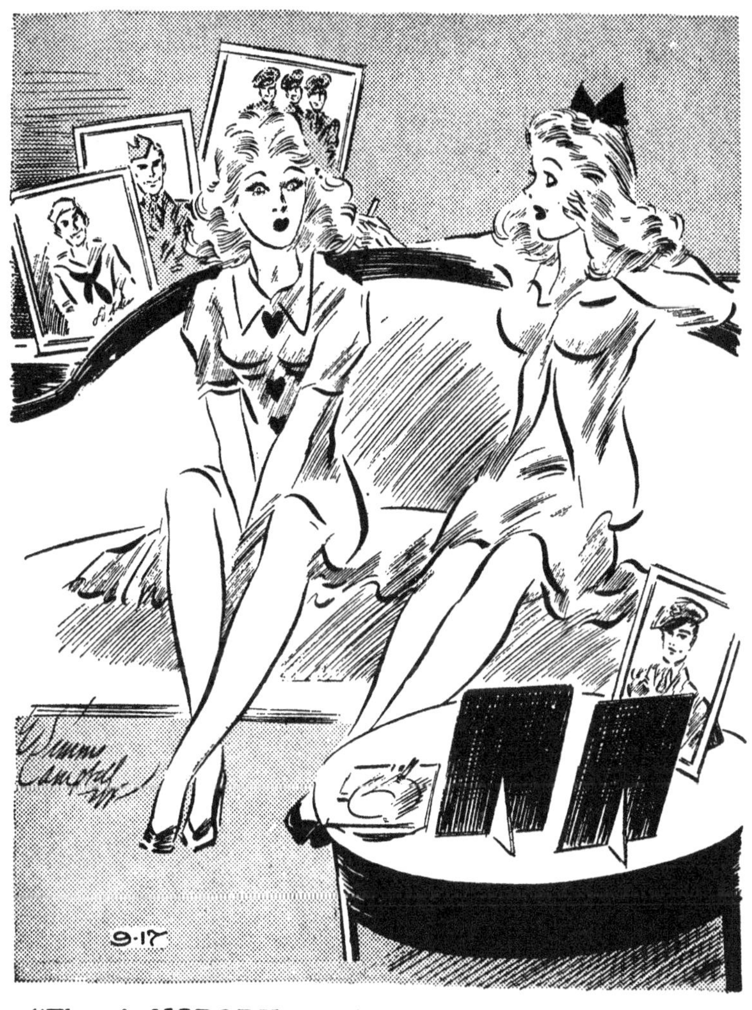

"There's **NO**BODY to call up. All the men **we** know are TOO physically fit!"

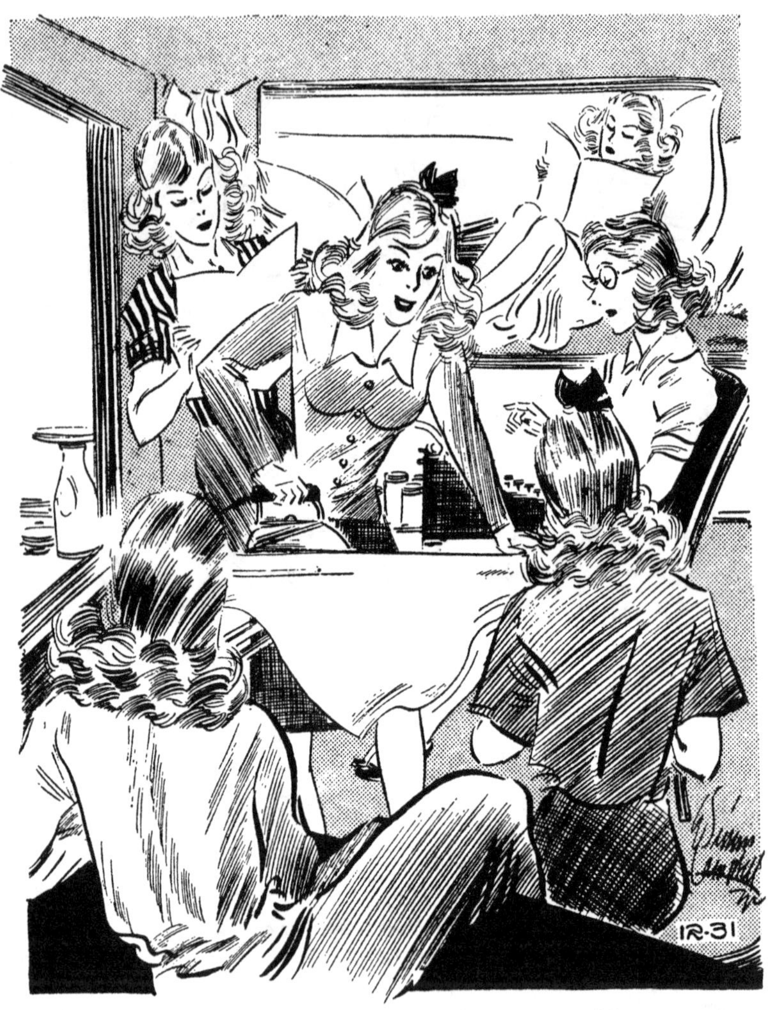

"The six of us were mighty lucky to get this room in Washington. They tell me SOME of the places are REALLY crowded!"

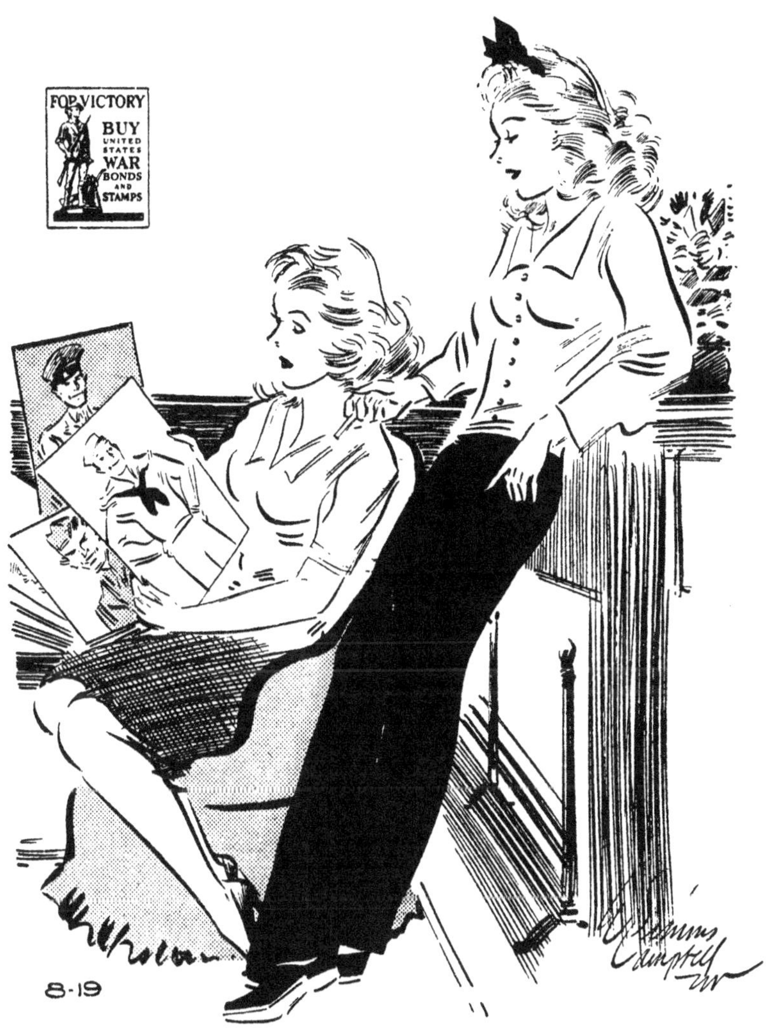

"You know the type, a heart of gold, lead feet and a head like ivory!"

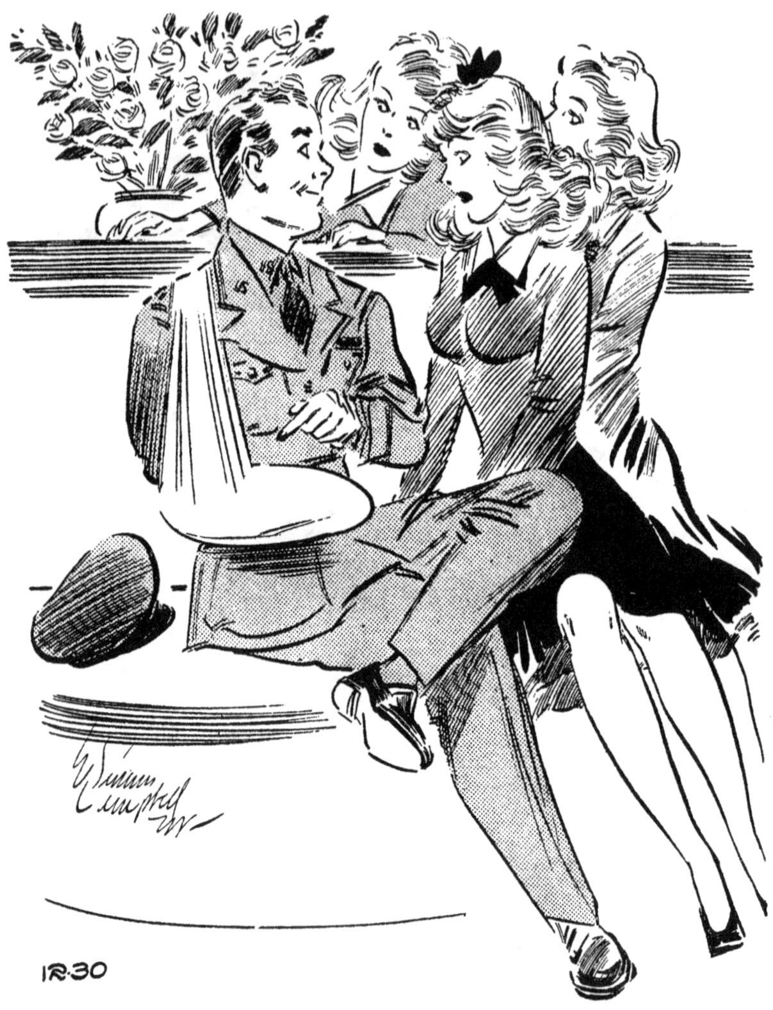

"I didn't get a scratch in any battle. It's from shaking hands with the Welcoming Committee!"

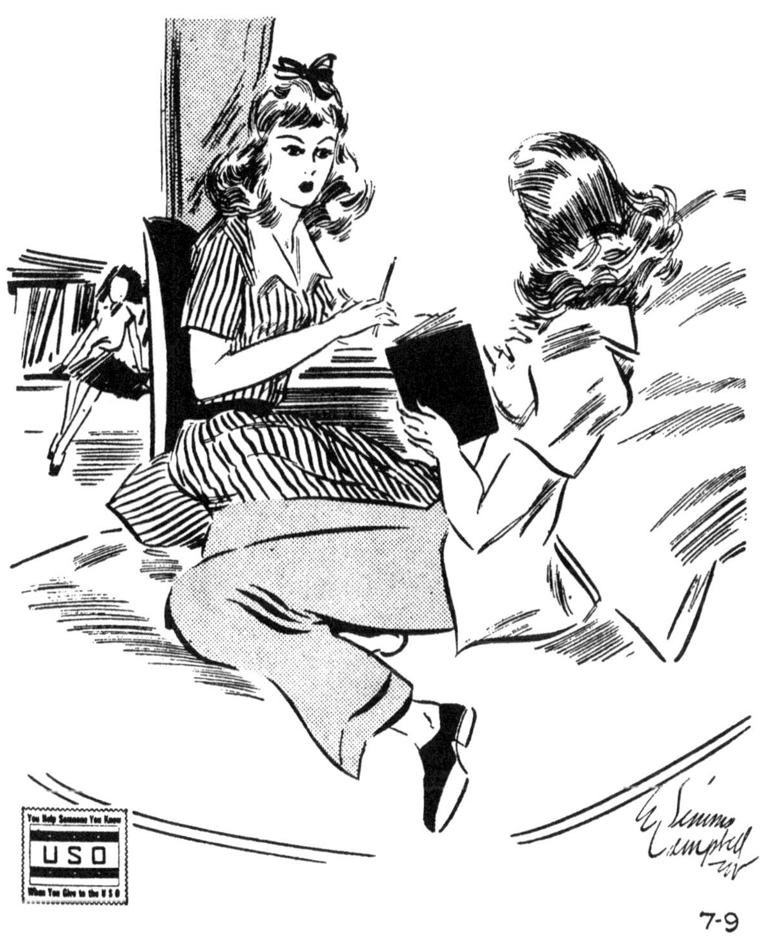

"The boy I went out with last night was awfully thoughtful. He rang up to see if I got home all right!"

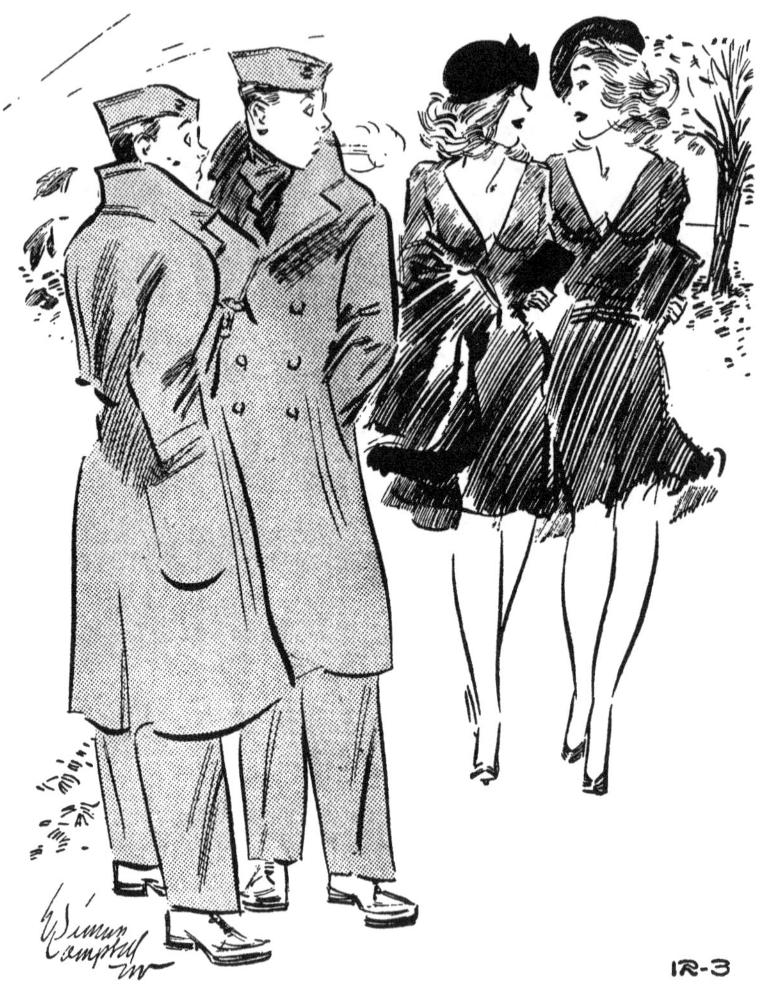

"Gosh! It must be wonderful to have a constitution like a woman!"

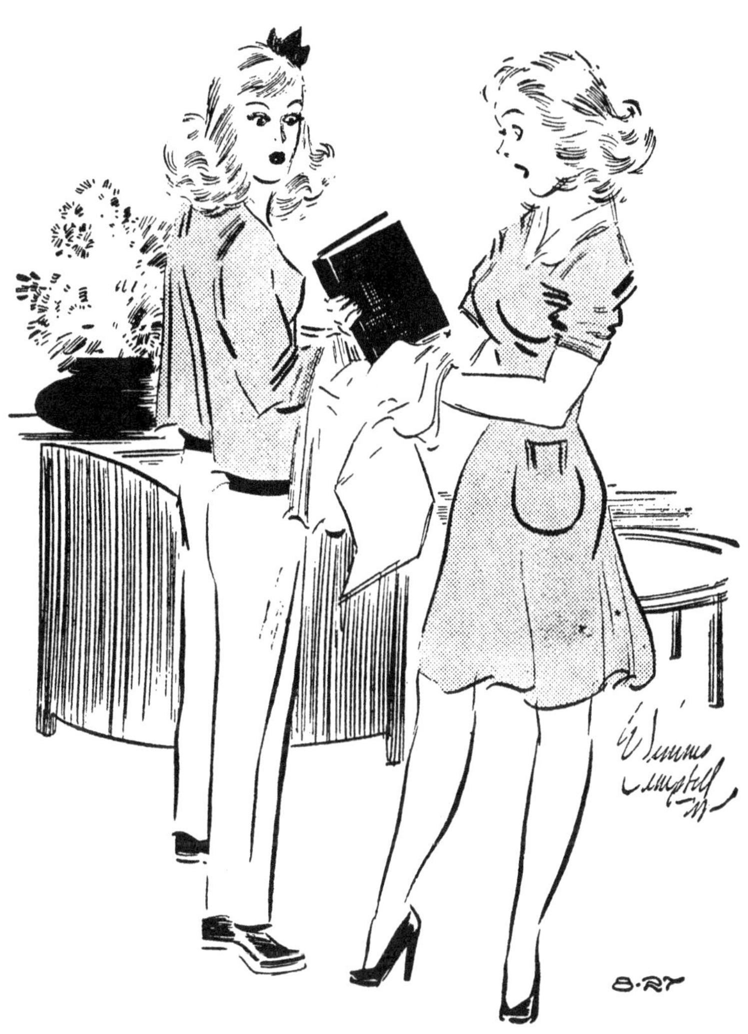

"Can you imagine! Of all the beautiful things a fellow can send a girl, he sends me a BOOK!"

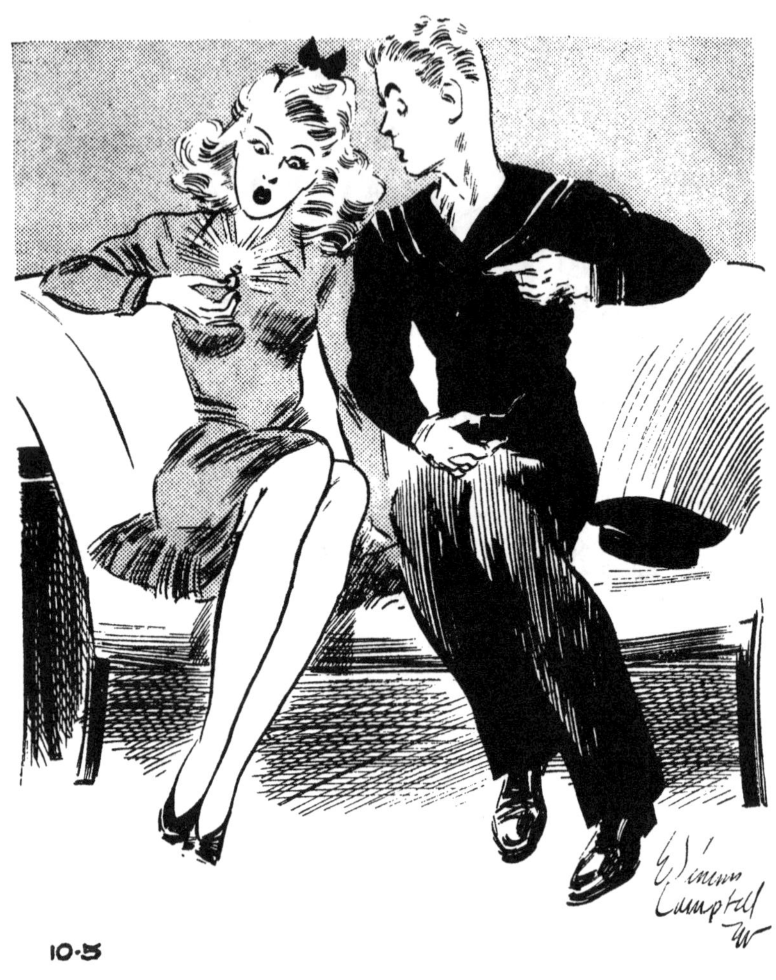

"Well, if it ISN'T a diamond, I've been gyped outa nine dollars and forty cents!"

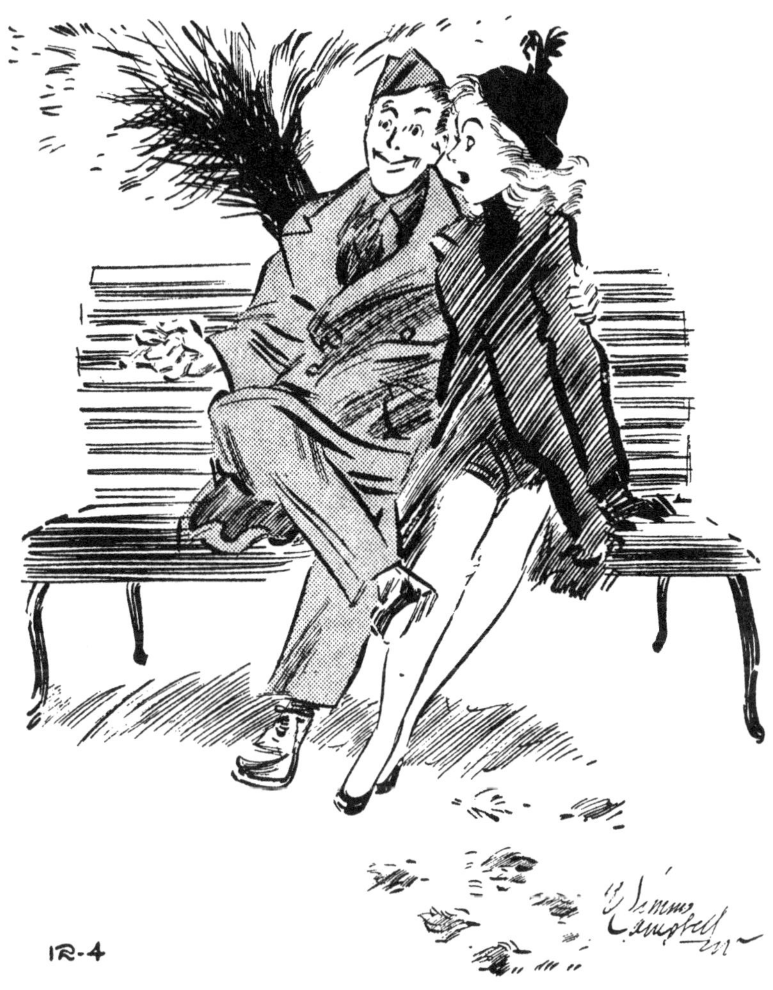

"When I'm with you, I almost forget that sweet, little, old tank I drive!"

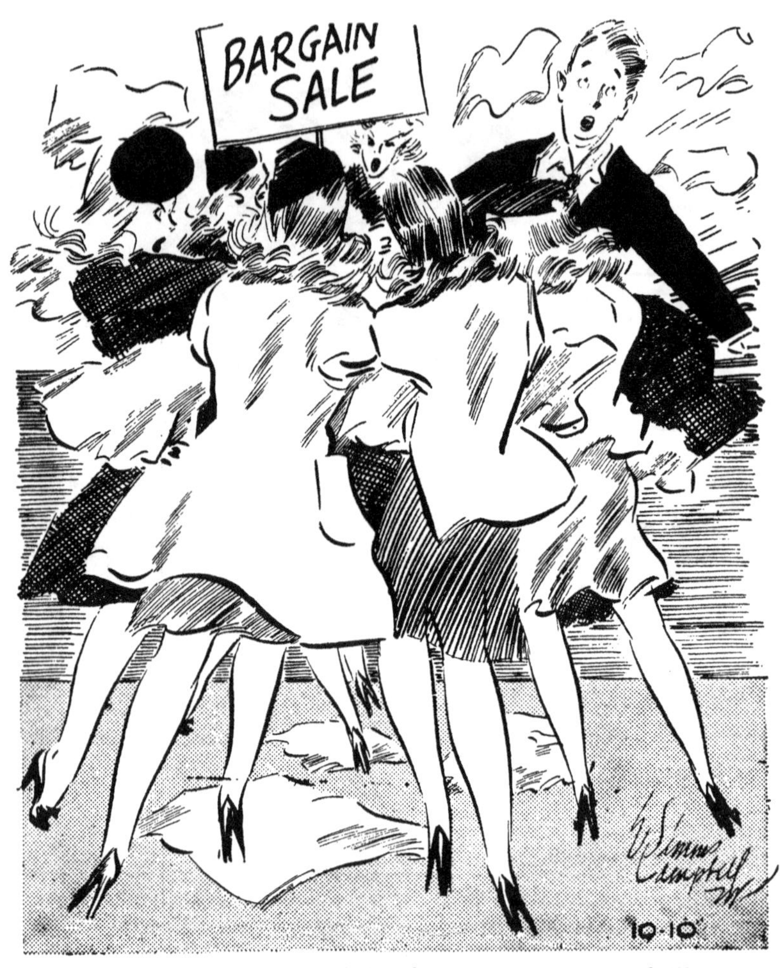

"Thank heavens, I join the army next week!"

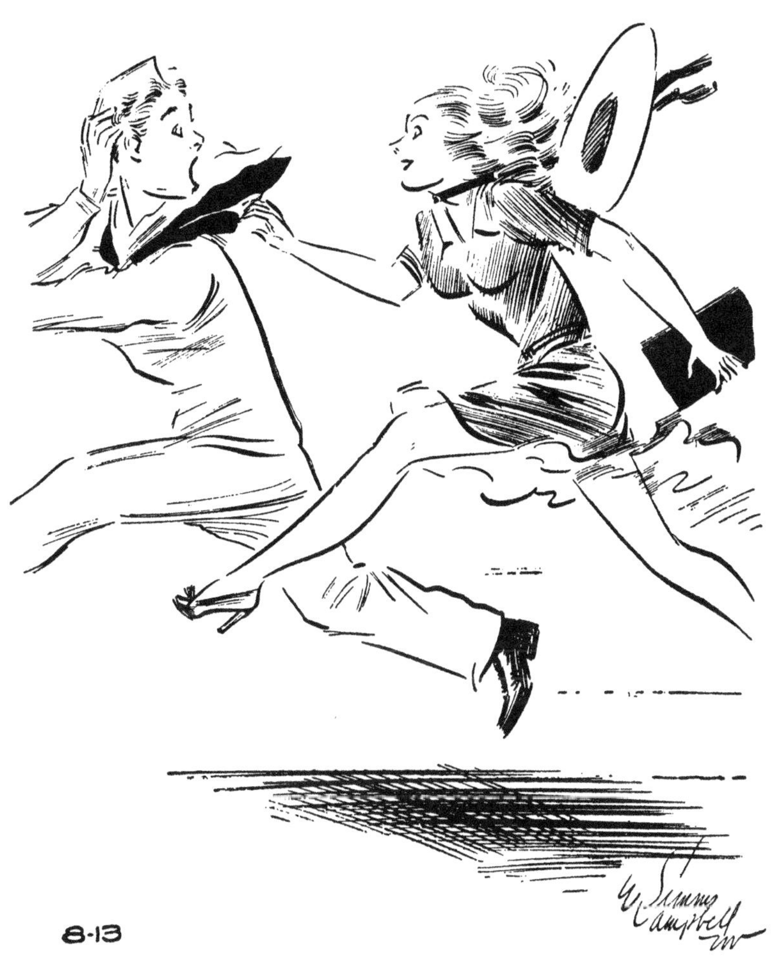

"—but I was only joking when I said, 'Let's get married'!"

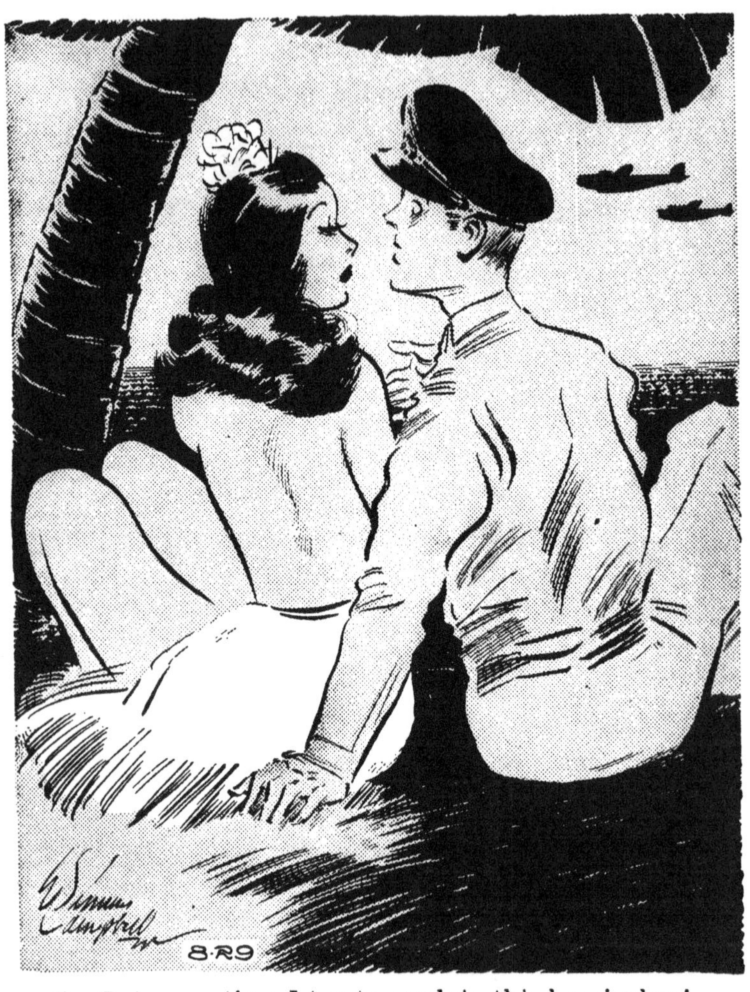

"—But everytime I try to explain this hemispheric solidarity to you, you get sore!"

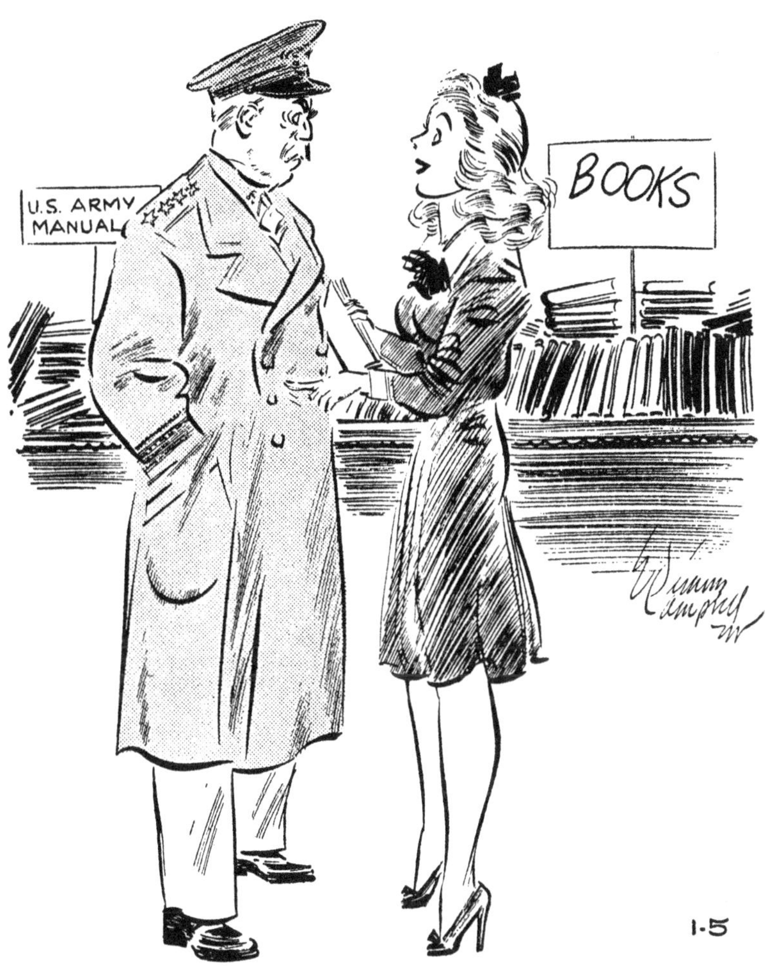

"Would you like something about the army? Army regulations, whom to salute and when?"

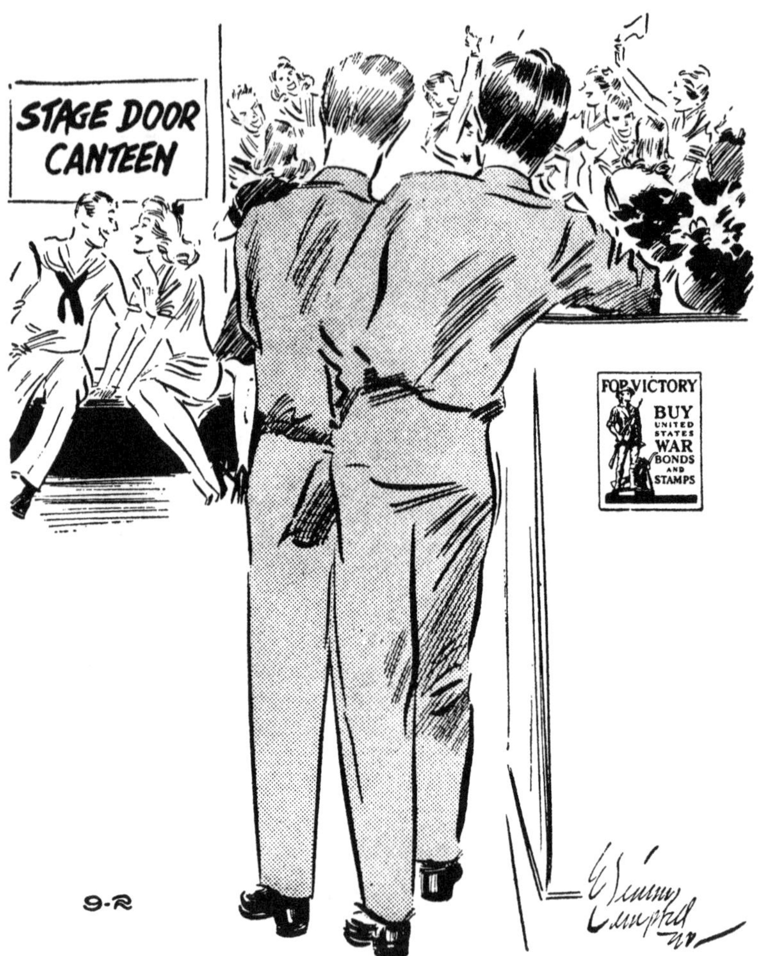

"I'll sorta be glad to get back to camp . . . for a rest, I mean!"

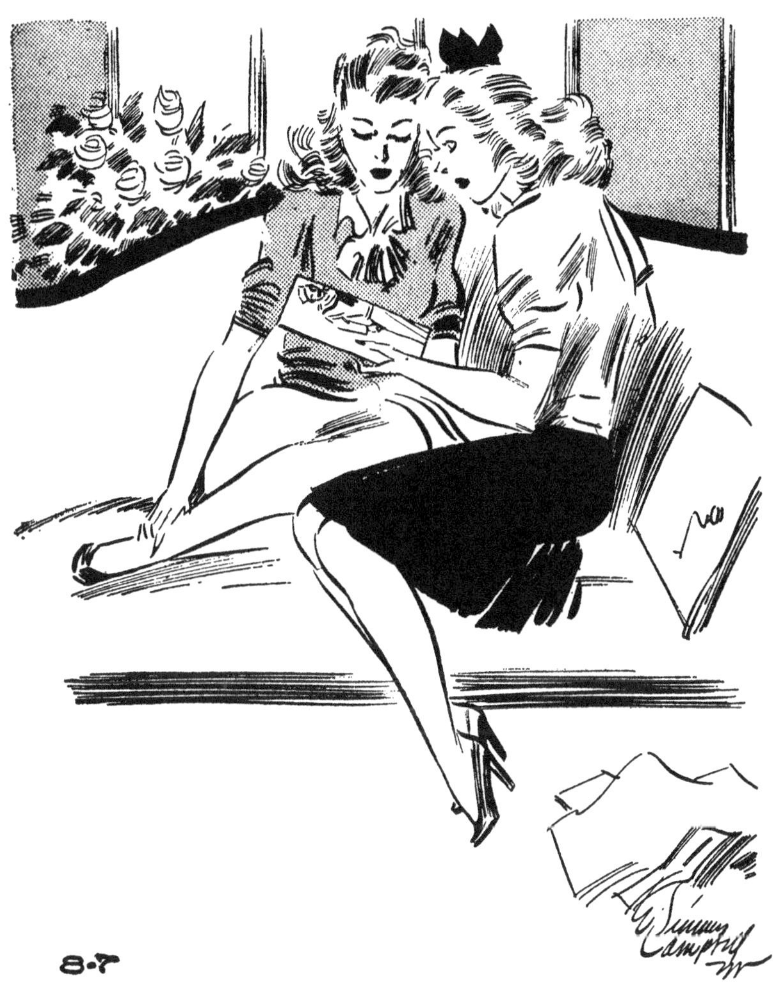

"He's sent me one of those cut-off photos of himself. Naturally, the half he's keeping shows **some** girl he was hugging!"

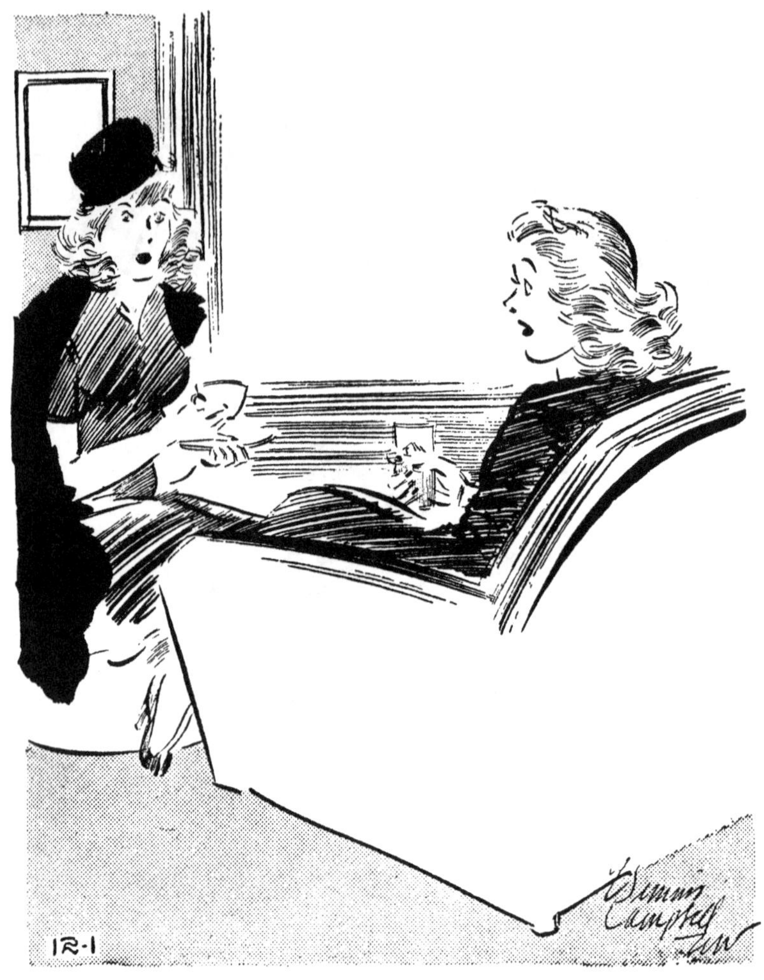

"Naturally, when he said he loved her family, she knew it was only a matter of time when he'd lie about OTHER things!"

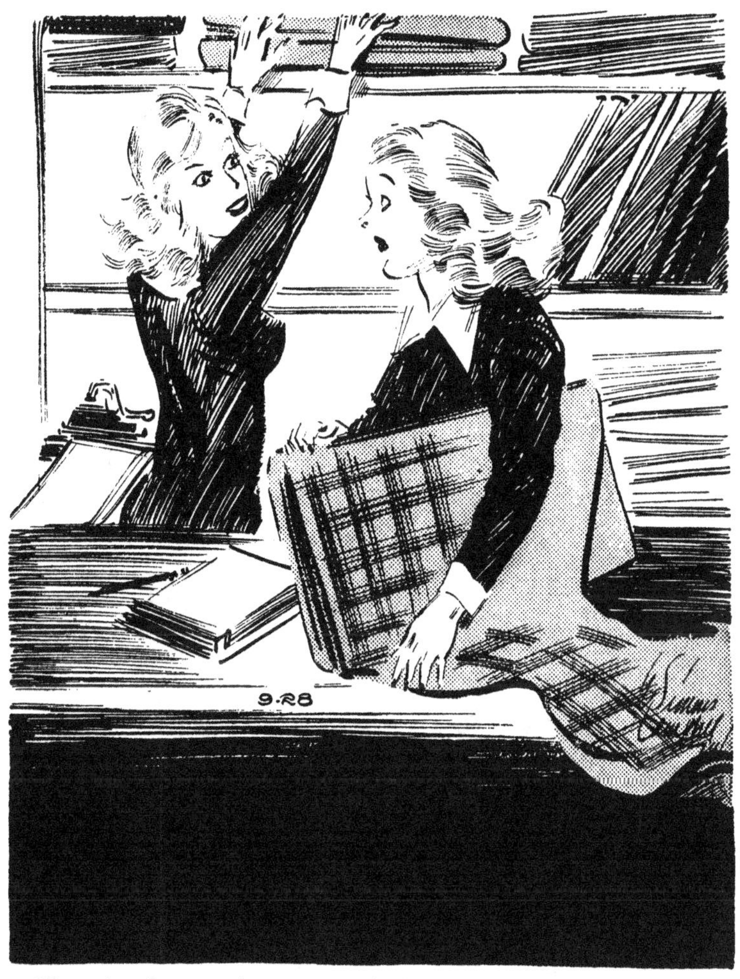

"Dearie, I met the cutest fellow on my honeymoon!"

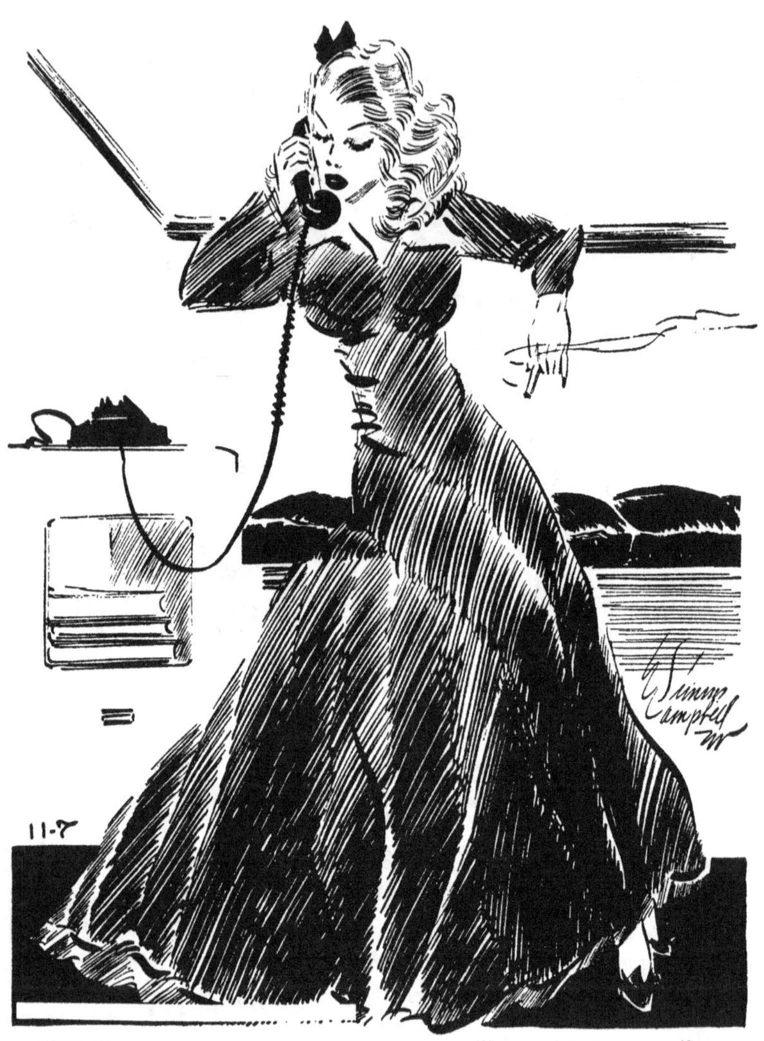

"Well, come on over, anyway. I've got two sailors here and you don't HAVE to know anything about boats!"

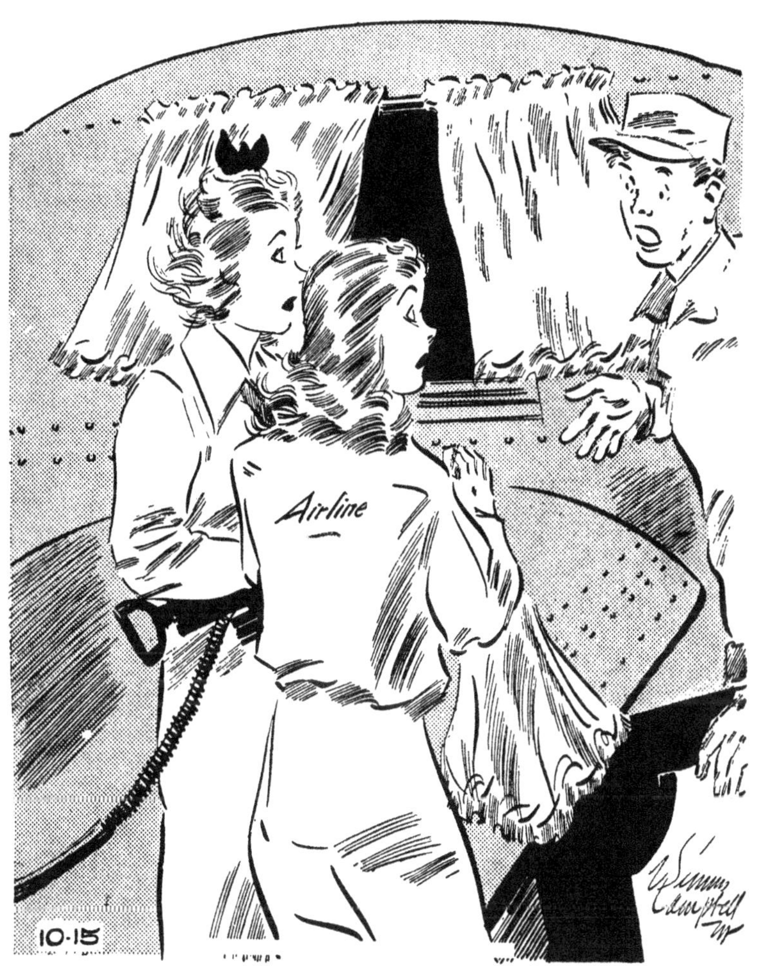

"—But we don't NEED lace curtains on bombers!"

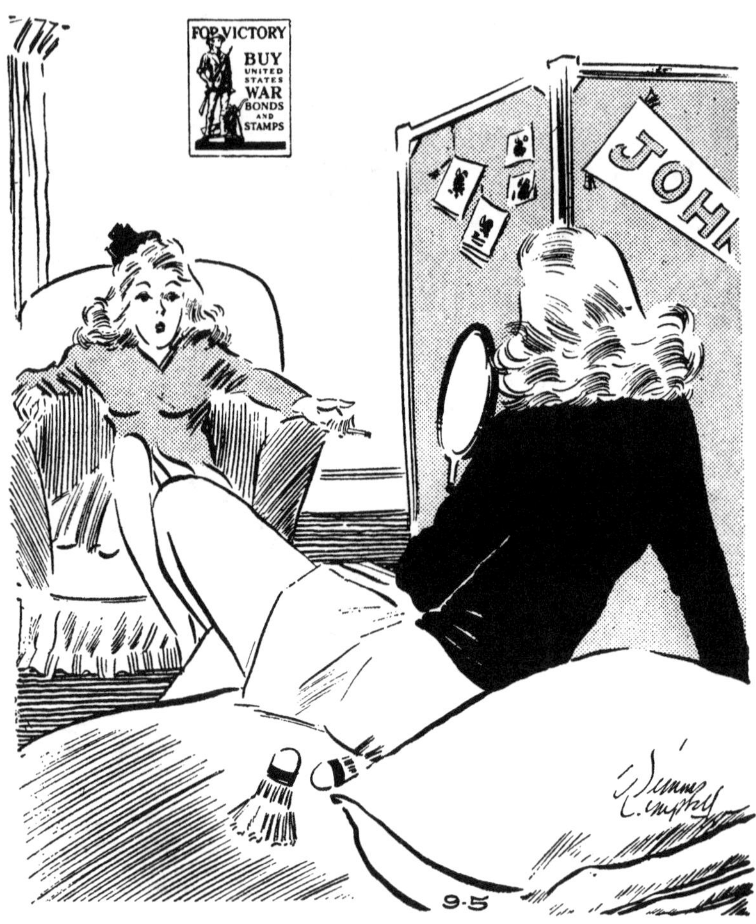

"I think he's training for the Commandos. Last night he jumped out my window when the doorbell rang!"

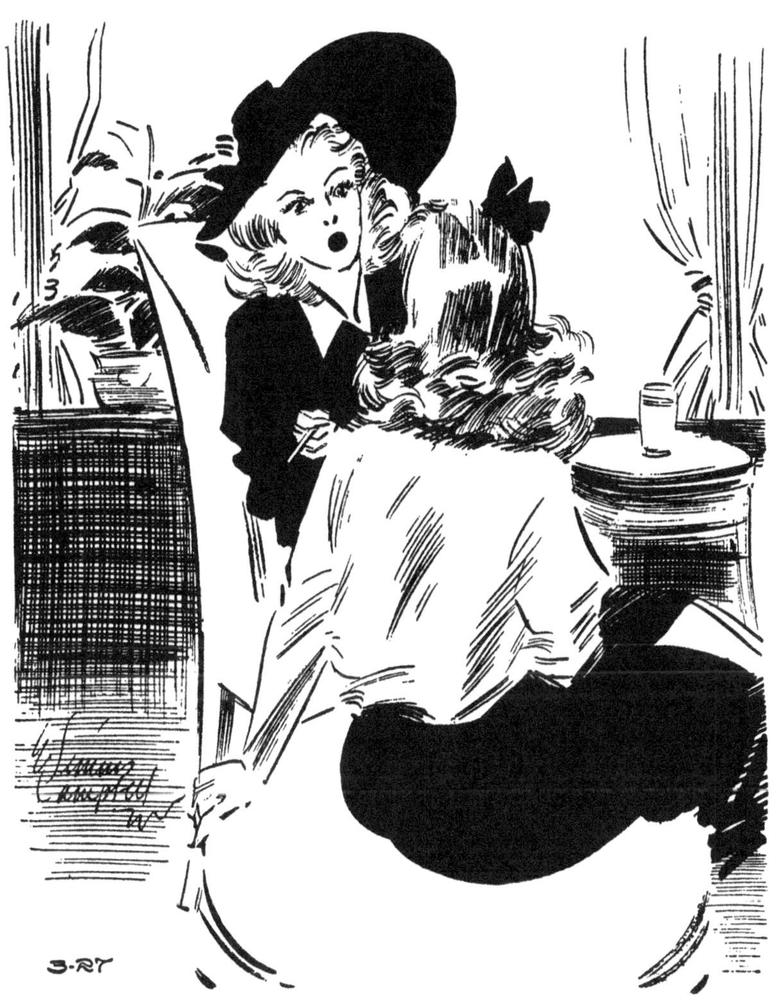

"He's the type who holds in the clinches! You need a referee when you go out with him!"

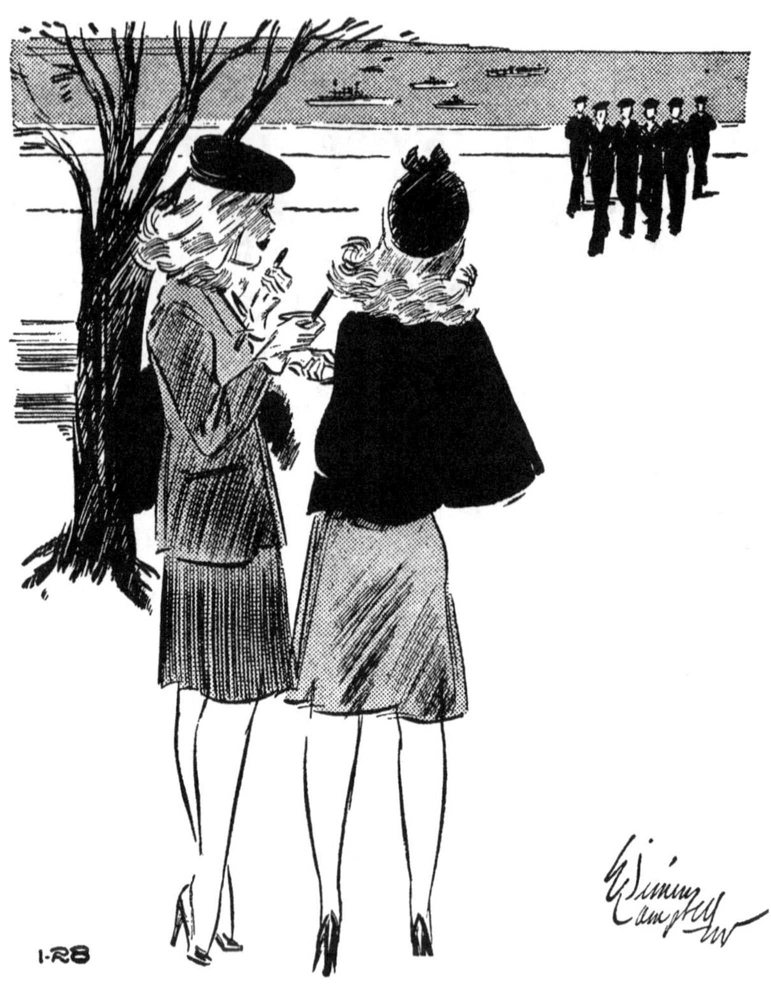

"Quick, your compact! 'Praise the Lord and pass the ammunition!' "

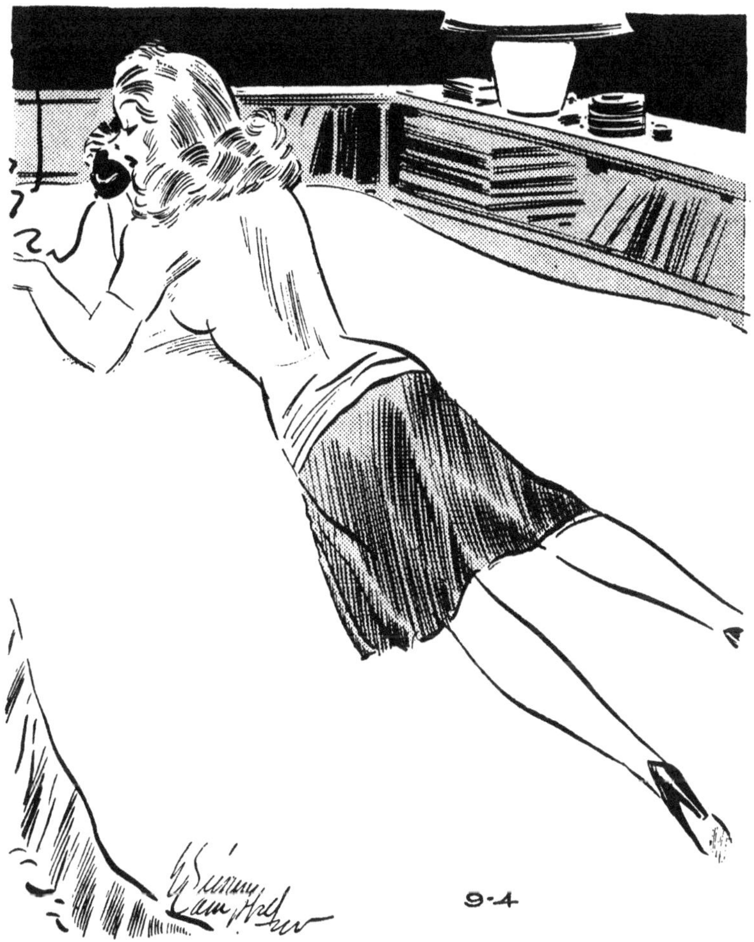

"He's been decorated by three different countries and last night I gave him a black eye!"

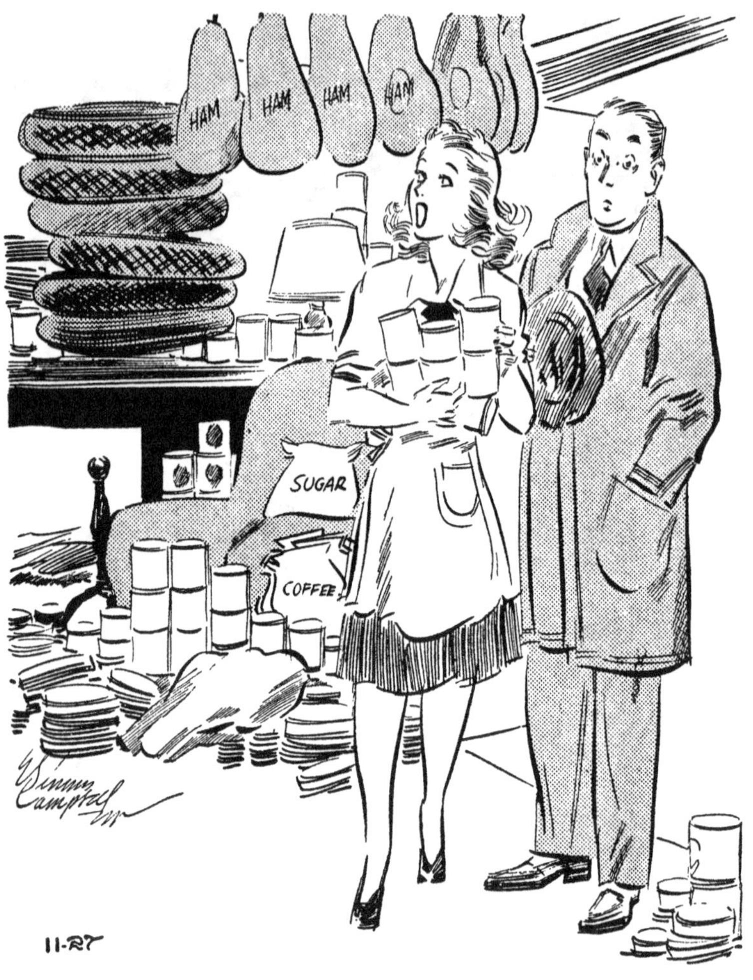

"Oh, darling! There's a man here from the government who wants to see you about something!"

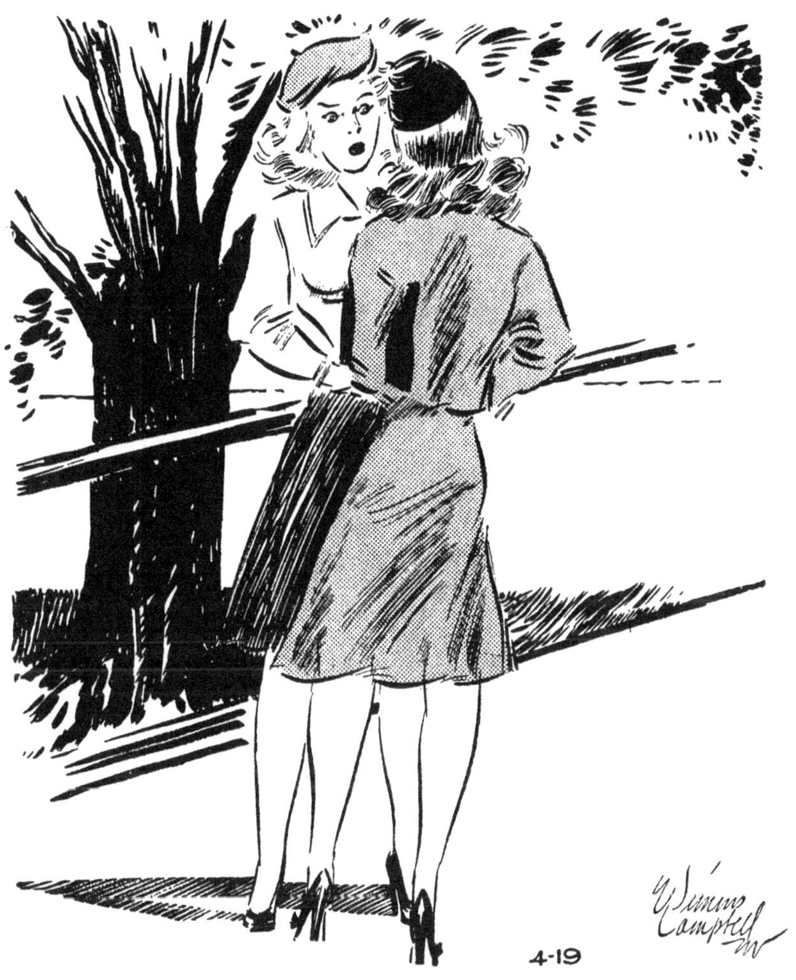

"It's a military secret where he is, but he's been sending me baby kangaroos and boomerangs from somewhere!"

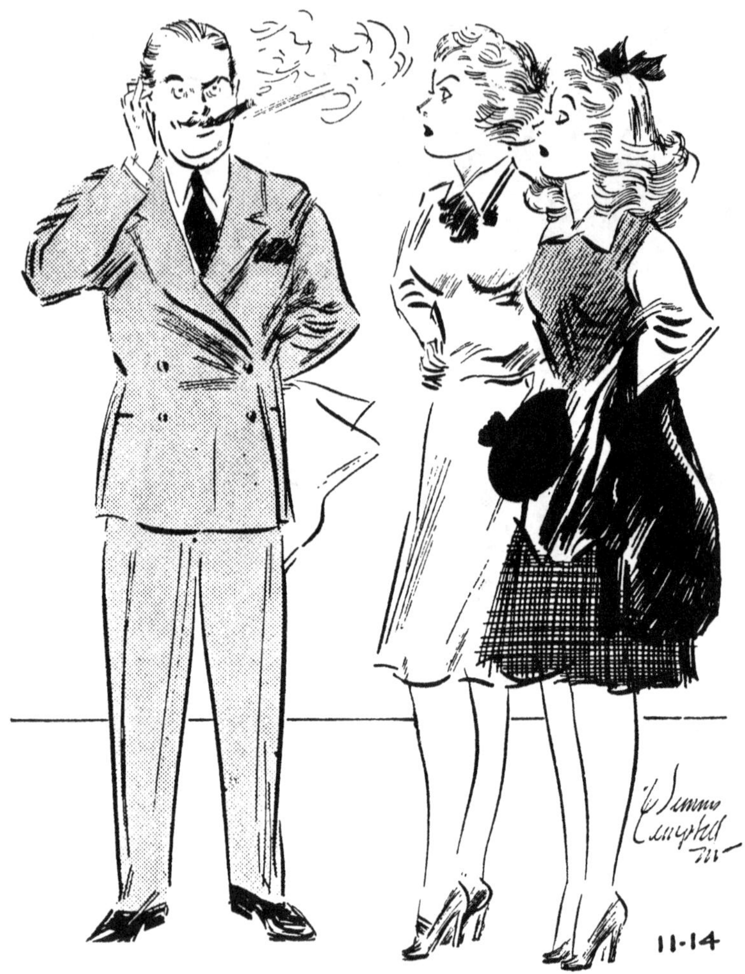

"M-mm-m—I don't know whether I'll let her go out with a Marine or not. I used to be a Marine, myself!"

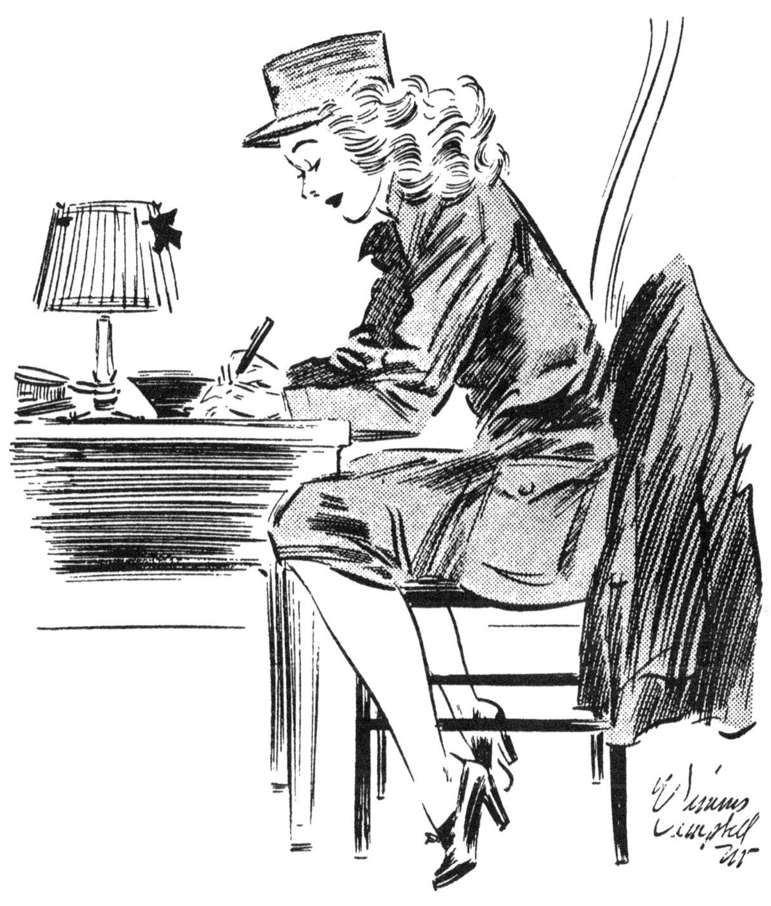

3-1

"Dear Diary—Life here at camp is no bed of roses, but we have the sweetest, loveliest captain you ever saw. He's a man!"

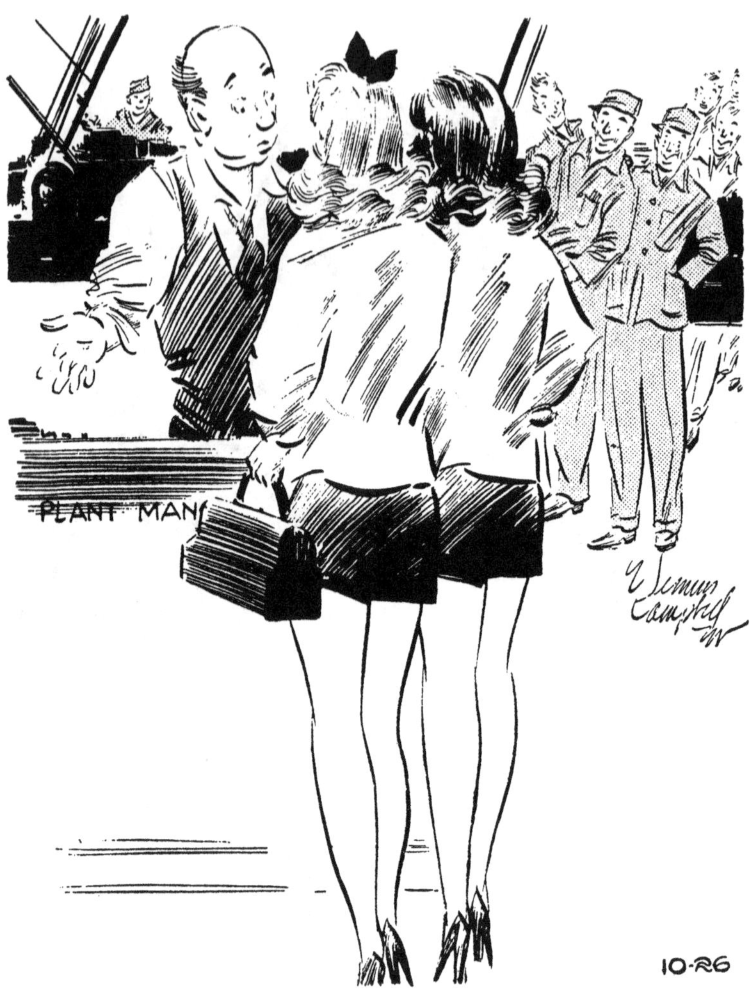

"It's a patriotic idea—your wearing shorts and no stockings to work, but we're losing 10,000 man hours a week from the MEN!"

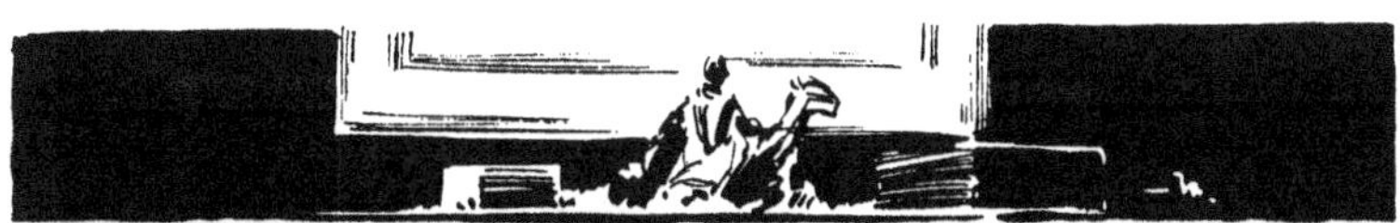

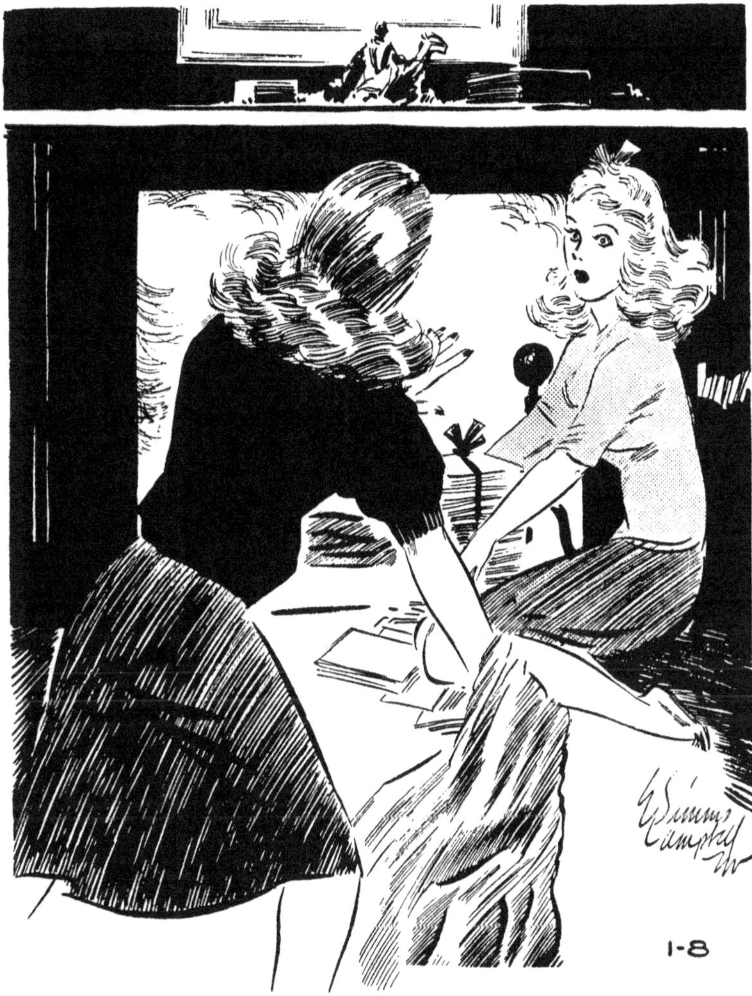

"My dear, don't EVER throw away old love letters! If you take good care of THEM, some day they'll take good care of YOU!"

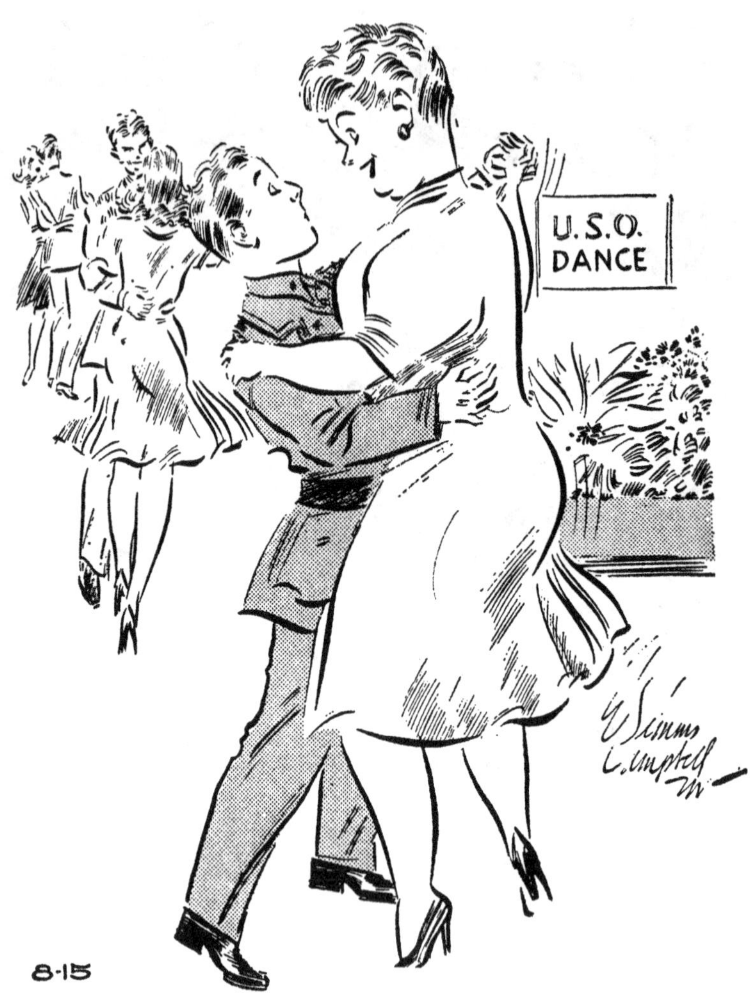

"It's incredible to believe you actually ferry bombers!"

COACHWHIP PUBLICATIONS
CoachwhipBooks.com

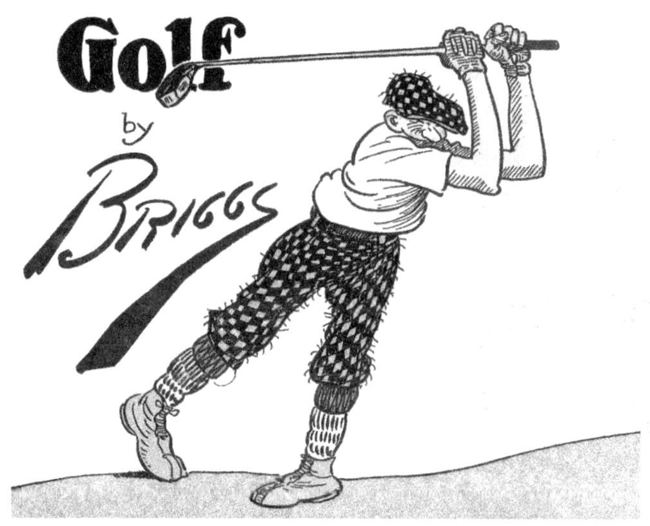

www.ingramcontent.com/pod-product-compliance
Lightning Source LLC
LaVergne TN
LVHW010616100826
845148LV00014B/2993

* 9 7 8 1 6 1 6 4 6 1 3 3 1 *